DARE

How Bowie And Kraftwerk Inspired The Death of Rock'n'Roll and Invented Modern Pop Music

David Laurie

First Published Something In Construction 2015

SIC: 94 Brackenbury Road, London, W6 0BD

ISBN 978-0-9933479-0-0

Printed and bound in Great Britain by
Berforts Information Press
www.bookprinting.co.uk

For Melissa, Joe and Sam; for everything, forever.

And for Himself.

Without whom...

The summer of 1982, when I bought one of your albums every week with my paper round money, changed everything for me. I learned the power of ideas and the freedom of change.

"In the seventies there were so many great bands in Germany that worked very intelligently and inspired to dissolve musical boundaries. Most people still think that there was simply Kraftwerk. Naturally. Kraftwerk are superhumanly good. You can describe my respect for them with the word "absolute". But there were others, many others, that didn't have the luck to become so famous so quickly like Kraftwerk did, but nonetheless made equally interesting music." **David Bowie, 1997**

With colossal gratitude, sine qua non, to

John Dore, Roberto Roda, Julian De Takats, Mark and Aimee, Kieran Breen, Ellie Velvet, Gary Cameron, "m", Dave Goddard, Neal Davies, Mark Bowen, Miki Berenyi, Keith Graham, Shawn Covell, Dominic Shales, Grainne Riley, Mark Williams, Alex Laurie.

And

for support, encouragement and ideas…

Melissa Laurie, Joe Laurie, Sam Laurie, Dave Roberts, Clare Britt, Keith Cameron, Matthew Hamilton, Richard King, Adrian Levy, Cathy Scott-Clark, Suzanne Cooper, Gavin Emerson.

Without whom, you would not be holding this book.

CONTENTS

INTRO #1

The Lunatics Are Taking Over The Charts

They say the music that surrounds you in your turbulent teens stays with you forever. Those sounds and sights are preserved perfectly in your mind, undimmed as the years fall away. The opening bars to dozens of favourite songs remain vivid enough to send Proustian tingles down your spine, flashbacks all the way back to your youth.

I was thirteen in 1981 when I heard *Ghost Town*; the game-changing swansong from my favourite band at the time, The Specials. As catchy as greed, it was a despairing state-of-the-nation address, set to wonky Mariachi Reggae. Britain made this eerie, doomy record #1 for a month that summer. Strong choice, Britain.

Terry Hall chose that moment in the spotlight to break up the band and launch himself into Fun Boy Three. Trying something new, colourful and fun was too much for many of the fans. Their hearts hung heavy at the Specials' demise and they just could not make the jump with Terry, Lynval and Neville – but such abrupt ch-ch-changes were everywhere at the outset of the Eighties.

Pulse-quickening Pop singles in the late Seventies' Top Forty had stood out like dayglo lifeboats in a sea of grey AOR but, starting in 1979 and building through 1980 and 1981, a synthesizer-led explosion of ex-Punks and oddballs with DIY attitudes and what-if ideas hijacked the charts. The lunatics really did take over the asylum, just as Fun Boy Three had suggested.

By the end of 1982, this creative quantum leap had changed Pop Music forever. This was not just the belated birth of "Eighties Music", it was the start of the whole modern era in music. A brand new timeline that had no roots in The Sixties.

Was the Sci-i Future we'd seen on TV for decades finally starting?

For the first time since the Sixties, Pop music was hip, experimental and unpredictable. The freaky New Pop stars, emboldened by David Bowie, empowered by Kraftwerk and embodied by The Human

League, Simple Minds, ABC, The Cure and Japan, spanned the covers of both Smash Hits *and* NME. Critically acclaimed and colossally successful.

I grew up in Cardiff, far from any of this musical upheaval. It rained a lot. All was grey. Back then, *Smash Hits* was my lifeline to somewhere more colourful and the evening Radio One shows let this new gold dream of Pop Music spill out into my world. Watching the new bands being fast-tracked from John Peel session obscurity into The Big Time was fantastically exciting to keep up with, full of life-changing moments and truly staggering records. I was entranced by the whole spectacle and drawn down a path that would lead me to London to try and make my fortune as an A&R man.

1981 and 1982 gave us *The Lexicon Of Love, Sulk, Dare, Architecture & Morality, New Gold Dream, Rip It Up, The Dreaming, Rio, Pornography, Combat Rock, Duck Rock, The Hurting, Tin Drum,* Movement, *Songs To Remember, Speak And Spell, Non Stop Erotic Cabaret, Nightclubbing* and *1999*. And *Thriller.*

This was music of quality and distinction with mass appeal that would restore the generation gap and be so unquestionably great that it would take over the world.

And for a time it worked.

Beautifully.

INTRO #2

Just Can't Get Enough: Record shops and me.

May I tell you about my problem? I am a pathetic addict. I can't walk past a record shop without wanting to go inside. Luckily, such shops are rapidly becoming fading memories now so my habit is much easier to manage. It certainly won't be a problem my kids have.

I am not one to make a big fuss about vinyl records versus CDs. I like them both. Records look and feel cooler but I listen to CDs more – but I will say this: Records are magical and they defy explanation. Surely they are proof of a Higher Power? I can understand how a song can be broken down to a 4Mb MP3. That is four million 1s and 0s and that is a lot of music DNA.

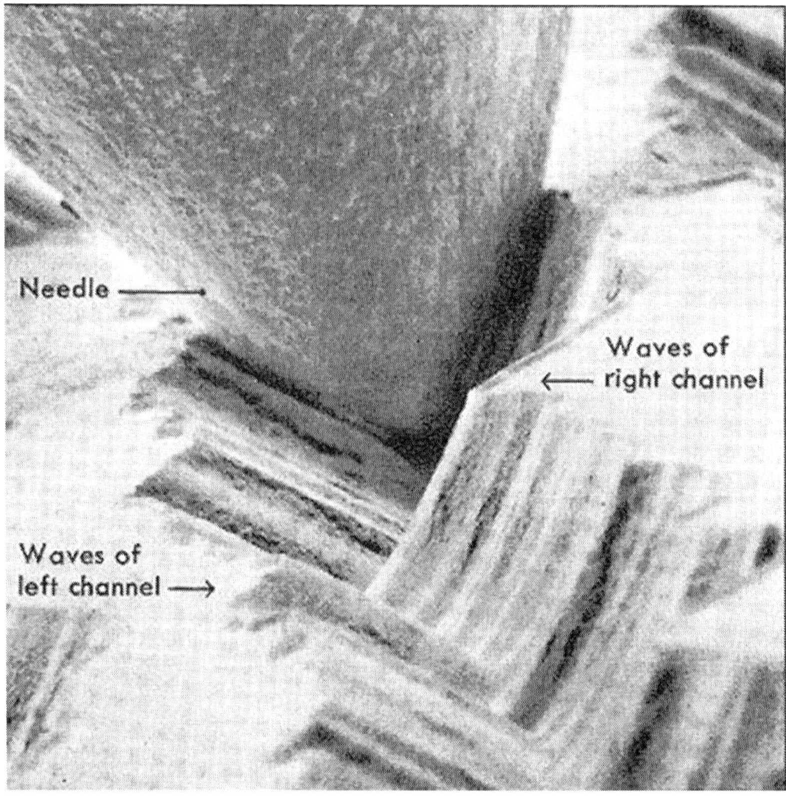

Just look at that picture. It's a close-up of a needle running through the groove of a record. The two sides of the groove are different because it's stereo and so there are two separate sets of vibrations are somehow passing through the same needle. I don't know if you've ever made a cone out of a piece of A4 paper and taped a pin or a sewing needle in the pointy end to play a record. Test it on a non-essential record if you are tempted – it does work. You can hear the music. It's a bit rough around the edges but – WTF! – that is an amazing thing. I find the idea that you can pass vibrations through a pin and play them with a piece of paper to hear the sounds from Beethoven's head or David Bowie's to be genuinely astounding. How do records do that? HOW? It's such an everyday notion that it doesn't get questioned but, c'mon, that is surely witchcraft, at least.

Of course, one can stand in a field and pluck music from the internet now and that is a modern miracle in a great many ways. If I fancy hearing a **Sparks** song, mentioned by someone I was just chatting to online in America, it's only a click away. This happened yesterday. It happens to me pretty much everyday, although not always with Sparks, obviously. Although, you'd be surprised how often it *is* Sparks.

It is a very efficient process. Very clean. No messing about, no delays. No sitting against a rain-soaked bus window, record sleeve on your lap, reading the lyrics, imagining what the music will be like and what it is going to do to your brain. There is less romance and foreplay in the 21st Century. On the other hand, if you are strapped for cash (ie young), it's pretty much instant and free now, which IS amazing but it's no coincidence that the culture of illegally downloading hundreds of songs at a time has coincided with the downgrade of music's importance to kids to something beneath their trainers.

If we'd had the internet first, there would doubtless have been no need for records but that was not how it went down and that is a good thing because records became Art. The music is the main part of a single or album, of course, but it's not complete without the packaging, which enhances and informs the music. It hints at subtext and lures the listener in, develops interest and strengthens the relationship and the message between the artist and the listener. It's a connection. A one-way connection perhaps but, done well, it's a profound one. It makes fans of listeners.

I run a label so, y'know, I would say that. But it's my love of music, of art and yes, of records that inspired me to do this job. That and an insatiable wish to be proved right.

Records expand the process from acquiring music to buying into it. Something as magical and transformative as music surely demands that you buy into it. If the mood took me, I could download the entire Sparks discography from a torrent. It wouldn't take long. Well, actually it might with Sparks there are 20+ studio albums. But would that immerse me in Sparks' world better than buying an album at a time? I don't think so.

Buying a record from a shop reflects a time and date in your day and your life. It's a unique combination of your knowledge, your mood, your finances, your passions and those of your friends, or sometimes it's a last minute choice, a risk, based on an intriguing sticker on the cover, or something you see or hear in the shop that joins the dots of disparate bits of rumours and knowledge you had lying around in your brain.

The **OMD** single ('Souvenir') that I bought in Paris on a school trip when I was thirteen, the **Cure** album I had to buy on cassette to keep me going through that summer job away from home, the **Young Gods** album that I bought and had signed at a tiny show in Hull, the giant **Motown** box set that I really couldn't afford at the time, the **Nirvana** album I was so so so excited to buy after seeing them change my life at a teatime Reading Festival slot, the surprise **Radiohead** 12" panic buying, the **Chromatics** LPs that I bought when I finally visited Amoeba Records in LA last year and, king of them all: the summer of 1982 that I bought a **David Bowie** album every Saturday with my paper round money.

So maybe the connection is not so one way. These links are part of *my* life, *my* memories and part of my record collection. They are human, emotional and way stronger than they are efficient.

Flicking through records – if I get a bit down, that is what cheers me up. Seeing a sleeve and knowing I just have to put that record on. And then that one. In record shops, at friends' houses and on my own bespoke, gorgeous, nerdy shelves. This simple pleasure has won me friends, started relationships, ended some too, and broadened my horizons more than books and films or anything else. Record collections and record shops are like brains. And flicking through the racks and shelves is like a thought process. Synapses link up and all of sudden you are considering Thai psyche music from the late Sixties or **Big Youth** or realising that **The Besnard Lakes** are amazing, or discovering that someone you least suspected has a full set of **Ramones** albums or, conversely, that someone you know likes **Maroon 5** and should possibly be treated with increased caution and/or contempt.

Scrolling through files on a hard drive is absolutely not the same experience, it is uninspiring and clean to the point of soulless. That hard drive is going to make for a piss-poor heirloom and it just doesn't cheer me up on a rainy day in the same satisfying way at all.

01. "HEROES"

Just who did invent the Eighties?
1974-1979: The Back Story Of Modern Pop Music.

KRAFTWERK, NEU, BOWIE, MORODER, SPARKS, BLONDIE

Let's look back. Way back when **The Human League** ruled the Earth. And then, back just a little further. The last couple of years of the Seventies. I had moved to Cardiff after my parents had divorced and woken up to Pop music and I absolutely loved it. Music was without doubt the most fascinating thing to me – better than toys and school and everything. Except possibly Batman. I really loved Batman.

There seemed to be an endless variety to Pop music and there seemed to be a lot more of it in Wales than there had been in Billericay but of course that was just my little world expanding beyond the back garden. I had an old school Dansette type of record player that you could load up with 7" singles and they'd drop down one-at-a-time in a very pleasing, automated and almost robotic fashion. In truth, after a few records were in play they would tend to skid over each other and not play at all, held annoyingly motionless by the needle. Such minor technological hiccups aside, the fascination with the many kinds of music coming out of these shiny grooves was strong. I had a handful of (mainly Sixties) singles acquired from jumble sales: The Beatles, Tom Jones, Cilla Black and, um, Meat Loaf. I made no distinctions between genres. It was all new to me.

I was aware of (and slightly scared of) Punk, having seen "it" gurning alarmingly from magazine covers in newsagents but had heard none of the records – partly because I was too busy playing with Batman and Matchbox cars and partly because I am not sure that I twigged "it" had anything to do with music at all. However, New Wave was getting through to me and I liked it; even if I didn't know what a New Wave was. The first album I bought was a Stiff Records compilation called Live Stiffs Live: **Elvis Costello, Ian Dury, Nick Lowe** et al. I bought it because I loved *Watching The Detectives* and *Hit Me With Your Rhythm Stick*, neither of which were on there but it did have an

Ian Dury song called *Billericay Dickie* and the record was a mid-price bargain. Let's just say that Ian's experience of Billericay and mine were quite different. I had never, for example, had a love affair with Lena, in the back of her Cortina, although I had kissed a girl called Lorna on the last day of school in Essex, so I felt we were broadly on the same page.

There were keyboards in most New Wave bands, just as there were with The Blockheads, The Attractions and indeed The Beatles but, for the most part, bands still looked like bands: endless varieties of "geezers with guitars". Bands looked much as they had in the Sixties, give or take a haircut and, due to my indiscriminate sampling of it, music was a thing that felt like it was growing from the past. But, as the Seventies breathed their last and a new decade was getting ready to reveal itself, a succession of records arrived that stood out a mile. As I moved up to Secondary School, **The Buggles, Gary Numan, Bowie, Blondie** and, yes, **The Police** and more had huge hits with records that sounded like they were beamed in from the future.

As 1980 landed, there was a full-on invasion of these alien, futuristic records, with more keyboards and space – and fewer guitars and less of rock's wall-of-noise. Synthpop had landed like a spaceship in the night. One day it didn't exist, the next it was hanging in the sky over your life, gleaming and throbbing. We couldn't fail to be seduced by its endless sleek lines, flashing lights and electronic bleeps.

We had seen the signs on the television. Tomorrow's world today. After years of tantalisingly notional science fiction, and with *1984* looming impatiently; space-age computer tech was finally here and you could touch it – and when you did, it bleeped appreciatively. It was in the home, on TV and everywhere: digital watches, microwaves, Sinclair computers, Space Invaders and synthesizers for all. Things started bleeping and flashing. Everything beeps and flashes now. You'd worry if it didn't. Your car bleeps if you get out and leave the window open. Your phone bleeps and flashes all day and night to update you on each infinitesimal change in your universe. Back in the late Seventies, we would not even notice a power blackout (and there were many) until it got dark; so when the bleeps and flashes first arrived, it was REALLY exciting. Tiny electronic brains in our midst alerting the world to new wonders of their own creation was very future indeed.

The microchip changed music forever and it all happened very quickly. It catalysed an incredible burst of musical creativity which refuses to stay buried in the past. At first, there were just those few alien-sounding hits that stood out a mile. **M**'s relentless, robotic *Pop Muzik*; **Gary Numan** at the top of the charts – motionless and deathly pale. He's a bleep, he's a weirdo. *Does he think he's a robot, or something?* More and more freaks and geeks arrived. Well, we couldn't help ourselves; resistance was useless and Britain fell in love with The Bleep. We opened our hearts to computer love. The Bleep was everywhere. Where exactly had all these keyboard wizards been hiding? Guitars were out – antiques overnight – and synthesizers were everywhere, sounding exactly like The Future.

The Sixties had grown up pretty seamlessly into the Seventies, had kids of its own and become very set in its ways. Despite Punk's angry noise stirring things up for a while, a musical sea change that everyone could get behind was way overdue and it needed to be convincingly different. By comparison, the Eighties seemed to have been designed in a laboratory and were delivered, straight outta the catalogue, ready to plug-in-and-play. It was clearly the start of what we had been waiting for. It wasn't altogether clear how long The Future would last – because we all lived under the threat of a mushroom cloud back then – but oh my, it was inviting and exotic and it dared you to push its buttons.

People started looking a little exotic. Youth fashion's eternal twin peaks, denim and leather, were finally losing the grip on teenagers that they'd held since the Fifties. Clothes and hair no longer looked natural. Everything was becoming synthetic and disposable as we entered the Age Of Plastic (not unironic – given plastic's endless half-life). After the long, unkempt hair of the early Seventies and the short, even more unkempt hair of the late Seventies, things were looking very Future up top. Hair was becoming sculptural, even architectural. The women wore bright, asymmetric clothes and ambitious sci-fi make-up and the men had asymmetric hair and wore even more outrageous make up. At least, the ones in *Smash Hits* did.

With each fortnight's new issue of the magazine, fresh Pop stars arrived with plumage to dazzle the eyes and exotic outfits to challenge the more conventionally dressed into doing something about that. Punk had renewed an interest in standing out on the high street and dropping jaws but that had degenerated into merely hanging around outside Boots, congealed in gangs, clad in the same sticky predictable anarchy. It was time for the individual to shine again. Post Punk's DIY Utilitarian Chic had been homespun and low rent, for the most part. It was time to be glamorous and fun, alien and sexy. Time to break out the glitter and draw birds on our faces. Wake up, time to dye: the hour of the peacock had arrived. But if not from space, where had this fashion courage, robotic muse and desire to shed the past and create something completely new come from?

Let's make like Sherlock and try to detect the roots of these ideas. Hidden among *Smash Hits'* colourful pages of **Duran Duran** posters and **Adam Ant** lyrics, there was a regular page called *Bitz'n'Pieces.* This was a repository for specialist charts, fan club addresses, pop stars' birthdays and an *All Time Top Ten*, with a different artist picking their favourite records each issue. More often than not (I counted), there was a selection from **David Bowie.** Although it would have made for a less snappy title, the *All Time Top Ten* really ought to have been called *All Time Favourite David Bowie Song And Any Nine Others by Mere Mortals.* Left to his own devices, that idea might even have found favour with the magazine's assistant editor; the starry-eyed and verbose, **Neil Tennant**. Bowie's name came up so often that His absence from a list often felt conspicuous; especially when Pete Murphy managed to forget that He might be an influence, despite **Bauhaus**' breakthrough hit cover of *Ziggy Stardust* being just weeks away from release. He didn't feature as often if Soul or Disco artists were making the selection: Bowie hadn't actually been in **Earth, Wind And Fire** or **Chic**, after all. However He *had* commandeered what was ghettoised or derided as Black or Gay Music, even after the Punk Wars had supposedly rendered us all equal. He had made synths, Soul and Disco just as cool and relevant as shouting and spiky guitars among the new crop of young groups. **Associates**' Billy Mackenzie, on his turn picking a Top Ten, knowingly described *Golden Years* as *"a real man's song".* Sexuality was coming to the fore once more and things got a lot more...relaxed.

Reading *Smash Hits,* or any of the many music papers I dabbled with in my quest for Pop knowledge, **David Bowie**'s name would come up again and again in interviews, invoked equally by new bands and old. It seemed that most contemporary musicians, regardless of genre, had had their life improved by something of His, and each time it was a different song or period in His career that was referenced. Sometimes it would be the early Seventies' ambisexual and glittery Glam posing, other times the Philadelphia Soul wiggling of *Young Americans* or the frosty synthscapes of *Low*. A distillation of all three of these aesthetics, in varying proportions, amounted to a blueprint for a great many of the exciting new bands that appeared between 1980 and 1982.

The debt owed to Bowie by these artists, and the depth to which it is felt, is evident in 2015 as lone Spider standing, Woody Woodmansey and David's longtime producer, Tony Visconti tour, playing Bowie albums to Bowie fans, featuring willing and enthusiastic guests like Marc Almond from Soft Cell, Martin Kemp from Spandau Ballet and Glenn Gregory and Martyn Ware from Heaven 17 among many others.

It became obvious that no other artist was as universally revered, except perhaps **The Beatles,** but as we were fast forwarding into the future now, it had become practical among the cooler new bands to keep quiet about them. Was it possible that this one man had affected the work of everyone in Pop? And just how many records had He made?

I knew some of them, of course. It wasn't possible to go through life and not notice **David Bowie**'s existence in the early Eighties, even before He came back, reinvented as a hit-packed, global stadium-busting brand, with *Let's Dance* in 1983. He had not put an album out for a few years, an occurrence not seen since the mid Sixties, such was his prodigious Seventies catalogue, but there had been recent hits with **Bing Crosby, Queen** and **Giorgio Moroder,** along with covers of **Johnny Matthis** and **Kurt Weill.** Who else could connect with such a broad selection of artists? His last album alone featured members of **The Who, King Crimson** and **The E Street Band**. Bowie's tendrils in Pop culture were everywhere – you didn't have to seek Him out. If one walked into a record shop, one would be greeted by a Bowie record without having to look for it in the racks, *ChangesOneBowie, ChangesTwoBowie*; iconic renderings of His face beamed down from posters and up from magazine racks, He was on the radio and TV, talking about his stage plays and films. If he wasn't doing the talking, then someone would be holding him up as an inspiration, sine qua non. What was the fascination with the man?

It was not ever so, nor had this endless kudos been easily won. **Bowie** had struggled to find his way musically throughout the Sixties, flitting from one trend to the next without making much impression but finally scoring a novelty #1 single, on the back of a global obsession with the space race in 1969, with *Space Oddity*. Novel it certainly was but this peerless song of dislocation, mirroring His own inability to connect with His Muse or find an audience, was the first time you truly felt magic at work on a David Bowie record. He clicked with Himself for the first time and the public felt it too. And so it began.

His peerless run of albums throughout the Seventies raised and reset the standard for Pop music, time and again. As an unfaltering body of work, it remains unequalled and seems likely to remain so. Starting out with literate and alchemical hippy music on *Space Oddity*, he moved through the earthy and epic psychedelic rock of *The Man Who Sold The World*, into the spaced out and very feminine sci-fi folk of *Hunky Dory*. His staggering, feline performance of *Starman* on Top Of The Pops in 1972 was the game-changing moment in which everyone in Britain noticed What Had Become Of David Bowie. Debuting proto-Ziggy hair and dressed in a skinny catsuit, seemingly made of curtains, with His arms draped around Mick Ronson, who wore the sort of blonde feather cut and catsuit combo that Charlie's Angels would later popularise, they made An Impression. Bowie was batting for both sides and knocking it out of the park, playing straight to camera. His voice dipped and soared again with total control; a consummate performance. You can't half watch its pure, devastating theatrics. Once in a while a singer can burn a song, every single nuanced word of it, straight into your memory, a sparkling, livewire connection, that is never forgotten. That is the magic of music and it's surprisingly hard to maintain that magic on television.

It's rare that someone who puts that much effort into making your jaw drop at their appearance can make it drop yet further with the music. He had been practicing being David Bowie for a long time and on that Top Of The Pops, He contrived to make it look easy. Bowie's slow burning superstardom, His love of and success with masks, make-up and characters mirrored that of a hero of His, Peter Sellers. They both insisted that they themselves were quite uninteresting and "had no personality" of their own and were thus willing, able and even desperate to fully commit to each role, each performance.

Bowie's next inspired decision was to allow each side of his music, of his mind, out at the same time; to meld the thrusting, riff rock of his imagined *Saviour Machine* into the receptive, circular ripples of *Hunky Dory* to create the two dimensional androgynous rock star template for *Ziggy Stardust*. A creature of pure ego, a pleasure seeker, neither bound by responsibility nor mired in routine. Then, just as predicted in His own lyric, *"making love with his ego, Ziggy sucked up into his mind"*, David was willingly subsumed into His own chaotic creation and fulfilled His stated destiny, as revealed in the slip from third person to first at the end of His theme song; *"when the kids had killed the man, I had to break up the band"*. David didn't just become Ziggy Stardust; at the same time He severed ties with the business of being David Jones.

Having ruthlessly discarded The Spiders From Mars onstage, He took his bold Psychological Rock experiment further out and made a bid to conquer the States, manifesting *Aladinsane*'s schizoid, ambisexual passions and riding *Diamond Dogs'* decadent cocaine tailspin deep into the heart of America. His fear of flying meant that he experienced the vastness of the country, gas station to gas station, at ground level. The endless highways dwarfed and consumed the overdriven ego of His sundry personalities, and brought his role as A Rock Star to a nominal End Of Part One; as Bowie Himself ran out of gas.

This period was captured perfectly in Alan Yentob's brilliant documentary, *Cracked Actor*. Bowie is seen as a man teetering on the fine line between confidence and collapse, stick thin and babbling about Aretha and the Soul Of America* [*just as Bono would do, somewhat less convincingly, ten years later], wide-eyed with cocaine and ambition. His rambling English tones hopelessly out-of-place on the long hot limo rides across the American desert, his monologues careering in and out of making sense. He'd have looked out of place anywhere and Nic Roeg, on seeing the film, saw that quality immediately and cast him as the Alien in *The Man Who Fell To Earth*. That "not quite human" quality was deployed again to great effect in the Broadway production of *The Elephant Man* a few years later. Taking leave of your senses is not without its own rewards.

No-one predicted the well-spoken Englishman's rebirth, a few months later as a *Young American* Soul diva, nor his succession of funky American #1 singles. After winning at Disco and planting His flag in the black music heartland of *Soul Train*, just as he had on *Top Of The Pops* a few years previously, David rounded up his few remaining unchipped marbles in an LA studio and let Europe seep back into his mind with *StationToStation*. The icy croons and machine-tooled sci-fi soundscapes, some of which had been conceived for his abortive *The Man Who Fell To Earth* soundtrack, were heavily influenced by the dehumanised noises of Germany's synthesizer pioneers, **Kraftwerk** and the snaking, locked grooves of **Neu**.

Between 1976 and 1978, Bowie was in mad professor mode, secluded away in studios in Berlin and the French countryside, aided variously by **Brian Eno, Iggy Pop** and producer **Tony Visconti**. Together, they rebooted and expanded Pop and Rock Music in ten different directions with each successive album. As Punk thrashed around lustily at **The Stooges'** old ideas at home in London; *Low, "Heroes"* and *Lodger*, along with **Iggy**'s *The Idiot* and *Lust For Life* drew upon and blended aspects of every genre imaginable to make A New Music.

These albums represented a masterful destruction of the foundations of the phallocentric Rock music that had powered Ziggy's swagger and strut. Bowie seemed to have prised His altered ego's grip from the reins and given the musical lead to His feminine side, allowing the glistening songs to pulse and grow, to draw the listener in, rather than batter them over the head. There was an introspective and self-critical aspect to the words and music; along with a slightly humbled sense of doubt and no little wonder. He took a step back and let the music find its way, no longer feeling compelled to preen and yelp all over the tunes. The albums sounded big, beautiful and eerie but accessible, filled with melody and bathed in light.

The "low profile" visual gag of *Low*'s sleeve, those important speech marks around "Heroes" and the impermanence of calling yourself a lodger are not bullish Rock Star statements, there's no more of The Big I Am. Instead they speak of questioning experimentalism, of breaking bad habits and learned megastar behaviour, no longer *"always crashing in the same car"*. Iggy's self-realisation was even more blatant and, not that the man had an excess of shame to begin with exactly, but calling your album *The Idiot* still takes balls. His rediscovery of his own *Lust For Life* just as transformative, and twice as infectious.

The results are stunning and gave life to the *"European Canon"* He had announced/imagined in *StationToStation's* lyric. A new music that had nothing much to do with Rock'n'Roll but still delivered thrills and sounded, if anything, bigger than ever. Stadium sized music that had not evolved from basement clubs. An alien, computerised music that practically demanded white lights and lasers onstage. *Close Encounters of The Third Kind* came out in 1977 and the aliens seemed to originate from the same planet as Bowie's grand, unfamiliar tunes, similarly dotted with machine-noises, pulses and throbs. These were tunes that often had no recognisable instruments and sometimes seemed untouched by human hands. If Ziggy lived and died as the ultimate Rock'n'Roll animal, then the second half of the Seventies saw Bowie bury Rock'n'Roll in the grave right next to him; and it seemed as though every cool band in Britain was attending the funeral.

He was pulling back the curtains on the sci-fi future that hadn't quite materialised after the space race in the Sixties. Each single sounded completely different to the last and the excitement to see what He'd do next made each one An Event. *Fame, Wild Is The Wind, Golden Years, Speed Of Life, Be My Wife, Breaking Glass, Sound And Vision, "Heroes", Boys Keep Swinging, DJ, Ashes To Ashes, Fashion*. A trailblazing comet, he was hard to keep up with but a source of constant illumination. His work rate gave drug addicts a good name and made bands who hawk around the same set for years on end look lazy beyond words. It also made sounding like Bowie virtually impossible. In the months it would take a band to dissect a record and spin it somewhere new, He'd have moved on, leaving them standing. The only thing that bands could hope to copy was his refusal to repeat himself.

This restless, inventive attitude to making music, and the freedom it engendered, inspired the thinking behind so many Eighties Pop groups. After *Low* and *"Heroes"*, all the cool Pop albums from then on had weird and unusual tracks among the Proper Actual Songs. I miss that a bit. Trying different things and leaving songs as experiments for the sake of it, without trying to force a chorus onto them, makes for deeper and more interesting albums. There is no shortage of invention today. Quite the opposite really, as the internet makes the all world's noises a click away, but it rarely troubles the Top Ten any more and those sonic adventurers have less time for Pop music…

…and yet Bowie's rampant experimentalism is now seen as His Imperial Phase. He tore up the rule book and refused to read it ever again. He wouldn't settle on his laurels for a minute but, at the time, this asked a lot of some of his fans. Not everyone likes ch-ch-changes; least of all his label who, on hearing *Low,* offered to buy him a big house in Philadelphia, where He had made *Young Americans,* if He would make another Soul album. Record labels really like it when artists repeat the winning formula because casual fans, who buy the bulk of the albums when an artist crosses over into the Top Ten, very often prefer repetition to *Repetition*, it seems.

A new and unfathomable record every few months meant that these European albums were not, by his standards, huge sellers at the time. Having pushed His creative impulses into virgin territories, He finished off the Seventies with the double tap of *Ashes To Ashes* and *Fashion,* which surfed the coming Synthpop revolution that he'd helped to kickstart, to be huge worldwide hits. They sounded like **David Bowie** songs, albeit unlike any that had come before, and were packed with unstoppable hooks and flourishes that made radios play them all over the world. They were set amid the otherwise quite dark and dystopian (and brilliant) *Scary Monsters,* which harked back to *Diamond Dogs* in terms of lyrical content and scraping guitar noise, and proved to be an equally crowd-pleasing move. Just as with 2013's grand comeback *The Next Day*, the sleeve of *Scary Monsters* features whited out versions of His older record sleeves, including *"Heroes",* and it makes the album feel like a wrapping up of the Seventies and the End Of Part Two for Bowie, just as *Diamond Dogs* had felt like and End of Part One.

The abundance of new noises on **Bowie**'s records were mostly out of the reach of the legions of bands who were following his every move. Early synthesizers cost as much as a Ferrari and so, during the Post Punk Years, bands looked to find DIY alternatives to Moogs. Recording studios looked more like workshops; with cumbersome homemade machines, oscilloscopes for monitors and modified tape reels contrived to make time-stretched clicks and pleasing whirrs, in order to render their own post-guitar landscapes. A lot of Post Punk's wonderful singles were inspired by Bowie's purging of rock'n'roll, the removal of ego and human warmth and the harsh industrial noises heard on sides two of *Low* and *"Heroes"*. These stark 45s are nonetheless alive with ideas and urgency; twitching with political unrest, their messages delivered mechanically and angrily but, as much as I love **Cabaret Voltaire**, early **Human League** and **PiL**, their spiky singles were quite intentionally not dripping with mass appeal.

If Bowie was the figurehead behind this change of attitudes and sounds, He readily acknowledged that He wouldn't have got there without **Kraftwerk** and **Neu**. The two German bands' roots intertwine and stretch back to the Sixties. Neu remained more underground due to their lack of structured Pop melodies but Kraftwerk had maintained a steady cult presence in the UK. *ManMachine* (1978) and *Autobahn (1974)* had been Top Ten albums. Bowie had asked Neu to contribute to *StationToStation* but they declined. Regardless, the first five minutes of its epic title song is a Neu track in all but name. Neu's music is less obviously electronic; using other methods to dehumanise it. Their long songs are largely instrumental and use endlessly repeating figures that develop very slowly. Klaus Dinger's drumming, while human, is very metronomic. The groove, once assembled, is adhered to with only the most subtle variations. Michael Rother's super minimal guitar playing bears shadows of Minimalist modern composers like Steve Reich and Terry Riley. The whole thing sounds clean and perfect. There is no suggestion of blood, sweat or tears on display whatsoever. Neu's slowly fluctuating, yet elegant and persistent tunes were not big sellers but came to be very influential, not just on Bowie but also Eno for his ambient albums and through those artists, a whole generation of Pop groups in the Eighties, Nineties and beyond. Neu's music is not difficult in any way and if you haven't, you should give them a listen. It's not too fanciful to extend the through-line from them on to the pulsing hypnotic soundscapes of modern electronic music.

Both **Kraftwerk** and **Neu** were not just distinctive musicians but also masterful conceptual artists. The reductively functional band names and utilitarian Pop Art sleeves, when coupled with the willing removal of their physical selves from the spotlight, speaks of trying to make a futuristic music that owes way more to the Avant Garde than it ever did to ego or Rock'n'Roll. Kraftwerk's willingness to be *seen* to relinquish the creative and performance processes to machines is a product of growing up in the Sixties with Warhol's Factory screenprinting mechanisation and their fondness for avoiding the indignity of labour displays knowing winks to DuChamp's Dadaist shortcuts.

Ralf Hutter and Florian Schneider-Esleben met in college in Dusseldorf in the late Sixties and were both in a group called **Organisation** (hence the title of that second **OMD** album) that released one album, *Tone Floats* in 1969. *Kraftwerk 1* appeared in 1971, followed by *Kraftwerk* 2 in 1972. These two records were more along the lines of **Can** or **Neu**, being instrumental live jams on traditional rock and jazz instruments, processed and distorted afterward in the mix. The band's revolving door personnel policy in these early years featured Klaus Dingle and Michael Rother from **Neu.** *Ralf Und Florian,* released a year later featured the drum machine that Ralf and Florian had used to play live, along with synthesizers and occasional use of what would become their trademark vocodered vocals.

The first time the world at large became aware of **Kraftwerk** was on hearing *Autobahn* in 1974. It was produced, as were the previous three albums, by Conny Plank, Krautrock's uber-producer who also worked with **Can, Neu, Cluster** and **Harmonia**. The format that Moroder would borrow for Donna Summer's records originates here on Autobahn. Side one is solely the title track; twenty two minutes long and is supposed to simulate the long whooshes and slow rhythms of a motorway drive. And it does. It turns the exquisite tedium, long slow curves and occasional interruptions of a lengthy drive into a stately and elegantly low key piece of music. It's worth noting, for what it's worth, that Germany's Autobahns were invented as city-to-city expressways and were built with no roundabouts, intersections or speed limits, for smooth, uninterrupted and, yes, efficient driving.

Autobahn is even, on its hugely truncated three and a half minute single version, Pop Music; a most unexpected development for the experimental young Germans. It helped that the chorus of *"Fahrn, fahrn, fahrn on the Autobahn"* sounds a bit like The Beach Boys' *"Fun, fun, fun"*, but the novel single was a Top Thirty hit in America and across Europe, hitting #11 in the UK in November 1974.

There are few vestigial traces of "real" instruments on *Autobahn*, mostly replaced by Minimoogs and primitive, self-built synthesisers and this is the first record that sounds like classic **Kraftwerk**. The success of the album internationally meant that the band were able to build their own Kling Klang studios and were free to push and develop the unique noises, tics and humour that make up their music. Accordingly, Ralf and Florian took their time and produced all the subsequent albums.

I've always seen **Kraftwerk** to be wry, and witty and a little silly, rather than po-faced, as they portray themselves; as evidenced by the thigh-slappingly titled *Ohm Sweet Ohm*, the final track on their next record, *Radio-activity*. The album is a study of sorts in English and German of sundry very loosely scientific ideas; or at least scientific puns. Indeed the surprise of hearing themselves on the radio while recording it, gave them the title's pun. Karl Bartos and Wolfgang Flur had joined for this album and filled out the classic line-up of the band. Their purple patch starts here for me.

I was, of course, blissfully unaware of all of this and didn't hear **Kraftwerk** at all until 1982, when a re-release of 1979's *The Model*, which had just been on the B side of 1981's *Computer Love* and had started picking up its own radio play and was itself re-released in the UK at the tail end of 1981 amid the Synthpop goldrush, hitting #1 in February 1982. Others, including OMD, had had their pivotal moment, akin to Bowie doing *Starman* on Top Of The Pops, when Kraftwerk first appeared on British TV, on future science programme, *Tomorrow's World* in 1978.

The first time you hear Kraftwerk, you will remember it. They are not as other bands. Not a bit. Appearing on their album sleeves like airbrushed weathermen gives you no clue as to what lies within. They look like robots or showroom dummies, as slyly hinted at in choruses like "*We are the robots*" or "*We are showroom dummies*". We are used to the idea that synthetic music is the dominant force in Pop today and will be in the future, and aware that 1975 is much closer to World War II than it is now, so it gets harder and harder to conceive that this music happened in the grey, rubble strewn, bombed-out Germany of the Seventies. It all happened in a bit of a bubble, in a quiet industrial part of West Germany too, rather than in the charged, creative atmosphere of Berlin; free of trends, the band were able to experiment.

Lyrics, if there are any, are often limited to a few spoken phrases or occasionally half sung, as in the case of *The Model,* sometimes in German, or French, or Japanese or English, often vocodered to sound like machines, or just phrases read aloud by machines. There is zero rock and roll. There is precisely no Beatles DNA here. There's no DNA at all, in fact; only machine code. This is a new parallel strand of evolution for Pop music. Music that has no need to spend three years looking for a good drummer to make it happen. It needs no drummer at all.

Having built the machines to make the sounds they wanted; having eventually rejected all Rock and Blues related influence and dispensed with traditional instruments altogether, along with any detectable signs of human life or input, often using the computers to "sing" for them; the band then set about eradicating themselves from the picture as far as they could. The press shots for Man Machine feature mannequins of the band and, when they play live, some of the songs are performed by motionless robots, torsos on sticks, in their image.

It's easy to bait dyed-in-the-wool musos about Kraftwerk playing live. They don't, really. It's performance art. Warhol would have been proud. Ralf Hutter was a fan of Warhol, judging by the contemporary (at the time) Pop Art sleeve that he designed for Kraftwerk 1. Once Warhol had created a painting, he was more than happy for someone else to reproduce it endlessly, screenprinting in his Factory, dispensing with the tools of his trade ie paintbrushes. Kraftwerk adopted the same reductive attitude to being in a band and similarly used a lot of purely functional terms to describe their artistic processes.

There is a cliché that follows electronic artists around like a tiresome dinner party guest, which tuts conspiratorially, muttering that they appear to be doing nothing musical onstage and "might as well be checking their emails for all the audience can see". **Kraftwerk** made a witty and artful riposte to such criticism, long before it was even levelled. They seem to enjoy the lack of effort that is required for them to play live. What started as airbrushing themselves out of their photos, ended up with the ultimate undermining of playing live, wherein the band are not even onstage (a trick **The Human League** would attempt a few years later to unpredictable effect). Amid the long-haired meritocracy that was rock in the Seventies, this was the final subversion. It was the absolute limit, guaranteed to piss people off. It was elegant Duchamp-inspired art terrorism on a grand scale and it makes the Punk revolution seem like a petulant playground tantrum.

Kraftwerk endure to this day, although Ralf Hutter is now the only original member. Such knotty notions of authenticity are possibly less relevant or highly valued by this band. They are allegedly planning a new album in 2015 but their run of records: *Trans Europe Express* (1977), *Die Mensch-Maschine (The Man Machine)* (1978) and *Computer World* (1981) contain their best loved Pop songs. *The Model, Computer World, Showroom Dummies, Numbers, Pocket Calculator, The Robots, Neon Lights* and *TransEurope Express* still constitute the throbbing electronic heart of their live set to this day.

These ARE Pop songs or, perhaps more accurately, Pop records, in their own way and on their own terms. Most of them are pretty and delicate melodies and very easy on the ear. Kraftwerk never copied anybody but it seems that all electronic pop music has copied Kraftwerk, wittingly or no. There are DNA strands in almost all electronic music, and thus almost all modern Pop music that can be traced back to Dusseldorf. The turn of the Eighties brought **OMD, Gary Numan** and the revamped **Ultravox**, along with brilliant solo records from their former singer **John Foxx** that all owe a debt to the Germans. **Afrika Bambaata**'s proto Hip Hop classic *Planet Rock* samples *Trans Europe Express* and Numbers and thus Kraftwerk were players at the beginnings of Hip Hop. **Joy Division, Simple Minds, Bjork, Radiohead, Depeche Mode, Aphex Twin**, every single techno artist ever and almost all bands signed to

Mute and DFA Records wear their mark proudly. Indeed Daniel Miller, the Boss of Mute bought the vocoder they used on their early records, likening it owning Hendrix's guitar. Basically anything with wooooshy noises or metronomic electronic drums wouldn't be here without Kraftwerk.

Trying to sound like Kraftwerk was all the more baffling in the Seventies because it was inconceivably hard to sound like Kraftwerk (no-one had bleepy machines of any sort, never mind wooshy ones). They had built much of their equipment themselves and there really was no analogue available to mere mortals. Synthesizers only became vaguely affordable at the turn of the Eighties and, even then, they were still out of the reach of most pockets. The spoiled brat in The **Undertones**'s *My Perfect Cousin* was so privileged that *"his Ma bought a synthesiser, got the Human League in to advise her"*. That couplet's two notions being equally far-fetched.

The process of conjuring sounds and then arranged melodies out of early synthesisers and Moogs was very technical, involving maths, dense bricklike instruction manuals, soundwaves and envelopes, whereas the assembly of the music was often primitive and Luddite, involving cutting and splicing of tape and endless arthritis-bating stab-stab-stabbing of single notes on keyboards. There were no sequencers, presets or samplers available. The first commercially successful sampler was a **Fairlight** and, on its launch in 1979, it did indeed cost about the same as a nice big house, so was only accessible in high end recording studios, and thus only to the biggest acts. Fairlights, for those had access to them, were a revelation. An Australian invention, these protosamplers created sounds from waveforms on a computer screen. Any sound has a waveform so if you could make the right shape on the screen you could make any sound at all. No instruments required. Such foul modern revolutions were spurned, at first, by the rock aristocracy (cheeky old curmudgeon, **Phil Collins'** *No Jacket Required* had the tagline "*there is no Fairlight on this record*"). The first purely Fairlight record was made in 1981 by **EBN-OZN** (Ned Liben, who represented Fairlight in New York, and Robert Ozn) and it was called *AEIOU Sometimes Y* and is brilliant computer disco, albeit with slightly underwhelming "singing".

The Fairlight was joined in the market a few years later by the rival Synclavier 1. Just to dispel your visions of future past, the Synclavier 1 looked like this. It's made of wood, mainly and resembles a 1950s telephone exchange. Sexy, right?

It's important to put these two devices and computer technology into context, relative to today's ubiquitous microchips. Computers were a bit crap at first. The first hugely popular home computer, the ZX-81 had, on its launch in 1981, a RAM capacity of just 1Kb of RAM. Your PC, even if it only has 1Gb of RAM, has one MILLION times more processing power. One million. A thousand homes with a thousand ZX-81s each to equal one bog standard out-of-date desktop PC. Sampling things back then was a lot slower but, given enough time, it could be done, which was nice. Synclaviers were later supplanted by the E-Mu Emulator, which was cheaper and more portable and relied on Floppy disks to load the samples. It looked like an only slightly bulky modern electric piano or synth. When combined with dedicated humans possessed of, let's not overlook, visionary musical talent, these machines shaped the Eighties. However, if you couldn't write a tune, the machines were not going to help you past that stumbling block.

Giovanni Giorgio Moroder released his first records in 1966 and had his first hit in Germany in 1970 with *Luky Luky* aka *Looky Looky*, from the brilliantly titled album *That's Bubblegum…That's Giorgio,* and it is a slice of Mannfred Mannish pop, every bit as atrociously good as you might imagine (Youtube is waiting for you). He made music for himself and others, including, I've just discovered, writing *Son Of My Father* by **Chicory Tip**, a UK #1 in 1972. Both that and *I Feel Love* were in fact produced with the same Moog (see below). Solid gold Pub Fact, right there. He remains best known for those songs he made with Donna Summer and you would be hard pushed to find a musician making electronic music that does not stand in awe of *I Feel Love*.

This single sounds completely fresh and futuristic to this day, after nearly forty years, so it's boggling to imagine the impact it had in the mid-Seventies. We are so used to samplers and modern digital production, which doesn't need any instruments at all, that music dedicated to genuinely novel sounds passes by unnoticed today, locked away in the Underground, monitored by Pitchfork.com, where competition for generating the most ear-shredding beat and harnessing the wildest glitch is like ye olde search for The Lost Chord. These sonic obscurists only trouble the outside world when rap moguls, like **Kanye** or **Drake**, co-opt the latest hot kid to be one of thirteen writers/producers to provide texture and grit on one of their new tracks. However, back then it was a breath of icy Alpine air in an analogue smog of drums, basses, guitars and vintage amps; alien indeed to the inescapable four-guys-in-a-room method of recording, which had dominated since the Sixties. Aside from the singing, *I Feel Love* has no discernable human element at all. Mind-blowing stuff in 1977 for the long-haul rock bands and bloated middle-aged session players of AOR.

Such was the novelty of *I Feel Love*'s textures that Moroder swiftly graduated to making film soundtracks, including 1979's *Midnight Express* for which he won the Oscar. His synthtastic scores are also heard in the

Eighties titans, of admittedly varying quality, that are *Battlestar Galactica, American Gigolo* (including *Call Me* by **Blondie**), *Cat People* (including the majestic title track by **David Bowie**), *Scarface, Flashdance* and the thankfully misleadingly titled, *The Never Ending Story*. If Eighties is going to be bent to become an adjective, then those are some of the Eighties-est films in the world. Alas Giorgio did not do the music for *Tron*. That would have been too perfect and would have had some nice **Daft Punk**-related symmetry too (they did the remake's soundtrack). *Tron*'s soundtrack was, of course, done by Wendy (nee Walter, long story) Carlos who also did the stunning *A Clockwork Orange* music.

The once and future hardline Christian, Donna Summer, deviated from her family's godly path in the Seventies and made some fantastic, timeless, peerless records with Giorgio. Leaving Boston for New York, she had tried her luck singing with a psychedelic rock band called **Crow**, before joining a touring version of the hippy musical, *Hair*, which rode the counter-cultural wave to enormous acclaim, scandal and success. It featured the sort of nudity and transgressive attitudes that would, and probably did, upset her parents somewhat. It also has some quite good songs and I do recommend you hear it, along with *Jesus Christ Superstar*, which appeared a few years afterwards, to get a full flavour of what passed for shocking around 1970. The latter has better songs, by the way. They were the *Jerry Springer: The Musical* or *The Book Of Mormon* of the day, I suppose. Funny how things change…or, y'know, don't.

Anyway, while in Germany with *Hair*, LaDonna Adrian Gaines met and married Helmuth Sommer, who provided her stage name. She also met Giorgio and his lyricist partner in crime, Pete Bellotte. They recorded Donna's first album, *Lady Of The Night*, which was released to muted response in Holland in 1974. On Donna's return to the US, she came up with the lyric hook *Love To Love You Baby*. Giorgio was so inspired that he built the track around it and Pete added more lyrics. Donna was initially unwilling to commit to singing the new words, which are pretty explicit, and were guaranteed to upset her religious parents, and to be fair, quite a lot of other people too. The song is written, none too subtlely, as a woman coming to orgasm, all lip-biting moans and gasps. Donna apparently overcame her shyness when recording the song by getting into character and pretending she was Marilyn Monroe singing *Happy Birthday Mr President* to JFK, which accounts for that breathy delivery.

Neil Bogart, the boss of the parent label, Casablanca, got hold of the single and played it over and over "at a party". A party made just for two perhaps. Inspired by its, um, durability, he encouraged Giorgio to make a long take of the song. A really long one. The result was promo'd as a twelve inch and subsequently took up the whole of Side One of the next album, running to just shy of SEVENTEEN minutes and giving the album its title (and raison d'etre). The cover is somewhat brazen in depicting what Donna might be doing with her hands, just out of shot, in the crotchal region. Holding a disco clutchbag, no doubt.

Pedants might take note that the track is credited to Bellotte as producer, with Giorgio taking arrangement and mixing credits. It was an instant dancefloor sensation and went on to become a huge hit all over the world, bringing and baiting controversy and notoriety along the way. This song is, for all that, quite a traditionally arranged Disco/Funk tune for real instruments, with some very nice jazz flute (man).

Casablanca squeezed another two cash-in "love" albums out of Donna the next year, 1976, marketing her as *the "First Lady Of Love"*. She felt increasingly uncomfortable with her role and people's preconceptions of her and began to feel somewhat exploited. The first, *A Love Trilogy*, has an even longer, Eighteen minute track (*Try Me, I Know We Can Make It*) as side one and four (whole) further songs. The second, *Four Seasons Of Love* manages just four songs, each based on a season. They are competent disco albums but not hugely remarkable, other than for the speed with which they churned them out and the thinness that the ideas were stretched out to. The idea of a single colossal song on one side of an album and four other derivative ones on the other owes much to Kraftwerk's *Autobahn* and Moroder borrowed more than that from his countrymen. He took their pretty synthesizer melodies, sexed them up on top of solid disco beats and squeezed them hard.

Never give up on a good thing is a solid disco motto and 1977 brought two further albums, making four in two years. The second of which, *Once Upon A Time*, was the first of three consecutive double albums, two of which topped the American Charts. The reason for all this hugeness was that Donna was hot stuff. Smoking Hot. And the reason for that was the last track on 1977's *I Remember Yesterday*, which was called *I Feel Love* and it's a track that remains Moroder's masterpiece. Little more than a slowly modulating rapid pulse, a few long slow synth string approximations and a metronomic drum machine that does not let up for a second. Oh, and Donna cooing bedward over the top. You know it, of course and it's utterly fantastic. The extended version manages a modest eight minutes but when I hear it in a club, I still want it to go on forever and, thanks to **Patrick Cowley**'s masterful remixing, it does sometimes.

I Remember Yesterday's songs represent music from the 20s, 50s, 60s, 70s and, finally, "the future". Can you guess which one was the future? Exactly. And it so was or would be. Its long slow pulsing and modulation, those fabled "Repetitive Beats" invented House, Techno and all modern club records. Yes, they did. Incidentally, Donna Summer went on to make a great many more amazing disco tunes and a great many rubbish ones. She became a massive gay icon and then had a breakdown and went back to loving Jesus again and told the gay community that God was not pleased with them and that her disco records were a mistake, neither of which is true, although that is being quite charitable to some of the mindless filler that pads out her catalogue.

It would be wrong not to mention *MacArthur Park* here also. It was a cover of a **Jimmy Webb** song, previously a gravel voiced hit for actor **Richard Harris**, who had promised Webb his Rolls Royce if it was a hit. The car had been a gift from Princess Margaret, who had engraved her initials on the bumper (as you do). The song was a huge hit but Harris reneged, the scamp. Anyway, Donna's Moroder-produced version was a massive hit in 1978 in its single edit form, and appeared as Side Four of her American #1 double live album *Live And More* (available at a boot fair near you for a pound, you lucky person), in an extended-suite-version running to a magnificent twenty minutes.

A band that also chose magnificence, fearlessness and Giorgio were **Sparks.** Two brothers, Russel and Ron Mael formed Sparks in 1971, after the demise of their Sixties band, **Half Nelson**. They were and remain a cult band despite breaking into the Top Ten now and then, in different countries, with different songs, in different decades. It's impossible to say they didn't influence the Eighties because in many ways, the Eighties just copied them. The combination of a disparate duo of a flouncy singer and a slightly bored/stoic-looking keyboard player upfront set the template for **Soft Cell, Yazoo, Pet Shop Boys, Blancmange** and many, many more. Such Eighties.

Their records are all the same and all different, (much like John Peel's assessment of **The Fall**). Except they were glam before glam, disco before disco, and electronic before electronic music was A Thing; and almost always all at the same time on the same tune. Their songs are witty, wordy, Wagnerian, and demented fun. All of them. Like sugar mice and champagne, you do need a sweet tooth and you can have too many quite easily, but oh my, they have some wonderful tunes. The one thing that none of their music sounds like is anything remotely American. Sparks sound French. Or Bavarian. Or English. But definitely and defiantly not Californian. Rock and Roll was not their thing. Oh, and like Kraftwerk, they are quite serious about their fun. Keyboard player Ron wore a Hitler moustache all through the Seventies. And the Eighties. That takes balls and persistence; qualities that Sparks possess in spades.

Forever promising and then failing to deliver huge success, they worked with every major record label in the Seventies and made records (separately) with the stellar likes of Todd Rundgren, Muff Winwood, Giorgio Moroder and Tony Visconti. There seemed to be no reason why each next record wouldn't be massive, but they never quite were. *This Town Ain't Big Enough For The Both Of Us*, produced by Winwood, was their biggest UK hit, peaking at #5 in 1974 (costing Elton John a few quid since he had bet Winwood that it would fail). My favourite single of theirs, *The #1 Song I Heaven (1979)*, was produced by Moroder and is as ludicrously skybound as the title implies and, while failing to replicate that chart success on Earth, was nonetheless a Top Twenty British hit. The album with Moroder, *Number 1 In Heaven*, also goes some way to explaining *Sulk* by **Associates**, of which, much more later.

Many years ago, I witnessed Sparks play a show to a superdrunk crowd at a genuinely decadent London showbiz party (whatever the received wisdom implies, these are surprisingly rare). Having drunk deep from the acid-spiked punch, cooked up in the snooker room by Primal Scream (who definitely have some Sparks albums in their collections), I became convinced that this song was, in fact, the pinnacle of all Pop music. Possibly the apex of all human achievement. I was perhaps taking the lyrics – and the punch – too seriously, but get me in the right mood and I may still argue this point. I believe it on some level to this day. It is pure fun and energy and colour and madness. Perfect pop's secret recipe.

Sparks continue to impress and make records. 2006's *Hello Young Lovers* was particularly wonderful and for a moment, it seemed as though there might be a career renaissance for them. Sadly, mannered Wagnerian Discopop is STILL not as popular as it should be. Heaven knows I'd love to see a stadium singing along to *Dick Around* from that record. "*All I do know is dick around, dick around, DICK AROUND*" go the massed choirs. As well they might, as well they might.

Another band who do not get enough credit for inventing what became Eighties Pop is **Blondie.** Their insouciant Punk Rock cool carried them through as they made the change to be the biggest, coolest, sexiest Pop band in the world for a few years at the end of the Seventies. They glowed white hot amid a supernova of magazine covers; dropping hit after hit, topping the charts, swapping styles, toying with them awhile and then tossing them away casually, like it was no big deal. And it IS no big deal.

It's tempting to argue that they were a Seventies band: New York, Punk Rock, leather jackets and skinny black jeans. And they were. But that run of singles from 1979 to 1981: *Heart Of Glass, Sunday Girl, Dreaming, Union City Blue, Call Me, Atomic, The Tide Is High, Rapture;* that refusal to be pigeonholed is just the definition of Eighties do-whatever-you-fancy Reinvention Pop. They skipped deftly through New Wave, Reggae, Rap, Disco, Rock, EuroPop and more and aced each one.

Let's not overlook that *The Best Of Blondie* came out in 1981 as the band were at the top of their game and it was a huge album. Huuuuge. Double Platinum on both sides of the "pond". There's a lag, isn't there, from when a record is released to when its impact is felt? Or for how long its impact is felt. Years, sometimes. As the Eighties were coalescing and feeling their way out of the Seventies' shadow, it seemed like everyone that I knew had a copy and it was top-to-bottom brilliance, each song bounced out of the speakers in its own unique way. There was little repetition of styles. After a certain musical austerity, through Punk, Post Punk and New Wave, this was fun music. Not light exactly but gleaming. A mini selection pack of cereal rather than porridge every day. The Best Of Blondie was a risk-free purchase and it did not date. Blondie were a beacon. They were not remotely a divisive band. How could they be? They were perfect and you wanted in. **Blondie** whipped up a perfect storm of hugely ambitious Pop, hard won critical acclaim and a colossal commercial payoff (albeit one that didn't find its way into the bands' pockets). They were proud to be Pop. There was no talk of selling out. They were just trying cool new things. Chris Stein told MOJO: *"We didn't expect the song [Heart Of Glass] to be that big (...) We weren't thinking about selling out, we were thinking about Kraftwerk and Eurodisco".*

Oh, and Debbie Harry was an amazing Pop Star. THE amazing pop star. She was ready for it. She'd been practising for years and it had been a long time coming. A Sixties Playboy bunny, she had been trying to find her way in New York for a long time, ever since being a backing singer on the 1968 debut album by forgotten folkies **The Wind In The Willows**.

It's confusing to remember that World War II was still going strong as she was born, when you are watching her owning the camera on any of the many 1980 TV performances of *Dreaming*. She was 35 (which is about 167 in Pop Years) and she turns each one into a masterclass in Pop, a masterclass in stardom, and a vision of the future.

Whatever the X Factor used to mean; it was this. She radiates. There is a Ready Brek glow around her. It was true love between her and the camera. Your dad loved her. Your big sister loved her. You loved her. I loved her. I met her years later, during the Britpop Wars, at one of her Jazz Passengers shows and she was sweetness and grace embodied; well-practiced at dealing with bumbling fools of men, and skilled at making them (OK, me) feel at ease. Forever, Debbie.

Blondie had come up, along with **Talking Heads** and **The Ramones**, in CBGB's arty Punk scene in the mid-Seventies, and, long before mainstream America caught on, they had a glistening run of hit singles around the world, starting with *X Offender,* previously known as *Sex Offender,* in 1976. These international hits brought them to Europe and the UK and exposed the band to all kinds of records that were not getting a lot of attention in the US.

So while they came to define New Wave's lean, house-trained take on Punk Rock, with clean, tight trousers, short Beatles-y hair and, of course, skinny ties, they were making ready to move ahead. Blondie were the ultimate Skinny Tie band and *Parallel Lines* was the ultimate Skinny Tie album, and sleeve. Those thin black parallel lines refer to the boys' trousers and ties and Debbie was the brilliant white light between them; at least I think that's what those white lines were.

Looking back, *Parallel Lines* seems like the New York Calling that precipitated the *London Calling* response from **The Clash**. Starting with a ringing phone, and Debbie Harry singing breathlessly, urgently *"I'm in the phonebox, It's the one across the hall"*...that is a call you were definitely going to take in 1978. Debbie was already the hottest girl in Pop and she was only just beginning to hit her stride on her march toward being *the* iconic Blonde Pin-Up, *the* iconic woman in pop. She channelled Marilyn through a street-smart New York girl and started a diminishing domino roll of inspiration that gave us Madonna, Lady Gaga, Britney, Shakira and Ke$ha, and whoever is next into the bleach.

Parallel Lines taps you on the shoulder, beckons you over and breathlessly knocks out twelve perfect songs in around forty minutes. *Hanging On The Telephone, One Way Or Another, Picture This, Sunday Girl, Heart Of Glass* are all meticulously perfect Pop songs. So far, so Seventies but something happened, both during recording and after the release of the album, their first produced by the pop hit machine that was Mike Chapman. Together with Nicky Chinn, their ChinniChap conveyor belt had written and produced hits for **Mud, The Sweet** and **Suzi Quatro** in the Seventies, and continued with **Altered Images, Pat Benetar, Tina Turner** and **Toni Basil** in the Eighties. Chapman was a logical choice for Blondie but clashed with the band over his perfectionist working methods and endless retakes in the studio. This was not the punk rock way. Proper Pop music, they found, is not easy to make.

Chapman turned them into superstars, but talking about his work with Blondie, in the *One Way Or Another* documentary, back when they were flush with money, drugs and celebrity, and assuredly not used to being criticised or bossed about, it seems they didn't quite end up lifelong friends. Chapman barely conceals his mixture of horror and disdain at the cocaine and heroin use that made the sessions a unique chore for him. The studio is a workplace and a very, very expensively hired one at that. The producer views it as his turf, naturally, and the band view it as their playground, where the bar never shuts and the slow shifts from day to night and back again are concealed in windowless rooms, evened out under the calming low lights and lamps. It is a place where the party need never stop and, frustratingly, very often only one member of the group (at most) is doing anything at any given point. There is a lot of downtime for each person. And downtime leads to idleness, idleness leads to boredom and boredom knows a really cool shortcut to the dark side. Especially when the rhythm section realises that the producer has no real need for them and the song will sound better with synthetic bass and drums. Equally, it is incredibly frustrating for everyone "behind the desk" when cosily sedated musicians can't keep it together, or play in time, or indeed remain sufficiently conscious when required and so the work then takes twice as long as it might.

In the end, of course, it worked out enormously well for all concerned and **Blondie** picked up their first Platinum album in the USA, where they had yet to have a hit, despite racking up #1 singles across Europe and a string of Top Ten hits in the UK. *Plastic Letters*, their previous album, had gone Platinum in the UK but barely scraped the Top Seventy Five at home. *Heart Of Glass* marks the turning point for Blondie. The Disco craze was at its peak in 1978 and Blondie were regulars at Disco's Mecca, Studio 54 in New York. However their output prior to *Heart Of Glass*, follows Ye Olde Punk Rock rules, more or less, which means it all sounds like a band in a room, playing their instruments. "Cheating" in the studio was very much frowned upon and most bands, who had proved their worth by cutting it live and learning their chops, wanted to proudly showboat their skills on their records.

Chapman thought differently and pulled apart a not overly promising demo, entitled *Once I Had Love* and turned it into a Disco masterpiece, a Pop masterpiece and one of the most recognisable songs in the world. But it's not just Disco, because most Disco records of that period were still recorded live by elastic-fingered Soul and Funk session players and were dripping in authentic sweat, flares and 'fros. *Heart Of Glass* sounded clean and synthetic and urgent and European and very future indeed. It also sounded white. Funk and soul had been the province of black musicians on the whole but disco had crossed over to whitebread America, and now the swing, the human element and the fancy basslines were being replaced with a metronomic groove that was much easier, for those less used to dancing, to click with. If your dancing involved hopping from toe to toe, then this was a perfect tune for you.

Giorgio Moroder (with whom Blondie would shortly work on *Call Me*) is very much in evidence in the sequenced (meticulously, by hand) electronic synthesiser throb running all the way through the song and, although *Parallel Lines* does not have an eyebrow or a hi-hat out of place anywhere, *Heart Of Glass*' dazzling plastic symmetry is a quantum leap, light years from their ragged, Punk Rock bar band roots. That futuristic, untouched-by-musicians, synthetic feel is very much the key component behind so many of the Eighties' genres and sub-genres.

It was the age of the two-fingered keyboardist on Top Of The Pops, frozen in a suitably decadent pose, motionless from the knuckles upward except for an involuntary flounce of the neck to waft the generous fringe away in the direction of your close-up shot. Posing, rather than performing, frozen proudly (and probably nervously) like Showroom Dummies. Human toiling could finally take a backseat and it was certainly not necessary for every (or any) member of the band to be "doing something" on every track anymore. Bands like The Human League had members whose jobs concerned the visuals rather than anything musical. Nor was it necessary to be a musician, a "performer" to be in a band. Boffins grew their fringes, practised combining sitting still and scowling and became pop stars.

Going disco was still very far from being acceptable behaviour in the Seventies in many circles; despite, and in some cases as a result of, David Bowie's efforts. The word faggot or poof was never far from being mentioned when talking about Bowie in a large group. *Disco Sucks* was the bumper sticker of choice among aficionados of real music (ie rock music), despite the passing of watersheds like the none-more-real **Rolling Stones** getting their hotpants on and circling the dancefloor for the peerless *Miss You* in 1978. Did you ever hear the eleven and a bit minute outtake version of *Miss You?* It's wonderful. Be happy and get your glittery hot pants over to Youtube right away and make yourself a cup of tea. Jagger and Richards improvise luxuriantly over the top and that liquid groove shows no signs of getting tired. Just magical.

In Punk Rock circles, going Disco was an even more heinous crime. Not so much for the sins against Playing Your Instruments, of course, but for the crime of Being Trivial and, one suspects, there was a sizable element of a condescendingly racist attitude toward black music, which was seen as vacuous, unimportant and appallingly fun by many uptight muso wankers.

Imagination, invention and re-invention were the three most appealing qualities that the best Eighties Pop bands had. They had to dream something new, then invent and perfect it, and then, having mastered it, discard it and try something else. Over and over.

That was the standard and it was set by Him. You are going to notice a lot of David Bowie love in this book. It's my first attempt at a book and I was sorely tempted to write one about David. He is my idol, my first and constant source of inspiration. However even I have not read all my David Bowie books and I don't feel the need to add to that epidemic of deforestation.

However I will say this: His run of albums in the Seventies defined the decade, inspired the decade and then, even more impressively, defined and inspired the one that followed. It remains untouched as a sequence of Pop or Rock records and will likely continue to be so. Bowie's is the single greatest, most consistent, yet varied, body of artwork of the Twentieth Century; running neck and neck with Picasso. Yep.

Is it too much to say that Bowie, Kraftwerk, Neu, Moroder, Sparks and Blondie invented the future of music? I don't think so. The changes that happened in music between 1980 and 1982 were total. Bands before and after that period are like chalk and starfish*. **[I've never* *understood that expression: chalk and cheese. It must predate feta settling in the UK].* It did not happen overnight, nor did it stop old fashioned bands existing. Lots of people like the hoary old rock clichés done with zero style and innovation; hence the, um, suboptimally unique majesty of **Kings Of Leon**.

Musicians were no longer limited by subtle variations and innovations in fretboard abilities. There was now a huge alternate musical universe that didn't exist and couldn't have existed before 1980, unfettered and powered solely by imagination, that didn't need any formal musical training at all. The possibilities were infinite and there was really no excuse to be boring ever again.

Blondie
HEART OF GLASS
RIFLE RANGE
HEART OF GLASS (Extended Version)
HEART OF GLASS (Instrumental)

Blondie
Sunday Girl
I Know But I Dont Know

Blondie
DREAMING

Blondie
ATOMIC

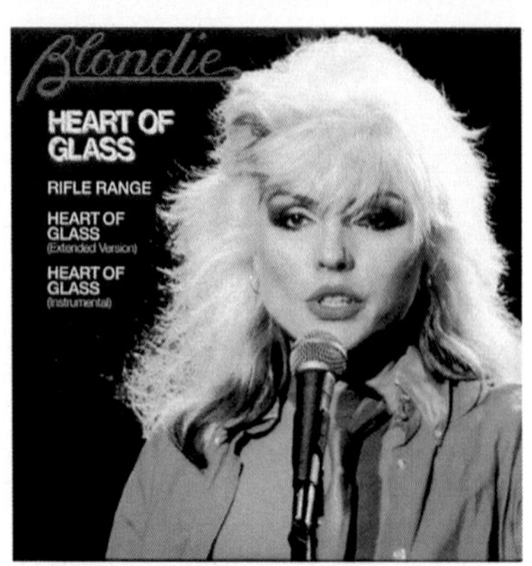

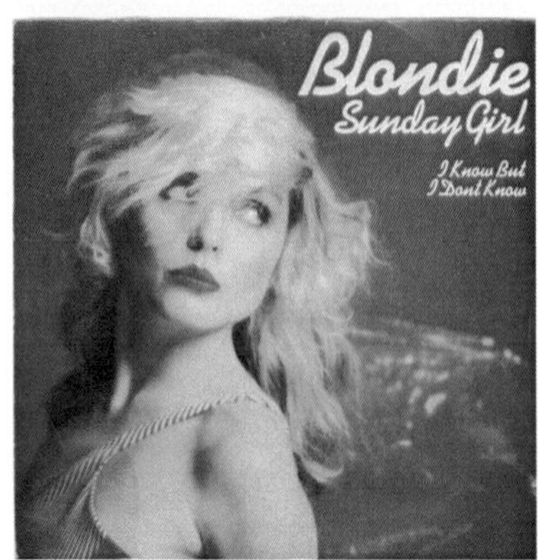

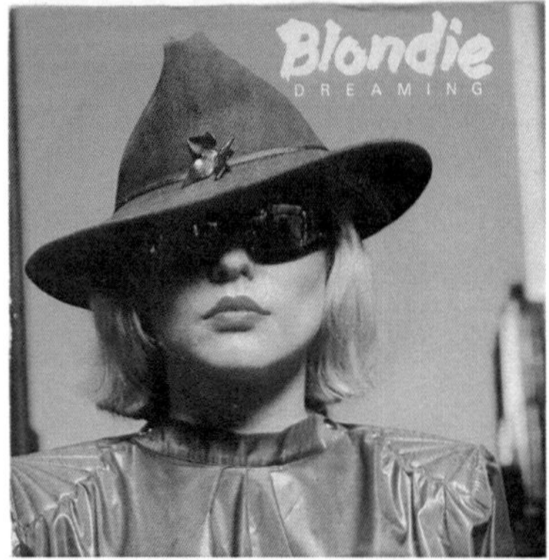

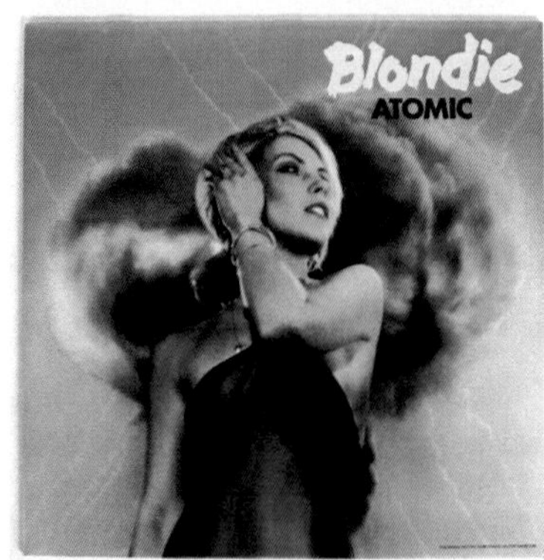

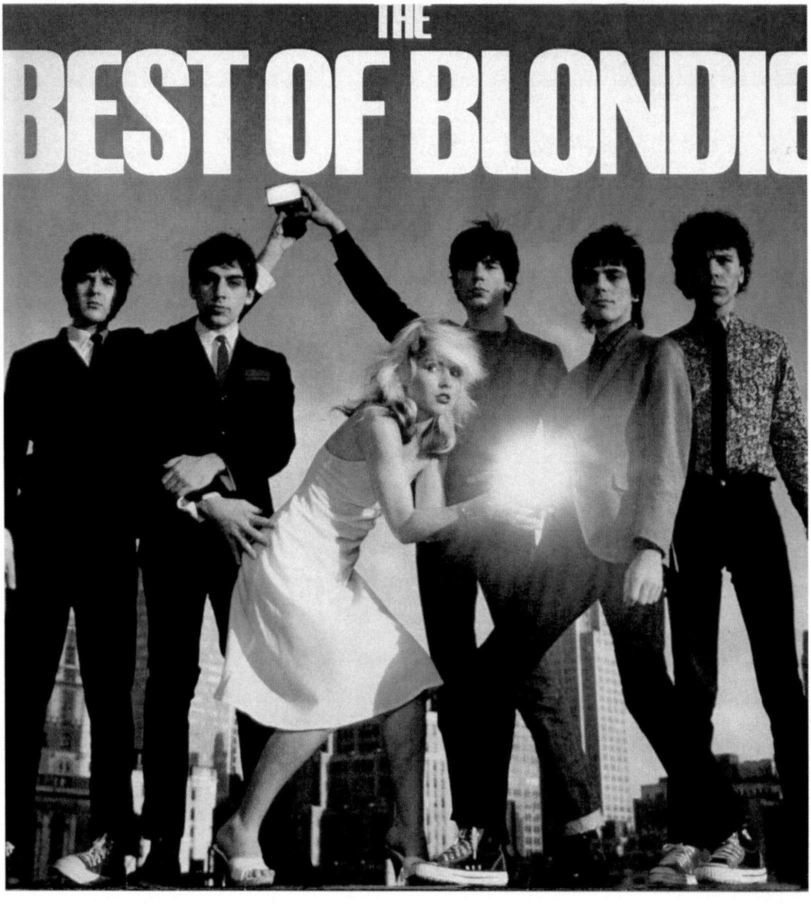
THE
BEST OF BLONDIE

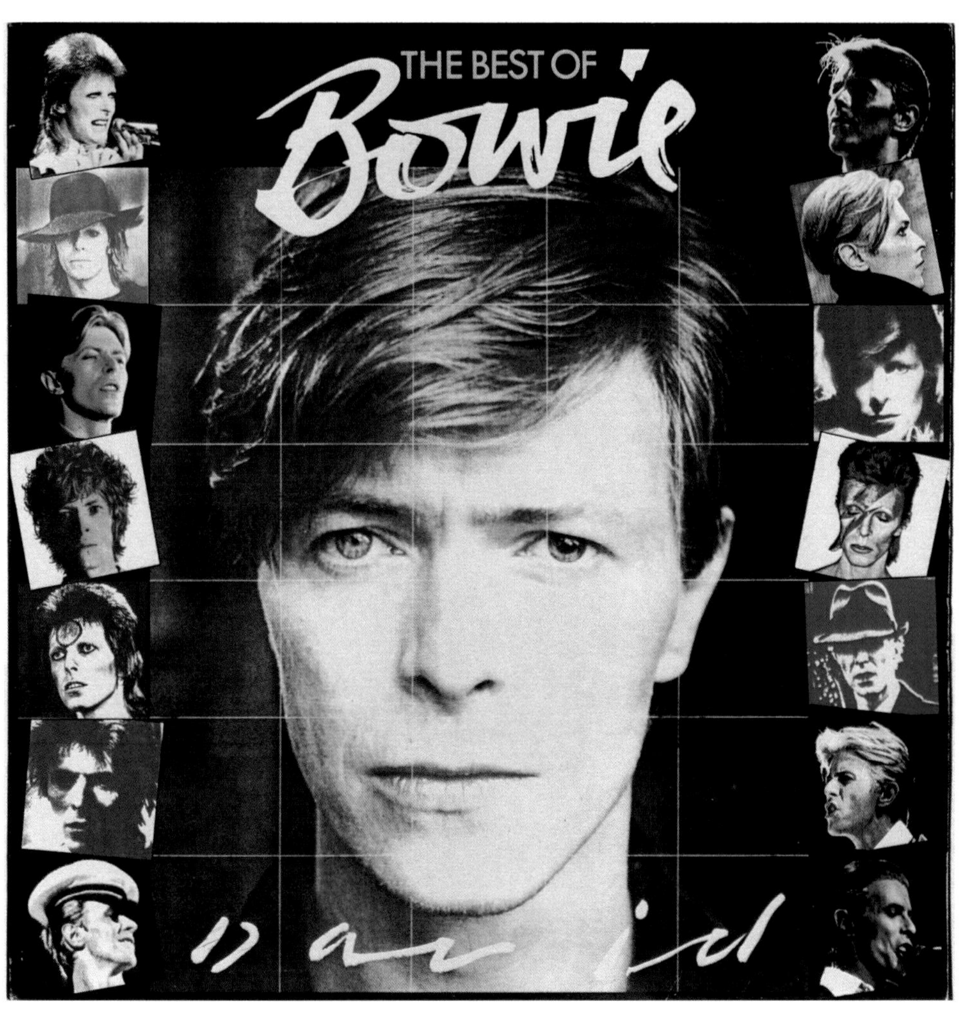

This was my gateway drug.

My first Bowie record.

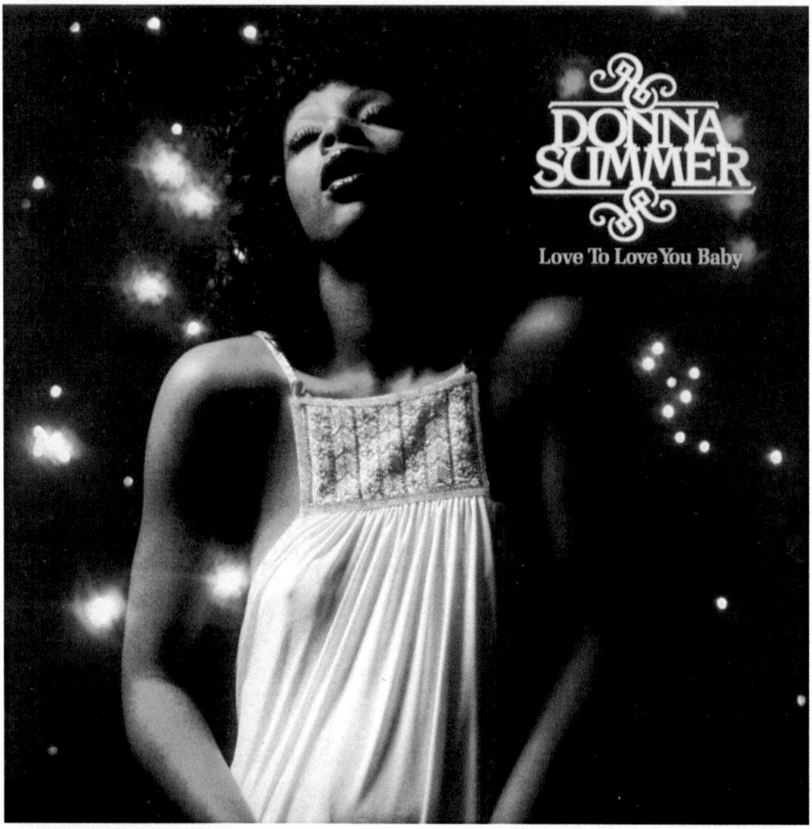
DONNA
SUMMER
Love To Love You Baby

DONNA SUMMER
I Feel Love
Casablanca
CA 501
Distribuzione DURIUM S. p. A. - Milano

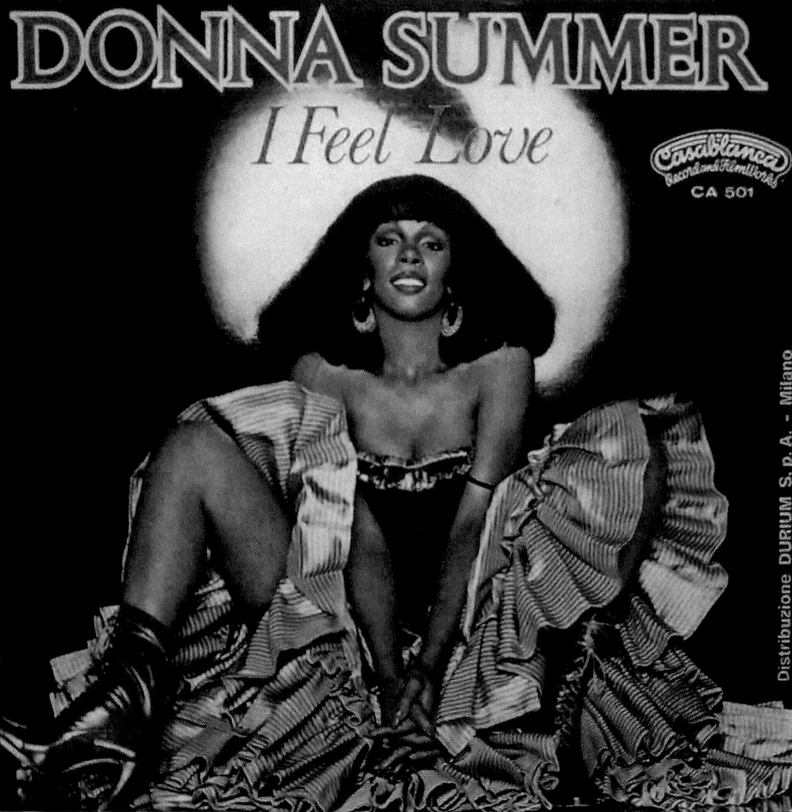

KRAFTWERK AUTOBAHN

KRAFTWERK
RADIO-ACTIVITY

KRAFTWERK
TRANS-EUROPE EXPRESS

KRAFTWERK
MAN·MACHINE

Dream machine.

A wild nobility.

This annoyed many Specials fans. Silly old them.

02 DAWNING OF A NEW ERA

1979-1980: After the grey Seventies, ch-ch-changes are afoot. English eccentrics start to reach for the fun, the colour and the glamour.

THE JAM, THE SPECIALS, ADAM AND THE ANTS

Decades are funny, wriggly things and they don't sit as neatly on the calendar as they ought to. In those pre-internet days, culture took its sweet time filtering down and out from London, Manchester and Glasgow; out to the market towns and especially to South Wales, where I lived. Like staring up at the distant stars, exciting trends had long since burned out by the time I got to hear about them.

Herds of Hippies, their heads stuck in the Sixties, were still very thick on the ground in 1973. The Seventies only really got started in about 1972 and its foolishly luxuriant sideburns were still going strong in 1981; as were its flapping flares. It seems that the visual shorthand for "Seventies" these days is a rainbow hued, be-afro'd disco dude in flares. This is just a tiny bit misleading for the world outside LA. Californian flares might have been sun-drenched and enticingly underwear-free but Welsh flares had three inches of gritty puddle at the bottom and smelled of wet dog. "Like Trouser, like brain", said Comrade **Joe Strummer.** Yep. Britain in the Seventies was so unsexy. What a swindle it was.

Alas, I remember the Seventies: it was cold and dark and strike-infested. And grey. The skies were grey, the roads and houses were grey. My school was smothered in one of those paints that local authorities buy by the lakeful that is almost but not quite a colour and soon fades to grey. There was a lack of colour all around. There were no bright ads on buses; no colour in newspapers. No colour in magazines past the front cover. Things were more solid and workmanlike, built to last, not dressed to impress. High street shop fronts were handpainted wood, announcing family firms, rather than today's endless backlit plastic Chicken Cottage signs that are visible from space. It still looked like the Fifties in Wales and fun was still being very carefully rationed.

Bands almost never played there, not that I was old enough to see them anyway, and nothing ever changed the shape of the cultural landscape ever. Except 2-Tone; a bit. That was big in South Wales but, being overwhelmingly white and quietly, um, insular, it didn't have the same "tearing down the barriers" reverberations, as were felt in the Midlands and London, so much as provide a suitable vehicle for cheerful, social aggression. It also briefly allowed being a skinhead to be a bit less threatening and more socially acceptable, although the local Skins were not like the enlightened, sardonic Terry Hall from **The Specials** or those nice boys from **Madness.** Not even a bit. But we were dancing and singing along to Ska and Reggae, so that was a bit different. Well, it was a LOT different, actually. It might have been rebooted from the Sixties but we had not heard those spiky, bouncing riddims before and they were FUN. A much needed tonic for the troops. The 2-Tone records were a bubbling hot mix of serious message and irresistible party anthem and they got people dancing, including a lot of people not used to doing so. Men. Yes, doing the stiff-limbed Madness dance was something we could all achieve. It was grim out there alright but that doesn't mean we can't have some fun of our own – thought the nation. Look how grim it was...

Very. As every teenager outside the Royal Family discovers, it's hard to connect with the world beyond home, school and your hometown. Cardiff seemed especially isolated, so God only knows what those tiny Towns Without Woolworths must have been like. The British riots of 1981 had seemed strangely exciting and empowering, showing that getting angry and sticking your neck out could get you "heard" (and, as it ultimately turned out, steamrollered) by the government. As a politically engaged teenager, and veteran of two whole CND protests, I had some of that feeling, although I had, of course, not joined in the riots. I am not even sure the riots made it to Wales. The free love of the Sixties and the groovy times of the Seventies and had not affected South Wales one jot. It still looked very post-war for the most part; and not any war in particular, either.

Except, oddly enough, Port Talbot, with its extensive beachfront refineries and chemical plants. At night, lashed with rain (and it never ever stops raining in Port Talbot), its dozens of huge steel towers with fire-breathing valves, looked staggeringly futuristic, and very LA 2019, just like we'd soon see in *Blade Runner*.

And, oh my, Seventies Pop music was very boring indeed, for the most part. Dull singer-songwriters, polite soul and bland cocktail cover versions sung by women in billowing white dresses. Of course, there had been fertile fiefdoms like Glam, Disco and Punk, but overall, the singles charts had become dull, family-friendly and very tame indeed. Punk had not changed anything very much in the world at large. The same dinosaurs still ruled the earth and all the teenagers had not been convinced to put safety pins through their cheeks en masse, although, being teenagers, they were still pretty vacant. The charts still looked much the same after Punk had ripped its last pair of trousers but the idea of Punk had lit a spark and begun to reignite the passion for being a teenager, for making noise and wrong-footing old people. After Punk, there seemed to be a surge in teenagers wanting to be different. Not necessarily to be Punks, but to be *seen* as different to their parents; to liking different music and films and clothes, re-establishing that all-important generation gap that allows culture to leapfrog forward.

If you need to wonder why that should be, ponder for a minute the many, many Seventies hits of **Brotherhood Of Man**. If you are unfamiliar with their Eurovision-slaying oeuvre, they sounded like what they look like in that picture below. Only much worse. They had skipped into view from a place without shame. Winning Eurovision actually granted you a career in those days. Nowadays it's all a bit of a laugh and the stupidest act wins...nothing. In the Seventies, winners were rewarded with a market for album after album of their soggy marshmallow drivel for years. Here's a quote from dear old mother Thatcher, being interviewed by the genius that was Tom Hibbert, formerly of Smash Hits, but this appeared in Q: *"Brotherhood Of Man? Lovely! Fantastic young group, really professional..."* Well yes, quite. If that was what a pop star looked like on the Telly and you were a young upstart about to form a band, you would be compelled to rebel, like your soul depended on it; which of course it did.

My beloved Post Punk and New Wave, jointly responsible for some of the most groundbreaking and difficult records ever created, often embodied this functional Seventies greydom as some sort of subversive suburban camouflage and were, for the most part, very much anti-starry in their presentation. They only rarely troubled the charts and when they did, it was usually a case of a single mention on Top Of The Pops' Chart Rundown: **Magazine** in at 37, and straight out again the next week. Simon Reynolds has written some truly excellent books detailing this era already. He has had the last word and I cannot recommend them highly enough. I am going to focus on Pop music and the Top Forty, which was on fire for a time at the start of the Eighties. There was a flood of ballsy English eccentrics, looking down from the Top Ten. Cool underground bands that had made successful bids for the mainstream, amazing new groups that hadn't existed a few months previously and salty old punks, resprayed and reinvigorated by the new sounds and technology.

I didn't buy music magazines in the late Seventies, except maybe **Look-In**, which was more for the *Sapphire & Steel, Six Million Dollar Man* and *Battlestar Galactica* cartoon strips. There were few videos, hardly any music on TV and the cooler bands' photos were rarely on their records singles' sleeves. So, for the most part, I had no idea what the bands looked like or got up to. The first time ever I saw Elvis Costello's face was on a badge.

For the most part, you had to imagine what the people who made all this strangely compelling new music could be like. Oh my, but they sounded fascinating and alien on night time Radio One, where your synapses sprayed arcs of colour across your mind's eye.

As it turned out, in real life, the bands were standard humans, often ascetically purged of Pop's rightful, righteous glamour and, in fairness, this suited the music, which often felt pleasingly DIY; fashioned in utilitarian chunks from bits of old radios, thirdhand instruments and modified machinery, all held together with rubber bands. As such, it was kept safely underground, away from the general public, who didn't listen to Richard Skinner or John Peel's radio shows. It might have been a tiny subset of the population but Peel would often pull in 500,000 listeners a night. His show was an antidote to boredom and an inspiration to all. It was also very, very funny. I think Peel may have taught me sarcasm. He often said that his show had the lowest average age of listener and that was why he was allowed to continue so long. Lots of teenagers; too young for pubs, too early for bed and too shy to go out getting into trouble; all huddled round a speaker or listening on headphones in bed.

Veterans of several Peel Sessions but long since gone overground, the biggest People's Band in 1980 were **The Jam**. The fucking Jam were gods. They were tough and danceable; exciting like Christmas, convincing as hell and dressed like the coolest things you'd ever seen. They delivered lean, anthemic choruses the size of tower blocks about how unrelentingly tough life was out there. Yay. These were the good times. The other thing **The Jam** were, in spades, was serious. As a heart attack. Po-faced even. Sharp, black and white suits; no messing around. Strictly business. So, if you found Pop music to be the precinct of teenage girls, and there had been much evidence to support this, then The Jam were *your* band.

The day in March 1980 that *Going Underground* entered the charts at #1 was a cause for national celebration. Records just didn't debut at the top in those days; they climbed, fell, rose, got on TOTP and soared again, all over a period of many weeks. It might take a single seven weeks to dent the Top Ten. Entering at #1 was pretty much unheard of. The day, a few weeks later, when Polydor re-released all their previous singles to capitalise on this national **Jam**-gasm and they all charted was another milestone. Seven cool songs in the Top Forty at the same time was enough to celebrate in itself but seven new entries from The Jam alone in the Top 40 caused amazingly exciting scenes. We crowded round inefficient static-riddled transistor radios in the playground to hear the Top 40 on Tuesday lunchtime, cheering through the crackles and static. It was like your team winning the FA Cup, only much more so, because it seemed like it was everyone's team. I don't know that there was another band that united the whole country like that until Oasis. The whole business of being in the Jam was getting to Weller though, and the stoic king was about ready to inject colour and fun into his music.

Angry, tense and political, *A Town Called Malice* was another very Jam song and duly went straight in at #1 in the charts. It was a double A-Side and the flipside caused ripples among the Jam fanbase. *Precious* is a funk song. No doubt about it. It's not Punky or Mod at all. The sixties Mods were very much into Ska, Soul and R'n'B, but the 1978 Mod Revival was whiter, more conservative and more allied to Punk. The Jam were pretty shouty when they started up, often lumped with the Punks, not least by **Bob Marley**, in his song, *Punky Reggae Party,* looking forward to seeing *"The Jam, the Damned, The Clash"*. Worse still, *Precious* was also just a straight ahead love song. Weller had not got time for this, surely? He had more important issues to attend to, surely? Man's work. A broken country was more important than a broken heart. Was Weller abandoning the fight?

Well, The Jam were massive now and Weller could do as he damn well pleased. They performed both songs on a very memorable Top Of The Pops; the first band since the Beatles to do so. Their next single was a soul ballad and the band's finale was an EP with covers of Curtis Mayfield, TheChi-Lites and Edwin Starr. Soul music was a frivolity and regarded with extreme suspicion by many of the Jam's hardliners. To them, Weller stood for something and, it being a Mod thing, it was all quite delineated and easy to follow. There were rules and there were a great many things that lay outside those rules which must not be dabbled with. Things like this being quite high on that list...

They were in for a massive shock after that though. Not least with this...

Having broken up the band, Weller relaunched almost immediately as **The Style Council,** initially with songs the other two in the band had not been comfortable with, because *"they didn't sound like The Jam"*. This was not a Mod band at all. Beatniks maybe, fops definitely. This was not real man's music and there was an outcry. Weller brought his love of soul, jazz and more into the mix and **The Style Council** were a freeform and really rather adventurous band, even going as far as making an Acid House album some years later.

I'll admit that I found it all a bit confusing too but I have always loved being confused and stretched by music. It's important to regularly tap into your childlike sense of wonder, after all. I sort of lost faith in Weller after **The Style Council,** when he started his conversion to becoming **Steve Winwood** in the Nineties, inventing Britrock, Britpop's chubbier, mouth-breathing older brother, along the way. It was a brave move breaking up the Jam and the further Weller pushed The Style Council, the more it seemed quite suicidal, and the more I respected him for it. Sales declined inevitably, the final album remained unreleased by Polydor and Weller was dropped.

Liking The Jam and The Clash prepared us for 2-Tone, the first craze I felt swept up in and, like a first love, it was very exciting, uncharted territory and came with a welcome frisson of danger and a good chance of getting hurt. The look was not hard to approximate: the hair as short as possible, an ironed school shirt and skinny black tie, in cotton or leather, ideally emblazoned with Walt Jabsco, the cat from the 2-Tone logo or the girl from the Beat's logo, or the democratic **Madness** M-man. In 1980, these ties were EVERYWHERE.

Trousers would ideally be Sta-prest, hems should be high to show off pristine white socks, just like Walt's. Shoes should be shiny. School shoes would do at a push, but ideally you wanted Doctor Marten Eight-hole boots, if loafers were unavailable or if, as in my case, you thought/think them a bit twatty. Topped off with a black Harrington or a woollen Crombie overcoat with a two-tone satin lining. Oh and monochrome badges. My word, 2-Tone and Ska gave good badge.

2-Tone was conceived and aesthetically overseen by **The Specials**' Jerry Dammers, and launched from Coventry. They released records by **Madness, Specials, The Beat, The Selecter,** ska veteran **Rico,** and later, the punk funk of **The Higsons).** The bands featured black and white members on an even footing, which was still pretty unusual. They recycled Sixties Ska, injecting its tight-or-nowhere riddims with punk's ragged energy and witty, direct socio-political lyrics that pulled no punches in stories about unfortunate characters that were half familiar and wholly believable.

Being a teenage craze, it didn't last forever but, for two years or so, it felt like a new **Motown**, with its own dances, clothes, slang, films, posters and records. And politics. It was a new kind of unifying folk music, seemingly spontaneous and not led by fashion or London. It was, on paper, extremely unfashionable music for the time but succeeded so swiftly and convincingly on the back of the song-writing of these amazing characters, all in their early twenties. The stories were easy to grasp and resonated with the audience, even if the point only lodged after you'd been singing them for a while. Or, y'know, not at all.

The first two albums each by **Madness, Specials** and **The Beat** were fixtures in the charts and in the windows of record shops non-stop for two years. The fact that the music was so digestibly relevant to kids in Britain, stacked with colossal choruses and bursting with angry energy, allowed it to sweep a nation, who knew almost nothing about Desmond Dekker or any of the original, more laidback, Sixties Ska bands. 1979 remains the only time I have ever had a Number Two haircut. It makes your head cold and people regard you a little more warily. Formative experiences indeed.

Elvis Costello produced the debut **Specials** album and set out to capture the ragged energy of their live show. He succeeded brilliantly and the album is crackling with Punk bile set to Ska rhythms and huge tunes; bum notes and all, the band singing over each other. It is all kinds of exciting – an angry party album, lashing out at the world, taking on targets large and small, from where they live (*Concrete Jungle*), the government (all of it, really) to girls who have slipped somewhat in the bands' estimation (*Little Bitch, Too Much Too Young*). I hadn't noticed that so many of the songs were covers until quite recently. They all fit so perfectly with bands' own songs that it doesn't really matter.

Anyway, after the brief, intense, imperial phase of **The Specials**, they went out with a bang and a shudder. Dammers had already been rocking the ska boat, (and cash cow) musically with the second album, the completely fantastic *More Specials*, much to some of the band's annoyance, by introducing Bossa Nova, Jazz, Muzak, and 60s Soundtracky burbles to the pot. This shuffling off of shackles, refusing to stand still and challenging the expectations was very much a theme throughout the early Eighties; as was breaking up a band at their peak, which **Weller, David Sylvian** and others also did, in order to break the mould and flex those innovation muscles. This was not like **Oasis** cleaving to make two more slightly rubbish Oases. Massive unpredictable right turns were all the rage. Bands weren't in it for careers. Careers were for old people. They were young and bored; making music for fun and to see if it could be done. And, having succeeded, they moved on. All this reinvention was invigorating Pop music. Kids were buying singles again and these records were selling in huge quantities. In 1979, a **Specials** Live EP had gone to #1.

Aside from being a particularly brilliant, and brilliantly timed, song, that absolutely captured the hearts and minds of a nation, gripped with riots and unemployment; **The Specials'** finale, *Ghost Town,* was an innovative blend of Crooning, Reggae, Music Hall, 60s Soundtracks and Brass, with hysterical backing vocals and fiddly chords; all twisted into a lopsidedly stumbling arrangement. Dammers has said, *"The overall sense I wanted to convey was impending doom".* Job done, Jerry. Atypically, all three of the weekly music papers made it Single Of The Year and it was #1 for three weeks in June. Dammers again, *"I can only write about things that make me angry".* It sounded totally unique and totally on point with how Britain FELT in 1981, even to my thirteen year old mind. *All the clubs,* as you'll have heard, were *being closed down*. In ghost towns, everyone was going to have to make their own fun, thanks to Thatcher making everyone poor and angry and sad.

After the majesty of *Ghost Town,* and a bust up with the main songwriter, Dammers, Terry broke up the band taking Lynval Golding and Neville Staples to form **Fun Boy Three**. For my money, The Specials had taken a left turn on their second album and the Fun Boy Three's debut was a continuation of the path marked out by Ghost Town, heading off into a cartoonish take on Dr John and Tom Waits territory. The three refugees wasted no time however, shaking off the shackles that remained, including Dammers' relentless, angry polemic and embraced fun, adventure and wearing silly hats right away.

Fun Boy Three still had plenty of that voodoo to their sound but this took a back seat to playfulness and increased band democracy, and thus a decrease in intra-band tensions. The writing credits for Fun Boy Three are spread equally with Hall, Lynval Golding and Neville Staples. The Specials reputation for seriousness and Hall's growing reputation for being morose (he was later diagnosed as bipolar) was probably getting a bit tiresome for these three men. Never had a group's purpose been more clearly set out with their name than **Fun Boy Three**. Witness the band virtually smiling on this front cover.

Their debut single *The Lunatics Have Taken Over The Asylum* is another really weird song. It starts with a few pips from a phone hang up, signalling a break from the Specials (to me, anyway). **Dr John**'s New Orleans records are about the closest antecedent to the noises that follow but even that is not too helpful. Bone-clattering tribal drums, crickets and chanting makes up the backing track. The song on the top is a fitting follow up to *Ghost Town* and covers the same disgust with those in charge of the country. It can also be read that the trio are the lunatics in charge of the band now. Clever.

The new band were meeting furrowed brows from the critics and fans alike over such issues as Terry's unusual palm tree hairstyle, not sounding like **The Specials** anymore and the new band's dabbling with Fun. And smiling. *Lunatics* stalled at Number Twenty, which was quite the drop-off after *Ghost Town's* reign of weary terror at Number One.

Terry is often depicted as miserable, and I am sure he is a bit but he is also bloody-minded and faced with such a lack of faith from the faithful, it must have been just too tempting not to go further away from expectation. **Fun Boy Three** teamed up with **Bananarama** for the next two singles *(It Ain't What You Do (It's The Way That You Do it)* and *Really Saying Something*). Both were completely brilliant and massively FUN Top Five Hits. Terry, Lynval and Neville had gone Pop. This might equal, in today's money, Thom Yorke and Ed O'Brien departing **Radiohead,** circa *OK Computer* to have hits with **Sugababes**, except Terry was still only 22 with a hugely successful band and People's Hero status behind him. Regarded as sacrilegious by many, it was in fact showing how absolutely on the money they were. Going fully Pop was the coming thing in 1981. It took people a while to catch on but the smart ones moved quickly and very happily.

Madness had obviously wanted to be a Pop band right away. They had started at the same time as The Specials (and on 2-Tone) and had almost immediately included Crooning, Reggae, Music Hall, 60s Soundtracks and Brass into their Ska music. And humour. And the kitchen sink. Not saddled with the granite-faced image of The Specials, they were English eccentrics and proud to be labelled Nutty from the outset. The songs covered the same topics as the Specials but in a more cheerful and fun way. Echoing the straight-hair/curly-hair grass-is-greener envy that keeps Boots in business, Madness craved to be taken seriously after a few years of coathanger smiles on children's TV, whereas members of The Specials, burdened with tombstone tendencies, had craved Madness' fun and freedom, which wishes were shortly to be granted. **Madness**' popularity was instant and huge. Their first single, *The Prince*, was a Top 20 Hit, as were the singles and albums followed in quick succession and without pause for about four years.

The Beat were the smallest of the Big Three Ska bands and the ones that devoted more time to playing in America, which paid off handsomely for them, where they are regarded as perhaps the biggest of the crop. They weren't as smiley as Madness, or as dour as the Specials, although they were perhaps more politically focussed than both. Their irresistible singles were always aimed at the feet as well as the mind, calling for the Prime Minister's dismissal on *Stand Down Margaret,* a double A-side with *Best Friend* and a Top Thirty hit. It was a pretty popular sentiment and sure to meet with approval and yet no-one else of their stature thought to do it. I don't recall the last time I heard such clear dissent in the charts, except for Thatcher's memorial, *Ding Dong The Witch Is Dead*, hitting #2 in 2013, which showed the country's long memories, when it comes to That Woman. They too split up shortly after 2-Tone faded, and David Steele and Andy Cox had regrouped with the polished Pop of **Fine Young Cannibals** by 1984.

I finally saw them play at Glastonbury in 2006-ish and even though some members had, mind bogglingly, been replaced by their own children (hello Rankin Junior), they were utterly fantastic and, while not a big draw at first, had pulled an absolutely colossal crowd by the end, purely on the merit of that string of perfect pop singles that they hit big with from 1979 and 1983. You can't hear *Best Friend, Mirror In The Bathroom, Hands Off…She's Mine* and *Too Nice To Talk To* without having a little dance. Particularly on a sunny afternoon, as you are pulled gently through a wormhole of reverie, on a chemical cushion. It is without doubt one of the best festival performances I've ever witnessed and one with no need for props or big screens or lights or anything but those rhythms.

Well after the peak of 2-Tone, most of the kids still wore black and white. We had to. School Uniform was almost fashionable for a minute there and we didn't want to let that go. In about 1981, I went on a school trip to Paris. Fifteen billion hours on an airless coach, there and back in a day; leavened by a non-uniform policy and, being foreign soil, a taste of the unknown and exotic. It was mine and many others' first time abroad. ALL of the boys wore black Harrington jackets, Sta-prest trousers in black or, for fashion reasons I (choose to) forget, burgundy, and, for the most part, loafers. We had never looked so homogenous. The teachers did not stop laughing at our hopelessly rubbish efforts at freedom of expression.

The unshowy, almost practical monochromatic 2-Tone look echoed Punk's DIY photocopied sleeves and art. It was cheap and readily achievable but still the charts were in need of colour.

Adam And The Ants' look on 1979's **Banshees**-esque *Dirk Wears White Sox* era was all black biker jackets and Post Punk scowls, with a hint of Westwood and McLaren's SEX shop S&M. S&M was the stuffy, boarding-school educated section of British society's guilty secret, kept chained up behind closed doors. The tabloid newspapers loved nothing more than catching some prim, outwardly asexual MP and Miss Whiplash having an afternoon spanking session before catching the 5.15 to Surrey. It speaks of the colour and excitement lurking beneath the placid surface. Adam wanted to tap into that and bring it out into the light. He looked cool as hell but, after Punk's outrage, it was not exactly an original idea and the Ants were still an underground concern.

Adam needed to overhaul the music, the look, the songs and start taking care of business himself. In March 1980, his independent label *Do It* released a new, feistier version of *Car Trouble*, from *Dirk*, with Culture Club's Jon Moss on drums. It went to #1 in the Indie Charts and spurred Adam on to form a new Ants. The old ones had been scandalously swiped by his "friend", Malcolm McLaren, to back up Annabella Lwin in **Bow Wow Wow,** after Adam had paid him a £1000 as a management consultant fee to get tips on breaking the Ants. Malcolm certainly broke them. What a swindler.

Bow Wow Wow also briefly featured Boy George on vocal duties alongside Annabella, in an attempt, by McLaren, to make her share the attention and to reign in her stroppy teenage diva demands. It all worked out for Malcolm and the very Ants-y, or was it vice versa, percussive hits like *Go Wild In The Country* and *I Want Candy* went on to be ballsy and colourful additions to 1981's charts. Meanwhile in early 1980, the public at large was still very much unaware of Adam's existence.

Adam is another classic English eccentric; theatrical, expressive and undaunted by failure. Later that year, after learning a lot from Malcolm's words and, more particularly, his actions, Adam exploded out of the dressing up box and into the country's living rooms, bursting with intent. He looked incredible; lean, mean, colourful and sexy. His clothes looked like a mixture of Jimi Hendrix, Siouxsie Sioux and Keith Richards that demanded attention. His appearance empowered Adam and yet, in truth, it was his eyes that demanded your attention and they promised that the music was going to be good. You HAD to hear it after seeing those pictures. He stood out a mile in the summer of 1980 – a photoshoot waiting to happen. In truth, Adam stands out a mile even now. *Kings Of The Wild Frontier* was a fully committed look. All in, and damn the consequences. After years of black and white and grey, it was as though British Pop music had burst into colour. Lots of colours.

Half of the population (mainly girls) thought he was about as gorgeous and daring a man as had ever been seen before, and the other half (mainly boys) thinking he was definitely "a poofter" and quite possibly a dangerous lunatic. No-one had seen anything like Adam before and, damn, that was an eye-catching look. It was enormous fun to try and copy but virtually impossible to carry off successfully. Of course, it was. How could you hope to copy Adam? You weren't supposed to. He was the star and you were the audience. These were stage clothes, not an outfit to wear to the shops. Glamour was back.

It was baffling to see him leap from shady S&M-obsessed ex-Punk also-ran to being The Star of the Royal Variety Performance, chit-chatting with the Queen, in a little over a year. **Adam And The Ants** had, by that point dominated the singles charts for about eighteen months. This was all achieved through sheer force of will. Adam had decided to step out of the shadows and make a break for the mainstream and he knew how it was going to work. The look and the sound were mapped out as clearly as his business plan. As well as taking charge of the music, he designed the record sleeves, the costumes and directed the videos. The holistic managerial approach is key here. He wouldn't be fooled again although he shyly told Smash Hits in 1981, *"None of the ideas are mine. It's just the way Marco and I have moulded them together"*. Adam took care of business like no other pop star before him. He wouldn't rely on managers or a label for his ideas. He would achieve fame and money by himself. Money made his world go around. He even made sure that, at the height of his fame, his publishers charged Smash Hits twice the going rate to print his lyrics. How had he achieved this drastic reinvention from Banshees clones to teatime favourites?

In the spring of 1980, the new Ants demo'd several tunes from what would become the *Kings Of The Wild Frontier* album and shopped around for a new deal. Absorbing some of Malcolm's chutzpah, self-belief, ideas and his obsession with Burundi drumming, the new band; featuring ex-Banshee and soon-to-be longtime co-writer, Marco

Pirroni on guitar and future uber-producer Chris Hughes as one of two drummers, played a national tour under the ludicrously ambitious title of the Ants Invasion.

By the end of the tour they had signed to CBS and rush-released *Kings Of The Wild Frontier* as a single. It was all still a little smoke and mirrors and the single got a lot of coverage but only reached #48 in August 1980. Although the rest of the year was spent recording the album, the next single, *Dog Eat Dog* came in October 1980 and did the job that *Kings* should have. It smashed its way into the Top Five and felt like a new Punk Rock that wasn't above catering for youngsters. It takes more than one hit to make a phenomenon though. *Antmusic* was released in December 1980, while *Dog Eat Dog* was still ambling out of the Top Forty and was another colossal hit, entering at #31 and then climbing and climbing, #16, #10# #7, #7, #4, #2, #2, only held back from the top by the recently murdered John Lennon.

Oh man, it was exciting to see the records getting bigger and bigger. Buying a single early meant you were involved in this growth. The single buyer was part of the process, not just reacting to marketing on the designated day, as happens now. *Antmusic* is a massive sounding single and its double drum beat was tapped out ad infinitum by pens on school desks up and down the land. As it sounds, it's a statement of intent from Adam, a meta-mantra on his new found sound and a self fulfilling prophecy, just as Bowie had done with Ziggy. It too has swagger. The guitars swagger, the drums are pure swag and **Adam Ant** is at his swaggiest, most confident and yes, most adamant. *Antmusic* has the most swagger of any song ever, in my view. Especially when you bear in mind that he had never had a hit single when it was recorded, had recently had the rug pulled swiftly from under his feet by the dastardly McLaren and was making somewhat unprecedented songs about pirates and red Indians, in costumes that wouldn't get you ten feet on any high street on a Saturday night. It required colossal balls on Adam's behalf and a maximum suspension of disbelief along from the audience. Playing it safe, he was not.

The album, *Kings Of The Wild Frontier* hit #1 on its release a week or two later. The album was pure gold. There is not a duff song on there. The next year or so was Adam's. Antmania came to town. Every town. The Ants Invasion materialised and a re-released *Kings* also hit the Top Five. I had always thought that Antmania was purely British but the album broke the Top Fifty in America too. The music was exciting and fast and not a little dangerously sexy. *You may not like it now but you will,* Adam told all of us attentive schoolkids. *Sexmusic for Antpeople, Antmusic for Sexpeople* indeed. Was I an Antperson? I liked to think so. Was I a Sexperson? I doubted that very much. There was a frisson of sex all over Adam and we all went along with it.

There were also a lot of re-released Antsingles shooting up and down the charts, including a xeroxed *Xerox* and *Cartrouble* (again), his 1978 debut, *Young Parisians* and later *Deutscher Girls.* Without pausing at all, a brand new single, *Stand & Deliver* debuted at #1 in May 1981 and sold over a million copies in the UK alone. The iconic and quite cinematic (for the time) video featured Adam as the Dandy Highwayman, crashing through windows and sweeping up girls like Errol Flynn. Adam had already done some low key acting, appearing in Julien Temple's punk's filthy fairy tale, *Jubilee* but the video's message was clear. I am, he was telling us, a fucking movie star now.

They repeated this feat in September with the panto-esque *Prince Charming*. This time the video featured all manner of campery, including homegrown erstwhile sexpot, Diana Dors as a fairy Godmother, who transformed Adam into ~~Cinderalla~~ Prince Charming (via Clint Eastwood and Alice Cooper obviously) in a costume that did not look anywhere near as cool as the Kings look, and was quite a bit more silly, and – most jawdropping of all, an actual choreographed dance for us all to perform along with the song. A dance that all who encountered it can remember but very few actually deployed, not least because it's not a particularly dancey single, but mostly because it was intentionally ridiculous. I found the whole thing fascinating and it gave us Adam's enduring motto, *"Ridicule is nothing to be scared of"*.

The album *Prince Charming* was in the shops for Christmas 1981 and I wanted it. It was that and the **Duran Duran** album that I wanted more than anything in the world. Yet, in an odd move, I changed my mind at the last minute in Spiller's records, not for the last time, and bought the slightly more expensive *Dare* by **The Human League**, which had the coolest gatefold sleeve and a midprice copy of **Japan**'s *Quiet Life* instead. I was a bit amazed at myself for doing this, upsetting my own plan, but I feel that I made the right decision, so y'know, don't worry too much about me. I am over it.

Adam's slide into panto and parody continued in 1982 with *Ant Rap,* and his career became a series of diminishing returns after that although not without some brilliant singles, with actual pantomime titles like *Puss'n'Boots* and *Goody Two Shoes.*

By that time, however, he had done it. He'd made it. Adam & The Ants were another People's Band. A craze, for sure, but a huge one and, while the streets were not filled with people dressed as pirates exactly, there was a surge of colour out there, and excitement. The idea of dressing up, had pulled us out of the drab Seventies. Things were looking up. He had exploded the charts with his noisy, exciting records. A riot of colour and a mix of the smart, the sexy and the dumb. And that, we all noted, was an excellent recipe for fun. David Bowie had shown the value of being different, the possibilities of reinvention – and the rewards. Adam had echoed that and made clear that following that path could be FUN and once ridicule is no longer a concern just what was there to be scared of? Have a go, all you latent British eccentrics, if you Dare.

03. THE SOUND OF THE CROWD

1980-1981: Synthpop arrives.
Pop Music takes a quantum leap into the future.

M GARY NUMAN OMD ULTRAVOX THE HUMAN LEAGUE

I was a Punk. I was a Mod. I was a New Romantic. All of these were true-ish at one point or another but one of them just sounds wrong. What the hell was a New Romantic? A New Romanticist? A Futurist? A Synthpopper? They each sounded faintly ridiculous when spoken aloud. It's just not on to say, "Hello, my name is David and I am a Futurist". It meant nothing to me. Even as a teenager with nothing to lose but my pocket money (and teeth), that was just not going to happen.

Looking the part was easy if you were a teenage Punk. Doing It Yourself was very much the idea there. Anarchy is an open forum, ruleswise, after all. There was an established subculture, with ample manuals and films, detailing what is required of Mods. And the devil is very much in the detail with Mods. An incorrect amount of buttons on your jacket cuff is seen as an unforgivable error in that mob. Both sub-cultures were suited to pack mentalities. Hanging around. Testosterone and street gangs go hand in hand, so the records had terrace chanted choruses so you and YOUR gang could bellow along to the measured socio-political bile of *Too Much Too Young, Complete Control* or *Going Underground.*

However, outside photoshoots for *The Face* magazine and the three or four clubs in the country that embraced and launched the New Pop groups like **Duran Duran, Spandau Ballet, Soft Cell, Ultravox, Visage** and **The Human League**, you just wouldn't see people dressed up like...Spandau Ballet. Maybe even Spandau Ballet wore jeans and a T-shirt to go out and buy milk on Sunday morning, although that revelation would have proved very disappointing. However, with the best will in the world, you were going to look a bit foolish if you raided your sister's make up bag and wardrobe, appending the requisite amount of tea towels to kilts and scarves to your jangling, bebangled wrists. It was probably for the best but this was music about dressing up not down and, after a few years of geezerish People's Bands like The Jam, Dexys and Madness, this Synthpop Explosion made quite a disturbance in the fashion Force.

e were used to identifying kids by their clothes. Here a squint of Punks, there a crease of Mods, everywhere a trudge of Metallers. However not only were the New Romantics not visible on the High Street, but, as a delineated scene, it barely existed at all. There were no roving squads of Futurists, alas. Can you imagine? For all the column inches that were written about the Blitz club, Steve Strange, Boy George and Marilyn; at best only a few hundred people were even vaguely involved. This music came with an impossible, impractical glamour but it was a fantasy. It was couture catwalk fare, never intended for the High Street. It wasn't supposed to be replicated. It was about being a lone ephemeral peacock not joining a flock of, um, seagulls.

It wouldn't be the first manufactured or, more accurately, exaggerated scene but it is one of the most enduring. Like the Pop stars who die young and stay beautiful forever, we never bump into old, fat New Romantics because there weren't any in the first place. The fantasy remains intact conceptually; with the exception of the occasional rumour of Tony Hadley denting the couch on a Morning TV show. Somehow seeing middle aged cider Punks, topping up their blood alcohol levels in the park; or a convoy of balding mods, pushing the capabilities of their Vespas' suspension, adds a taint to the memories of those scenes. And a human distance. Youth culture just does not look good on old people. But the Synthpop records that were scattered across the charts, starting with **M**'s *Pop Muzik* and **Tubeway Army**'s *Are Friends Electric?* in 1979 and moving through *Love Is A Stranger, Enola Gay, Girls On Film, Tainted Love, Just Can't get Enough, Sound Of The Crowd, Fade To Grey, Vienna* and more seem immortal now. At least once a year they are gathered together for the nth time in the latest definitive Best Of Neon Eighties Electric Synth Dream Anthems 3CD compilation with a suitably eye-worrying retrofuturist cover. There isn't an annual Punk hits compilation. Or a Ska one. Or even a Britpop one. So how come these records have lasted so well? On paper, they should not. Nothing gets old faster than the future, after all.

Well, let's not overlook the elements of surprise. And timing. Digital watches and then home computers arrived in short succession and Britain fell in love with buttons that make Bleeps. The Bleep sounded like the future. *Alien, Buck Rogers* and *Star Wars* had reinforced the idea that that the Bleep was the language of advanced technology, so this music was the sound the future arriving in our homes. A Bleep of our own. The first digital watches made about 4 very similar beeps but that did not stop people from mashing those buttons endlessly, really giving that microchip a workout. The bleep was new and sci-fi and very addictive.

If you can afford a truck,
you can afford a Synthesizer

The Clash had sown seditious seeds with talk of *"No Elvis, Beatles or Rolling Stones"* but they had remained a guitar band, for the most part. Now the new groups could reject Rock'n'Roll completely. No guitars at all. The European Canon was becoming real and spreading like religion. As synths became more affordable almost overnight, a generation of groups was finally able to emulate **Bowie** and **Kraftwerk**'s noises. The New Pop records were minimalist in arrangement and the new synths made very pleasing noises right away. Not that they could write a tune for you – that came from within but being able to commandeer the new noises, gave those songwriters with imagination a huge head start.

The new groups were feeding on influences that the public at large had not heard. The noises of *Autobahn* or *Warszawa,* concealed in a couple of fading Kraftwerk hits or the under-explored sides of Bowie's less commercially viable albums. They joined the dots between those records and songs that might have been regarded as novelty hits, like *I Feel Love* or *Pop Muzik*. Those ingredients amounted to a soup base and many groups replicated the recipe precisely to no great effect; because no-one really likes generic vegetable soup, right? However, viewed as a base, a blank canvas upon which to let your imagination and your sounds out to play, well, therein lies the path that raises mere soup to Pop Art.

It was a new artform, a new medium. This was a pristine and stunning music with crystal clear colours and immaculate lines that, like the Autobahn, went on forever, describing endless planes of sound. It no longer needed four brains to be moving their respective hands in perfect synch to make something sound pleasing. If you needed the drums speeding up, you turned a dial; rather than sobering up a drummer. The sounds and the records were hypnotic and entrancing. Startling and novel, they jumped out of the radio. Lyrically, they moved into new territory too, ranging from the profound to the pretentious; leaning somewhat on the side of pretension. I've always quite liked pretentious things – it's a side-effect of ambition, in my view. Sticking your neck out is never safe but there is no shame in failing; only in not trying.

All the new groups had read about David Bowie's cut-up lyric method, wherein he would literally cut up lines from different songs into thin paper strips, then shuffle and juxtapose them to make new ones. It's a system he had copied in turn from the novelist William Burroughs. I suspect Bowie put a lot more effort than many into writing the lines in the first place and, if you are choosing to use this technique, you are going to have to accept that you will wade through a great deal of gibberish for the odd bit of revelatory truth or sufficiently artful mystery. It was however a reliable way of avoiding workaday songs of boy-meets-girl or tales of life on the streets or any mundane instances of reality puncturing the fantasy of this futuristic pop. There was no need to "keep it real". Quite the opposite, in fact. Music this new and futuristic needed a new lyrical counterpart. Tales of chip shops and getting off with girls at local discos were not going to cut it. The transgressive sex, mind control, exotic-sounding foreign countries, machinery and high speed travel of a JG Ballard novel were much more suitable subject matter and if the words sounded a little ineffable or impenetrable – so much the better. These songs were supposed to be beaming in from the future. Of course they were hard to understand. The Futurist tag was a nod to the Italian poet Filippi Marinetti, who wrote the original Futurist Manifesto for art back in 1909, urging painters to reject the old masters in favour of depicting and referencing speed, technology and the cult of the machine. Compared to life beforehand, the Industrial Revolution must have felt way more radical and inspiring than the arrival of microchips and bleeps. Notwithstanding that, Space Age tech at your fingertips meant that everything was going to be different and it warranted a complete makeover for Pop.

Adam Ant had injected a hefty dose of showbiz and theatrics to the charts across 1980 and 1981; much needed after Punk's dressing down and Post Punk's utilitarian anti-fashion. He had been labelled as a faggot or poof by many, just as Bowie and Bolan had been previously. Britain was quite a huge bit less tolerant or indeed understanding of gay people in those days. Homosexuality was illegal in England until 1967...and, unbelievably, until 1981 in Scotland. A man under sixty ordering a half pint of beer in a Yorkshire pub might still be hilariously taunted as "a bit borderline" even to this day. So back in 1981, men wearing make-up was going to get your band attention, one way or another. Adam had done it but, whilst he was dabbling in subtle eyeliner and lip gloss, the attention was focussed on the white stripe across his nose, which was more warpaint than actual girls' make-up.

Upping Adam's ante over 1981, **Marc Almond, Duran Duran** and **Phil Oakey,** materialised on *Top Of The Pops* and caused more tea to be spat out in front rooms up and down the land than the Sex Pistols, Thatcher and the TUC combined. Most homes still had only one TV and the whole family would be watching *Top Of The Pops* together, which meant there was going to be reaction and discussion. These were not isolated instances. There was an epidemic of Goths, gays, freaks, weirdos and men in make up on *Top Of The Pops.* And it was spreading rapidly. This was unheard of and unpalatable and it brought back something that had been missing from Pop music for too long – a generation gap.

I thought it was amazing and completely natural that this brilliant and colourful music was being made by equally colourful people. The older generation, not so much. Things were afoot and they sensed it but they didn't understand the appeal of said things. Why, they reasoned, would you do THAT to yourself? Alternative comedy was bubbling up at the same time and getting on television too, causing similar outbursts and confrontations. It's vital to remember that in 1981, the pre-internet days of three channels broadcasting for only some of the day, appearing on TV was the only way of launching or communicating anything nationwide in Britain and it worked overnight. Well, it worked instantly but we didn't share the experience until the next day, using the old school IRL "talking face to face" app. Bear in mind that at least half the TV that was on was outrageously boring. BBC2 seemed to show a LOT of Open University programs, mainly about geology or drainage, or both. So ANYTHING remotely exciting was seized upon. There was so little on TV of interest to kids that anything new and odd was BIG NEWS. Anything that was new and odd and annoyed your parents was like gold dust. *The Young Ones* (RIP Rik Mayall) launched in 1982 and most parents hated that too. They were supposed to. That was half the point. It went off like a nuclear bomb to instant and total (and utter) effect. When these things happen, youth culture moves forward in quantum leaps. The generation gap encourages creativity. Drawing a line in the sand creates a void that must be filled with new things, better things, *your* things. Your parents *should* hate your music and the films you like. If you all cosy up together on everything then nothing will ever change and it's the same with music. So it was out with *The Good Life* and The Three Degrees and in with *The Young Ones* and **Soft Cell.** How brilliant is that?

Leeds' **Soft Cell,** emerged sweaty and smiling from the sleaze of their adopted home in Soho's clubland, with their massive, massive #1 single, the cover of Marc Bolan's girlfriend **Gloria Jones'** hit *Tainted Love*. Prior to this colossal breakthrough single, which was a #1 hit in seventeen countries, including America; they had released a couple of cool but low key electro club singles, produced by Daniel Miller, MD of Mute records. They followed *Tainted Love* with the unglamorous, unstoppable and not un-Smiths-y, *Bedsitter* and the epic torch balladry of *Say Hello Wave Goodbye.* These were, and are, three spectacularly great songs, built for the radio. Soft Cell, fronted by the overtly bisexual and leather-clad Marc Almond, and backed up by the motionless Dave Ball on a small, solitary keyboard, were something else we had not seen before. Previously, gay or partly gay people in the media had, for the most part, either kept that side of themselves hidden or adopted a Kenneth Williams / Liberace-style overly camp, so-gay-he-can't-be-gay manner, that worked so well for Freddie Mercury for reasons that look rather quaint now. It was a convenient shorthand that skirted the issue by, um, painting it pink and covering it in glitter, I suppose. If you were appeared to be gay, then you couldn't be gay because if you were, you'd hide it, wouldn't you? Stout thinking.

Marc, however, was dripping in sex and the debut album, *Non Stop Erotic Cabaret*, from its title alone, caused a lot of "conversations" in Britain's households. Songs like *Sex Dwarf* and *Seedy Films* opened a door to a world unfamiliar to many outside That London. I remember being a bit shocked when I first heard it at a friend's house. What on God's green Earth was a sex dwarf? The music was a smart blend of cabaret show tunes, which seems Marc's preferred style, and calculated-to-shock pervy electro pop. Many of their more commercial and less cum-sodden songs have since been adopted as standards now.

Soft Cell have since been adopted by the industrial world, having been covered by **NIN** and **Marilyn Manson**, both of whom have shady pasts as New Romantics, or the American equivalent thereof. Their further adoption of and by clubland is exemplified by the follow up record, *Non Stop Ecstatic Dancing*, inspired by visits to New York and encountering Ecstasy in the clubs out there, wayyyy before it took off here. This early example of a remix album was really no such thing and in fact was more of a mixed bag: three older singles or B sides, a filthier rework of the already quite filthy *Sex Dwarf*, a hornier, (as in, yes, more horns) take of *Non Stop Erotic Cabaret's Chips On My Shoulder* and the brilliant and not unHumanLeaguey electro of early song, *A Man Could Get Lost*.

Soft Cell managed five consecutive Top Five Hits but their popularity fell away a bit by the third album, appropriately titled *The Art Of Falling Apart*, which is less synthpoppy and more amazing. It did reach #5 but the singles failed to chart. The next album, with the lets-not-beat-about-the-bush-at-all-this-time title of *This Last Night In Sodom* is also particularly great and Marc continues to have a glittering solo career.

Prior to this epidemic of British Synthpop fops, two other groups had made breakthroughs in 1980, OMD and Ultravox. Both bands were light on natural glamour and big on Computer Instruction Manuals. They had both been at it for a few years in the Post Punk wilderness, beavering away under Kraftwerk's neon lights. Liverpool's **Orchestral Manoeuvres In The Dark** (OMD) released their first two albums in 1980. A nippy, eponymous debut followed eight months later by the muggier *Organisation;* its title taken from an older incarnation of **Kraftwerk**. Their sparkling debut single, *Electricity*, was powered by a simple drum machine of Paul's making. It was released on Factory records in 1978 and the band borrowed (and kept) Factory design genius freak, Peter Saville, for their first five albums.

Born out of Post Punk's backroom industrial experimentation but with the chops to "accidentally" write massively hooky Pop songs when the mood took them, **OMD** were not and did not need nor seek to be "Pop star material". They considered themselves experimental, bewitched by the dystopian drones of the soundtrack to A Clockwork Orange, conjured by Wendy/Walter Carlos. Andy McLusky and Paul Humphreys both sang and played keyboards. They were geeks by Pop star standards. Normals. Their lives changed by a Kraftwerk gig in Liverpool, after which they doorstepped the Germans in their dressing room, announcing to them that *"You have shown us the future"*. They performed as an experimental duo initially, backed by a reel-to-reel tape recorder called Winston (after the character in Orwell's *1984*), playing up their tech/geeky aspect and Kraftwerkery by writing songs about machines, vehicles and, in *Stanlow*, an oil refinery, as was the custom.

Enola Gay, the beautiful and incongruously supercatchy single from *Organisation* made a slow but steady climb up the charts, peaking at #8. A Synthpop classic now, it concerns the early morning drop of an atom bomb on Hiroshima. They focused on a technological, rather than human, aspect of that tragedy. Many clocks were found in the aftermath of the attack, stopped at the same time *("It's 8.15, that's the time that it's always been")*. *Enola Gay* was the name of the plane that dropped the bomb (code name: Little Boy) and also the mother of the pilot of the plane. This colossal ambassador of death reminds me, in some way, of my mother, he no doubt thought.

One of the more interesting traits of the initial wave of Synthpop groups, carried over from Kraftwerk, via Post Punk's year-zero austerity, was this tendency to avoid (or conceal) old school boy-meets-girl lyrics, rejecting the past and embracing the gleaming, dynamic future of technology and, particularly, travel. Vienna, Cambodia, Tel Aviv, Prague, China, Berlin and Japan were all plucked from travel agent's catalogues and taken into the charts.

Kraftwerk were the key influencers of the budding Synthpop artists (via **David Bowie**, of course). Their output by that point was exclusively songs about computers, machines and vehicles. Oh, and one about a model, although that is a low-key joke about a new model, a new product. Although their records mostly dated from the Seventies, they felt very futuristic. They still do now. I took my kids to see Kraftwerk play in 3D in 2013 and we all loved it. They are still quite the trip. Funny guys too, those Germans. No glitter or leather here. They dressed as businessmen and factory workers. This functional utilitarian aesthetic was a Kraftwerkmanlike, Socialist and anti-pop-starry statement. It elevated the music, the process and the product above the artist or worker. It was also a very cheap and effective stage gimmick, even in 2D. Boiler suits were a convenient look if you didn't have Elton John's wardrobe budget. It's not possible, or it wasn't then, long before Primark's One Thousand Pence Reich, to buy cheaper stage clothes. It's funny, I hadn't really noticed until now but, since the Cold War packed up its gas masks and colossal tank regiments, you don't see as many Army Surplus shops anymore. They provided super-cheap utilitarian stage clothes for a generation of bands.

Despite *Enola Gay*, **OMD** were still far from being a proper Pop Group. They didn't find a follow up hit and looked uncomfortable in the charts and awkward on TV. However 1981 saw them start a run of three quite different singles, each of them masterpieces. *Souvenir* was a massive worldwide hit and they followed it with a brace of singles; one slowish, one slow and both called *Joan Of Arc*, which was typically abstruse for the times and something that I had always assumed hadn't filled their label, Virgin, with much hope, especially at the expense of *She's Leaving,* which remains one the decade's greatest unreleased singles. Yet it seems that the label were behind the singles choices, after all. Brilliantly, all three singles were Top Five hits across the world and their third album, *Architecture & Morality*, sold three million copies and endures as one of the best loved records of the era.

OMD were not pinups and the wonderfully stark artwork, designed by Saville, was not constructed for mass appeal but the nine perfect Pop songs within *Architecture & Morality* were impossible to argue with and the album kept selling and selling. There's a dreamy and slightly mournful feeling throughout the record, even on the more upbeat sections, with choirs and organic instruments, like piano and saxophone, working very much in harmony with the synthesiser, drum machines and, um, radios. Paul Humphreys is quoted in the liners notes of yet another reissue, *"[it]...was a culmination of everything we had learned to that point about song writing and sound textures...to me, this is our finest hour"*.

This is exemplified on the second *Joan Of Arc* single with the helpful, bracketed addendum *(Maid Of Orleans)*. It starts as a sort of abrasive tone poem, with slabs of *music concrete,* and then gently lilts away in waltz time again, until marching drums and what sounds like synthetic bagpipes come in. The whole thing is mournful, weird and slow and completely wonderful. The lyrics are pretty minimal and seem happy to idly muse on the personal sacrifices Joan made in her life (obviously). It sailed into the top shelf of the charts in January, 1982. The sleeve of the 12" was a graphic representation of a stained glass window rendering of Joan on silver foil and it I have it framed on my office wall.

Even more brilliantly, they followed that album with 1983's *Dazzle Ships,* which is one of the oddest records to ever grace the Top Five. It's barely half an hour long, half of its twelve songs are not songs at all but instrumental experiments, speaking clocks, talking toys, snatches of radio broadcasts, jarring submarine sirens and sonic mood boards, with loose Cold War slash Communist Eastern European themes.

The band employed an Emulator for the first time. It was an early, primitive (by today's standards) and massively expensive sampler. I can picture them, ensconced in their own Gramophone Suite recording studio, ignoring their self-confessed writer's block, mildly cursing their status as Actual Pop Stars, and sampling every little discordant bump and clang they could think of, retreating into boffin mode.

The lack of new song-type-songs necessitated the inclusion of two previous B-sides on the album, *Of All the Things We've Made* and *The Romance Of The Telescope*. *Dazzle Ships* was produced by Rhett Davies, who had worked with both **Roxy Music**, on the smooth *Flesh & Blood* album *and* **Brian Eno** on many of his sonically adventurous Seventies albums. Eno was still shocking people in 1981 with his stunningly prophetic collaboration with David Byrne, the world-music-sampling, proto hip hop classic *My Life In The Bush of Ghosts*, which sounded like nothing anyone had heard before (and if you haven't, you really should). Andy McLusky very much comes across as the one pushing the experimental envelope after the Pop perfection of *Architecture & Morality*, and is quoted as saying *"it's taken Paul twenty five years to forgive me for Dazzle Ships"*. Paul does like a pop song, as one can surmise from his masterminding and song-writing that propped up (and thought up) Atomic Kitten. So we must thank him for Kerry Katona. From *Sealand* to Iceland.

Isn't *Dazzle Ships* just a brilliant, evocative, combative title? It's a way of camouflaging the silhouette of warships with paint. It was suggested by Saville after a 1919 painting "Dazzle Ship In Dry Dock At Liverpool" by Edward Wadsworth. He also suggested they write a song based on the painting, which the duly did on the title track.

I bought *Dazzle Ships* on the day it came out, from an Indie record shop (whose name I cannot recall or discover but I also met Orange Juice there round about the same time) on Albany Road in Cardiff, and from the moment I saw the fantastic gatefold sleeve, which opened upwards (such innovation!), I knew it was going to be a bit weird and hoped it was going to be brilliant. When I got home and put it on, I absolutely loved every weird second of it and I still do.

I am in something of a minority though and it sold about a tenth as much as its predecessor, despite leading with the colossal, barn-storming, typewriter-percussion-led, proto-industrial-sounding single, *Genetic Engineering*, which was a deserved Top Twenty hit, but one that I had assumed was going to be #1. Forever. Not the first and, by no means, the last time that has happened to me. It was succeeded by the super poppy *Telegraph*, another holdover from *Architecture & Morality* album, and one whose presence you might think would surely have added another million sales to that album. Except, oddly enough, the initial Manor Studios 1981 version of

Telegraph is discordant, abrasive and angry and indeed much more in keeping with *Dazzle Ships* than the smoother version they went with. Bands, eh?

The band's experimental side had been suppressed with *Architecture & Morality* and their pure Pop songs had since captured huge chunks of the world. However, it resurfaced with a vengeance on this record. I had never heard anything like this. The **Stockhausen** references went sailing high over my head (and still do), as did many of the **Kraftwerk** ones too. Andy McCluskey recalled, "*We wanted to be* [both] **ABBA** *and* **Stockhausen**. *The machinery, bones and humanity were juxtaposed*" (wiki). This might be true but, aside from on *Genetic Engineering*, those two titans were not really combined as much as laid out side by side and OMD and Rhett Davies' trick was not making them sound too jarring when alternated across the album.

The remainder of the songs on the album are all completely wonderful. The grace of *Of All The Things We Made*, the stately sci-fi **Joy Division** of *Silent Running* and *The Romance Of The Telescope, International*'s waltz and the single-in-waiting that was never called to battle, *Radio Waves* are bold, confident brilliant songs that sounded weird then and utterly timeless now.

I got a lot of stick for defending the album at the time but its perverse and brave, OK bloody-minded, ways have clearly resonated with **Thom Yorke** and a whole generation of electronic musicians with whom **OMD**'s critical stock has always been buoyant. Radiohead's unwillingness to produce *OK Computer II,* opting instead to pull themselves apart and cybertise their sound, ending up with the experimental and abrasive noises of *Kid A*, and somewhat similar synthesised voices *("Fitter, Happier"....."Butcher, Engineer")* is very familiar indeed, in the context of *Dazzle Ships*. Both records got a pasting from the mainstream media at the time, both pruned the bands' fanbases back to a more, um, manageable size and now both albums are continuing to grow in stature, appreciation and sales, ahead of the rest of the bands' catalogues. Definitely two of my favourite records and I urge you to wrap your ears and slide your minds around *Dazzle Ships* and *Kid A*, together in one sitting. As with so many game changing records, I'd so love to be able to experience them anew, together. Do it for me. Let me know how it goes.

It would be unfair to talk about OMD in 1980 and 1981 and not mention **Ultravox**. OMD made some quite dull records later in their career and, atypically, have sort of returned to form or at least their roots, in the 21st Century, and now bask in the warm all-worth-it-in-the-end glow of having albums accepted into the critical canon of groundbreaking music alongside continued royalties from massive hits.

No such fate for **Ultravox** alas, which is a little sad but not altogether unfair. After three weird and mostly unsuccessful, glammy New Wave albums with initial singer and later cult synthpop god, **John Foxx,** they had split up. Foxx went on to record a series of icily melodic electronic albums and, throughout the Eighties, he released some fantastic Pop singles, none of which seemed to quite capture the imagination and all of which stalled just outside the Top Forty. So, despite Virgin Records' efforts, he never became a Pop star but singles like *Underpass, No-One's Driving, Europe After The Rain, Endlessly* and *Your Dress* are connoisseur's dystopian Synthpop choices and strongly recommended. He continues to plough this furrow to this day and is a cult figure among fans of electronic music.

Midge Ure had tried a lot of things on the road to Vienna, from trying to blend synths and guitars in **The Rich Kids** with Steve Jones from the **Sex Pistols**, to having a mid-Seventies #1 single with **Slik**, a band created by the **Bay City Rollers'** puppet masters to being in, of all things, **Thin Lizzy** for a spell. His other (other other) role was in **Visage,** which Ure had formed back in 1978 with singer Steve Strange and then added three of the gents from **Magazine** and Ultravox keyboard player, Billy Currie. **Visage** would finally blossom with 1980's *Fade To Grey* but in the meanwhile, Midge and Billy had resurrected the Ultravox brand, with Midge replacing Foxx. That is quite the odd history, isn't it?

Ultravox 2.0 were one of many bands that had a bit of a stylistic rethink and emerged as pure synthpoppers. It was less of a leap for them and the new look suited them. Like OMD, they were not a natural pin-uppy band, although they did their best to look cool and sophisticated. They always struck me as trying to be quite grown up (and Kraftwerky) in their dress, all suits and ties. And moustaches. Midge's efforts to look like Bryan Ferry were quite sweet but a little comical. So much so, that Smash Hits made Midge's tidy moustache into an actual cartoon character for a time.

The new band's first single, *Sleepwalk* was a Top Thirty hit but the second, *Passing Strangers*, failed to make the Top Forty, despite being seemingly tailor made for the charts. The album was not much of a success at first and things looked bleak until the title track, *Vienna* was released. It's long since been admitted by Ure that this billowing and portentous-sounding ballad is about nothing very much *("it means nothing to me...")*. It's easy to mock **Ultravox** now, and I am certainly not above doing it, but you would have had to look very hard to find someone who didn't like that song at the time. It succeeded in seeming to be sophisticated, foreign and cool. Britain did not feel remotely exotic back then and it was exciting to aspire to be *New Europeans* in some way. *Vienna* is beautiful and huge and infernally catchy; as perfect and empty as a ping pong ball. It became a massive global hit, aided by a particularly brilliant and expensively monochrome video from Russell "Highlander" Mulcahy, which cast the band as trenchcoated spies from the film, *The Third Man*. *Vienna* does sound quite a bit like **OMD**, actually, with minimalist intro and the way it gracefully layers on the arpeggiated pianos and synths. It also does that trick of speeding up halfway through which is always fun.

Vienna was a victim of its own massive success, attracting mockery for the serious-face acting in the video, which is both justified and a little unfair. The clip was cool at first but rapidly seemed to become clichéd, then almost a pastiche and remains the butt of many jokes. Despite all this, it also served to inspire a lot of serious-faced imitators in the years to come. For a good while, Ultravox were an influential band and I am only slightly embarrassed to say I liked them quite a bit back in the day. The music and particularly the howlingly bad lyrics have just not stood the test of time however. So it goes. The New Romantic overblown video aesthetic was nailed at the time by *Not The Nine O'Clock News'* mercilessly accurate parody, *Nice Video, Shame About The Song*.

Very, very unjustly *Vienna* didn't hit #1, spending five weeks at #2, which I believe is a record of some sort, at the start of 1981. It was held off the summit by one of the many, many one-off Novelty #1 Hits that regularly befouled the charts in the early Eighties (especially in 1982). This one was the singular, stupid, slightly racist and, oh go on then, quite fun-at-the-time, *Shaddup Your Face* by **Joe Dolce**, whom I do hope was not actually Italian. Ultravox went on to have another three huge hit albums, dress as pilots (not pirates) and, in *Hymn*, release a single that I thought was jaw-droppingly incredible at the time and that now I see is arse-clenchingly terrible and makes me look hard at myself with crossed arms and a disappointed, raised eyebrow. Such is pop music.

With a playlist of Ultravox, Bowie, Sparks, OMD, Kraftwerk, Cabaret Voltaire, No Wave and Disco, 1981's New Romantic movement, centred on London's Blitz and Billys clubs, pushed new bands like **Duran Duran, Visage** and **Spandau Ballet**. Duran Duran is something I'll get to later but I was very taken with them. Their three triumphant singles of 1981, *Planet Earth, Careless Memories* and *Girls On Film*, all of which I bought on the day they came out, sounded like the most exciting music ever. I am not sure they achieved their stated aim of sounding like **The Chic Pistols** but the singles were bold and glamorous and exciting, boasting a sizzling production from Colin Thurston, who'd worked with Bowie, The Human League and Magazine, which is a much better comparison for Duran. They were sci-fi, disco and a little bit rock and they had committed to looking the part. They exuded total confidence and I love those singles dearly to this day, B-sides and everything.

Visage gave us *Fade To Grey*, probably the most perfectly realised New Romantic single, combining all the tropes of romance, mystery, travel, exotic Europeanism, wearing make up and sounding very clean, precise and synthetic. Oh and it's the dictionary definition of pretentious. Opening with a whispering drum machine, a repeating Moroderish acid squiggle, and then layering on the whooshes and a synthetic kick drum, until a French lady sings, in splendidly bored tones, what I have only just noticed is the same lyric that Steve Strange later sings in English: brilliantly ridiculous.

New Romanticism was all about pretence, dress-up and escapism and, through that, it was about reinvention, about starting over. These were David Bowie's children and no mistake. As an AceFace in the New Romantic scene, Steve Strange had featured in Bowie's most recent reinvention, in a meta-role, playing himself in the groundbreaking-at-the-time *Ashes To Ashes* video, which took place in an apocalyptic dreamworld, where Steve Strange made way more sense than he would queuing in the Post Office, which is a different kind of Hell.

Reinvention was a challenge, a will-to-power that required a burst of creativity. If you could go from being a Normal to dressing up, getting on stage and getting away with it, surely there was no limit to what you could do. I am forever gutted that I was five years too young and 200 miles too far from these clubs that I would read about in Smash Hits. As a fantasy, I could imagine going to Blitz, checking in your coat with Boy George, looking to see if Bowie or one of Duran Duran was hiding in a corner and hearing these songs and seeing all the kids in their peacockery and finery. Fantastic.

Now, hear me out on this. If you approach **Spandau Ballet**'s discography backwards, then their music is relentlessly horrible, with a curiously redemptive final lap, and seeing Tony "Orwightmaaate" Hadley, huffing and puffing with the band now on breakfast telly (the foul incubator for the most unwelcome of comebacks, it seems) is just plain embarrassing. Faced with a tough choice, they have, probably quite sensibly, chosen to re-emerge as a facsimile of their own insipid yet hugely successful *True*-era selves over recreating the initial flash of inspired carefree weirdness. Their later albums are so thin and bland, that even the titles have slipped from my mind, which is usually an unwilling haven for such minutiae. The empty wine bar noodling of the *True* album is, and always was, completely horrific and diabolically successful. Going back further, their second album, *Diamond*, is frankly a bit of a pup too, with the exception of the truly exceptional *Chant No.1 (I Don't Need This Pressure On)*, whose taut and weird funk is genuinely brilliant. It still sounds incredible and makes my feet twitch, whenever I hear it played loud. It belongs on the debut, really. It would feel more at home there because, prior to Diamond, I am going to have to insist that Spandau were a little bit amazing.

They were ex-Punks and an early Hadley-free incarnation of the band (as **The Makers**) claim the solid gold Punk-cred of having played at The Roxy. Spandau were the princes of the original and best London New Romantic club, Blitz, where they rubbed shoulders with Visage and anyone else who had the balls to look like they ought to be let into the place.

A buzz band, packing them in to the hippest club in town, and getting features in magazines, before releasing anything will always have all the record labels queuing round the block. And nothing drives labels wilder with excitement than not being able to get in to see the hot new thing, whatever it is. If they can't hear the band's demo and can't see them play but keep hearing how amazing they are, then you have a winner. The songs that made up their set and went on to be the bulk of debut album *Journeys To Glory* were so unusual and so strong that Spandau sparked an A&R bidding war, which was won by Chrysalis, who duly put the debut single *To Cut A Long Story Short* straight into the Top Five in 1980.

Alas, they were quickly eclipsed by Duran Duran's debut single, three months later. Spandau had the advantage, being closer and more closely tied to the media, the style press, Robert Elms and The FACE magazine, but, being first out of the traps, caught the flak first for their appearance. Unpopular though Duran Duran were with a great many (boys mainly), there was always an extra fistful of vitriol reserved for Spandau Fucking Ballet. That extra word in their name seemed to be used more frequently than not.

They had raided very similar dressing up boxes to Duran Duran, or vice versa, and clearly had listened to the same **Bowie** and **Chic** records and were encouraged by the media to be fierce rivals for the title of Hottest New Five Piece Dandies Wearing Tea Towels (And Eyeliner). Spandau had carved out their own slightly confusing sub-aesthetic too. There were tribal, Glitterband drums and Hadley's earnest and almost operatic baritone, booming out from videos with a lot of primitive and decadent types, roaming around purposefully in the darkness in bunkers with fires burning and flags flapping. Oh and kilts, lots of kilts. Hadley carries a pair of vintage binoculars throughout the *To Cut A Long Story Short* video for no obvious reason. Such Eighties.

Lyrically they were on a par with Simon Le Bon's wordsmithery; in that no-one had much clue as to what any of the songs were about. The words were (at least) faintly comical but it didn't matter, and at least it wasn't boring or secondhand. The whole package of words, music and expert posing was irresistible though, catchy as hell and, for a year or so, they were a magnificent pop group.

Musclebound, Glow, Chant No.1, The Freeze all rode along with big (relatively anyway, for New Pop) drums clanging out and colossal, opaque chanted choruses on top, twitchy funk bass (of course) and skeletal Durutti Column /Chic-y guitar lines here and there. *Journeys To Glory* (and *Diamond*) was produced by **Landscape**'s Richard Burgess, whose big fat one-off 1981 hit, *Einstein-A-Go-Go* remains one of the early Eighties weirder and more wonderful hit singles, resembling Talking Heads on disco pills, musing about the Theory Of Relativity. Their debut album *From The Tea Rooms Of Mars...* is fully wonderful and includes the near hit single, *Norman Bates,* based on Hitchcock's *Psycho*. I have some strong affection for singles from their next record too, especially the beautiful, ambient lilting electronics of *So Good, So Pure, So Kind* but I seem to be about the only person who has, and is prepared to admit liking, this. So it goes.

THE HUMAN

LEAGUE

DARE

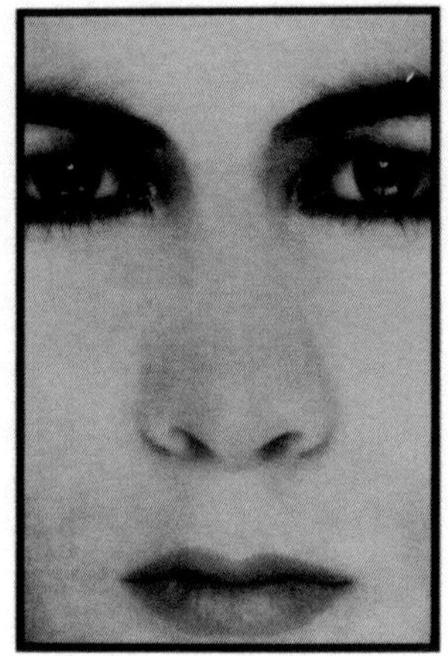

A perfect 10

This was Phil talking.

& MORALITY
by
Orchestral
Manœuvres
In The Dark
ARCHITECTURE

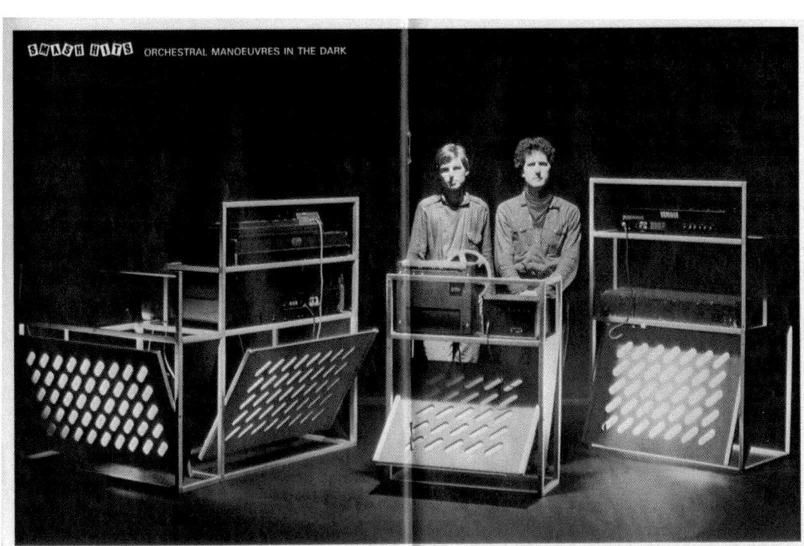
SMASH HITS
ORCHESTRAL MANOEUVRES IN THE DARK

Teen Idols.

DAZZLE SHIPS
OMD

Nice and Sleazy.

SPANDAU BALLET
TO CUT A LONG STORY
SHORT

MUSCLE BOUND
SPANDAU BALLET

JOURNEYS TO GLORY
SPANDAU BALLET

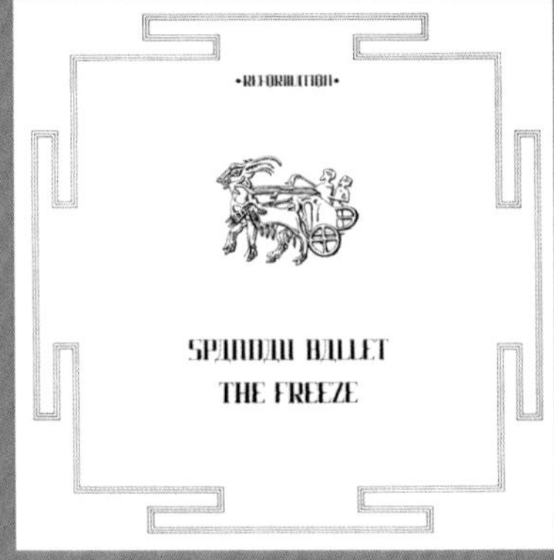
SPANDAU BALLET
THE FREEZE

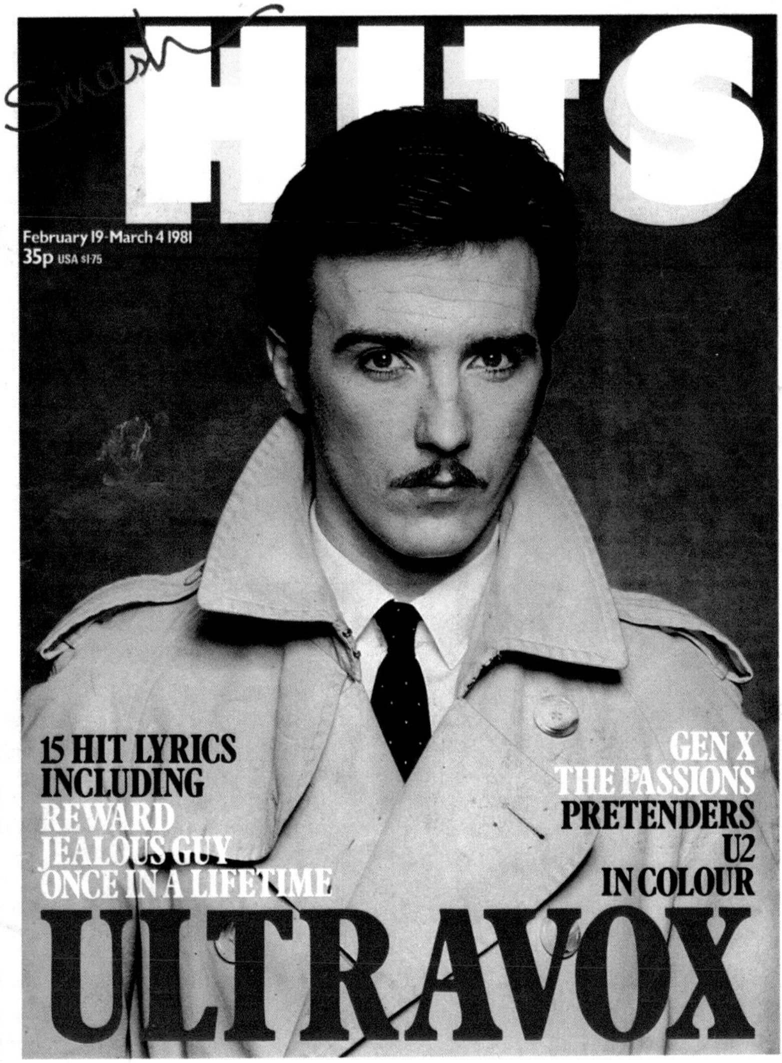

Smash HITS

February 19-March 4 1981

35p USA $1.75

15 HIT LYRICS
INCLUDING
REWARD
JEALOUS GUY
ONCE IN A LIFETIME

GEN X
THE PASSIONS
PRETENDERS
U2
IN COLOUR

ULTRAVOX

Smash HITS

January 22-February 4 1981
35p USA $1.75

THE LOOK
BAUHAUS
THE BEAT-
photofunnies

HIT LYRICS
including:
SCARY MONSTERS
YOUNG PARISIANS
IMAGINE

HAZEL
O'CONNOR
XTC
in colour

Steve Strange & Visage

There really hadn't been anything like these bands previously and I could not get enough. I love that first Spandau album and play it to this day and yes, the remastered bonus tracks version is worth getting, if you are curious and bold. Their look got them attention, quite often negatively so but that was very much the point. A nice suit and a haircut would just have been letting the music down. Ridicule was going to come calling and it would get them the coverage they needed. They knew it and threw the gauntlet down.

To many, Spandau were the ultimate worthless band, singled out among a swathe of allegedly worthless bands, undeserving of the attention; lacking in any talent or point, a decadent and risible product of That London's poncey club and A&R scene, who were more into pouting than playing and, of course, had that suitably stupid name. They were...twats, to many. The "kilts as fashion item" alone turned Scotland off en masse. Me, I loved them for exactly the same reasons. They understood how Pop works and that flouncing and rehearsed pouting had been a little thin on the ground during the Post Punk years.

The rules of pop are very strict however and if you stray too far from the reservation and achieve significant levels of subsequent awfulness, then you are retrospectively tarred (and feathered) with your own brush. You only have yourself to blame. For a long time, I wanted to call this book *New Gold Dream* because it's a brilliant phrase that sums up how I felt about this music as a teenager. Both Spandau and Simple Minds got bigger and bigger with worse and worse subsequent albums and both came masterfully unstuck when they felt the need to write actual songs addressing Important Things. No-one needed either band's inept analysis of decades of sectarian violence in Ireland. *Belfast Child* and *Through The Barricades* are the two worst singles of the Eighties. Despite Simple Minds' subsequent stadium status, it's the earlier, pre-fame albums that are the ones that are gaining critical momentum. I am still waiting for the reappraisal of *Journeys To Glory* but it will come. Won't it?

Professing to liking these bands did not make life easy back then, especially in South Wales. If Britain was not, by some distance, the tolerant, metrosexual cosmopolis it is (becoming) today, then Cardiff was, well, let's just say it was a bit further behind. It was rougher out there. Quite a lot rougher. Men were men and took to their fists to celebrate that fact at the drop of a pint. Looking different was not an invitation for trouble in Cardiff; it was an absolute guarantee of a visit to the Infirmary, if you were cornered alone. God help you if you had a pierced ear too, *"ewe bluddy pooftah"* (to be read in a Tom Jones voice).

Watching the teams of lads swarming through town on a Friday night was like watching a nature program. You could almost hear David Attenborough narrating. They all looked and dressed completely identically: stripy shirt and "slacks", for those who were aiming for ten pints and then a visit to the Ritzy (and the women within); or rugby top and jeans, for the less romantically gifted. No jacket required, obviously; "S'only a birrah bluddy rain, mun". These clusters of drunken landmines, down on day release from The Valleys, often collided in the dark along St Mary's Street, damaging anything and anyone within ten feet.

Notwithstanding those prevailing caveman attitudes, I don't think Marc Almond was really seen as a threat to the collective national manhood; and Adam had basically been a dress up pirate, which was not entirely unacceptable on paper. He was obviously one good exfoliatory scrubbing away from looking "normal" and the music was respectably rowdy.

However Phil Oakey felt a bit different. He was a veteran of the Post Punk dungeon, and knew what was cool and what was not. He knew he didn't have to leap about on stage to command attention. He just stood his ground on TOTP, looked the nation in the eye and dared you to blink first. A big, booming Northerner, singing songs about girls to girls but wearing lots of actual MAKE UP on his eyes and lips, rather than across his nose, and rocking THAT haircut.

It is amazing to think that a lopsided ladies' bob was such a big deal in those days – but it was. People hadn't adopted the permanence of tattoos in such great numbers and that lopsided haircut represented A Commitment. He was STUCK looking like that; when he went to the shops and....everything.

But, I thought excitedly, a Commitment to what? And was there a way I could join in, or at least sidle in closer, because it all looked like massive fun. Very slightly scary, transgressive fun perhaps but definitely fun. Oakey says of his appearance then, *"it wasn't really a gay thing. It wasn't effeminate – it was somewhere in between. I did have about ten or fifteen years where I didn't wear any men's clothing, but it wasn't really women's clothing either. It was just... somewhere else." (© BlindYouth.co.uk)*

The Human League had previously embodied the cold, flat Northern machine funk of the Post Punk era, derived in part from songs like Iggy's *Nightclubbing*, but had always had a beating heart of Pop, albeit one that was not totally realised and was kept underfed in an ironic cage, as exemplified by covers of **Gary Glitter** and **The Righteous Brothers.**

At the outset of 1981, however, I had no idea they existed. By the end, they seemed like the biggest and best band in the world. The Mark 1 Human League had been going since the late Seventies, to solid critical acclaim. *Being Boiled* had been a critical hit, when released on Fast Product in 1978. The band had toured the UK as support to **The Rezillos** (featuring a young future member in Jo Callis) and **Siouxsie & The Banshees.** By the end of 1978, they had been feted by **David Bowie**, who showed up at The Nashville in London to see them and paraphrased the description applied to one of His heroes, Bruce Springsteen, describing them thusly *"I have seen the future of pop music"*. Clever old David. He could see that The Human League were taking his industrial noises, and those of Kraftwerk and slowly kneading them into the shape of actual Pop songs.

By 1979, helped by Bowie, they'd supported **Iggy Pop** across Europe and also been mentioned by **The Undertones** in their 1980 single, *My Perfect Cousin ("His mother bought him a synthesiser/Got the Human League in to advise her*"). A band feted by Bowie, who hadn't had a hit, being mentioned in another band's big hit is indicative that their star was rising and they were making their presence felt. They signed to Virgin in May 1979 and had taken their A&R's advice to try something more commercial, albeit somewhat unwillingly. "I Don't Depend On You" was, rather oddly, released under the pseudonym, **The Men**, and was lifted up by a couple of female backing singers. It sounds more like something from *Dare* than anything they'd release for two years. Main songwriters Ian Marsh and Martyn Ware hated it. Just too damn poppy for industrial pioneers, I expect. It seems likely that Oakey disagreed somewhat. It failed to capture anyone's imagination and the band went back to their ever-so-slightly lumpy synthpop.

Meanwhile **Gary Numan** took over their title as the "future of pop" and scored two fantastic #1 singles in 1979, with *Are Friends Electric?* and *Cars*. Numan had also gone a bit Synthpop overnight. He had borrowed so much disconnected sangue froid chic and Velvet Underground love from David Bowie that he was singled out for abuse, if the rumour is to be believed, as *"One of the new wave boys, Same old thing in brand new drag"* in the lyric for *Scary Monsters' highlight, Teenage Wildlife*. Watching interviews with Gary back then, his spoken voice does sound very like fellow Londoner, Bowie's.

His use of synths was groundbreaking and seemingly a happy accident, resulting from a spare day messing around with new toys, found in the studio, on what was to be a *"punk album"*. The way he combined the new technology with live drums and bass made for really phat sounding recordings, which still sounded very futuristic and yet trampled over many of the early, feeble-sounding attempts at doing the same.

So, let's say we all agree on those two songs being amazing. We do, right? I am happy to go further and say that the first batch of albums are pretty, if unevenly, great too. *Tubeway Army, Replicas, Pleasure Principle* and *Telekon*, and, oh go on then, *Dance* are all a bit special. For all that Gary may have borrowed elements from anyone, and this book should demonstrate that critically skewering everyone who stole from Bowie is asking for trouble; he carved out and strongly defended his own musical corner. Each of those albums stumbles along a fine line between ballsy individuality, self-parody and nonsensical drivel. It's both unwise and impossible to go along with all of it with a straight face. *"I Nearly Married A Human", "Stormtrooper In Drag"* and *"Remember I Was Vapour"* were wincingly silly titles even then, when pretending to be a robot was the height of fascism – I mean, fashion. Gary didn't seem to know or possibly didn't care about such things. Almost immediately he was his own most sincere parodist. There are a handful of grotesquely bad songs on each of those records and there are also a handful of really quite inspired, beautiful, clever and dazzling Pop songs too. He didn't make it easy for anyone. It didn't help that Gary Was a self-confessed Tory, much opposed to Labour's ideas on taxing his royalties. Such self-sabotage grew to be very much part of his schtick.

Undeterred by their new rival, **The Human League** released their debut album *Reproduction* (1979) and its big and *"tall, tall, tall"* single, *Empire State Human, which* again failed to capture the record buyers' imagination, selling in modest numbers. They allege that Numan stole their moves in an interview for their one TV appearance from that time on a program called *Mainstream,* promoting *Empire State Human* and also debuting Oakey's lobsided haircut and, it's hard to ignore, his quite badly flat singing.

Reproduction is a pretty good album, although much of it comes across as a little dated now. Such is the durability of the prototype future. Their cover of *You've Lost That Loving Feeling* is kind of fun though. They were lined up to support Talking Heads that autumn but were booted off the tour before it began on account of the reaction to this Press Release, issued by their manager, falling on less enthusiastic ears than they had bargained for: *"The Human League, intrigued to experience their own performance themselves, have designed a remotely controlled touring entertainment. Therefore, 30 Human League minutes will be available on the upcoming Talking Heads tour. The League themselves may well join the audience on some evenings to savour the occasion. The arrangement will allow them on other evenings to continue working on their second album in their Sheffield workshop."* This is both pure Kraftwerkian thinking and controversial to a degree they hadn't quite anticipated. It probably didn't sit too well with the Musician's Union either, who were already sniffing around Numan, with mutterings of his synthesizers putting real musicians out of work.

1980's *Holiday '80* EP got the band onto Top Of The Pops, performing the third track, a quite faithful cover of **Gary Glitter**'s *Rock'n'Roll Pt.1* and they scored a minor hit. Produced by Richard Mainwaring, who went on to produce **OMD**'s *Architecture & Morality*, the more commercial and dynamic second album, *Travelogue* was released in May 1980 to better reviews and reached #16 in the UK charts but yielded no hit single, despite containing a new version of Being Boiled. It stands up way better than the debut and if you like *Dare*, you should give it a go. And if you don't like Dare, then I am not sure we have all that much to talk about. Listen to *Travelogue* if only to hear their cover of a Gordon's gin advert, written by Jeff Wayne (of course). Their perky cover of Spider From Mars, **Mick Ronson**'s *Only After Dark* is absolutely amazing, and really paints the song in a more apt setting. It should have been a hit but was relegated to being included with the re-release of Empire State Human, which still only reached #62. Re-releases and cover versions failing only added to the band's internal problems and by the end of 1980 they had fallen apart extremely acrimoniously. The main song-writers Ware and Marsh left to continue their electronic experimentation, with singer Glenn Gregory, whom they had originally wanted instead of Oakey, as **Heaven 17** and later, with a host of singers, including **Billy MacKenzie** and an out-of-favour **Tina Turner** as **BEF,** the **British Electric Foundation**, which was conceived to truthfully portray Pop as a business. Oakey says, *"I think they were finding it a bit embarrassing, what we were doing. They thought it was too poppy or something, and they were happy to go and look like backroom boys somewhere else. Whereas, you know, all I ever wanted to do was be Donna Summer."* *However,* as Martyn countered, *"Heaven 17 is a 100% serious attempt to be incredibly popular, whereas B.E.F. is no less serious but tends to be involved with more experimental projects."*

Phil Oakey kept the name, **The Human League**, fired up by his ego, his ideas and his desire to be a massive pop star. The name came saddled with various incumbent debts and problems. Quite a gamble. It seems that all concerned thought that he would fail miserably and that the talent had left the band. He recruited a new band with ten days' notice to fulfil touring commitments and avoid being sued by promoters. It's a lovely thought to believe that he recruited teenagers Joanne Catherall and Susanne Sulley, whom he spotted dancing in a nightclub, on a whim, in the hope of injecting some glamour into the band, and who knows, he was desperate enough to try such a thing; maybe it's true.

What is definitely true, however is that it is an amazing and resonant story, that Oakey has told and retold for decades now, that mirrors the lyric of the band's biggest hit. The first single the new **Human League** released together was their catchiest yet. *Boys And Girls,* produced by John Leckie, was their biggest hit thus far, charting at #48 in February 1981. It's fine enough, the vocals soar away but the music remains earthbound, held back by a flat and mechanical groove. This was progress but it was as nothing compare to what was to follow.

Two months later in April, the first single from The Human League 2.0 emerged from their recent sessions with Martin Rushent, who'd worked with **T Rex** and **The Stranglers.** The recording was aided right at the crucial moment by the acquisition of the newly invented Linn Drum. It was the missing piece of the puzzle. *Sound Of The Crowd* was stunning and undeniable. An instant classic. It reached #12 and took the new Human League back onto *Top Of The Pops* and into my life. Rushent's minimal, sexy production was what was needed to contrast with the occasionally flat tool that was Oakey's voice and the relentless groove, and beautifully panned drums of *Sound Of The Crowd* were a revelation. The arrangement was perfect and, although nothing much was added to the recipe, other than a deft touch and some sparing FX, all of a sudden The Human League made sense. Producers can do the most wonderful things.

The feline follow-up, *Love Action (I Believe In Love)* was another triumph and a massive crossover hit that went to #3, and was one of the many great singles of that era (that employed (vaguely pointless) brackets (that I love and still miss (sometimes))). They were Pop stars now and there was no denying it. Your mum knew their name. *Love Action* in turn was followed by *Open Your Heart*, which hit #6 with its surging crystalline synthpop and huge multi-tiered and uplifting choruses. It had to be the peak, surely. I had never heard anything I loved more in my life. Way more disco than anything the band had released before, there was nothing of their whirring, clicking Post Punk roots left and Oakey was actually singing in different keys, aided by the girls' backing vocals.

Their third album *Dare* was released to inevitable and universal acclaim in October 1981 and went straight to #1. NME's Paul Morley said it was *"the first* ***Human League*** *greatest hits collection"*. A fairy tale pop ending and a brilliant story of balls and belief, setbacks, near ruin and triumph. It's pure Hollywood, right? It is a perfect pop album in every way and, along with *Architecture & Morality*, released a few weeks previously, was the first to convey the wonder of the synthpop singles into the album format with total success. I've played it a thousand times and if you have not heard it, I suggest you throw this book down and go and fix that disastrous flaw in your character right away.

Opener The Things That Dreams Are Made Of is a list song, detailing "....all the things you ever dared". *Do or Die* blends just a hint of synthetic reggae into a spiteful song about an Ex. They stuck with covers, this time including the much cooler theme to *Get Carter* by Roy Budd. *I Am The Law* is about Judge Dredd, of course, and *Seconds* is an (only very slightly trite) effort to write about JFK's assassination. *Dare* sold bucketloads all over the world and was still buoyant in the charts in 1983, dipping out after a very impressive seventy one weeks. The logo was swiped from the cover of Vogue magazine and the faces were close cropped because, as Sulley explains, "*we wanted people to still be able to buy the album in five years, we thought that hair styles would be the first thing to date. We had no idea people would still be buying it 25* [now 35] *years later.*"

The rise of **the Human League** was only just getting started. The brave choice to release *Don't You Want Me* in December, happened against Oakey's wishes, who thought it the weakest track, hence it hiding at the end of the album. Its autobiographical-ish story of plucking a girl to make her a star, was coupled with a moody and quite Hollywood video, with the band acting out the lyrics and a strong performance from Susanne Sulley, playing out her real life role. It was just too much to resist. It became a global hit, topping the charts all over the world, including America and selling over 1.5 million copies in the UK alone, stayed at #1 for five long brilliant weeks in the UK.

The massive momentum of *Dare* even dragged **The Human League**'s early single, the bizarrely brilliant *Being Boiled* in to the Top Ten too. It sounds like (and is) a different band playing archetypical post punk electronics; all whirring, clicking and impenetrable of lyric. It is something of a primitive pop masterpiece but even dialling back the calendar six months, it would seem ludicrous to suggest that this was a crossover hit bound for the top end of the charts. Yet it really did seem as though someone had broken out the fairy dust over

Christmas and there it was; arms folded and bewildered, just above **Altered Images** *I Could Be Happy* and **Dollar**'s *Mirror Mirror*, looking up knowingly at **Kraftwerk**'s *The Model*, and *Don't You Want Me,* above it.

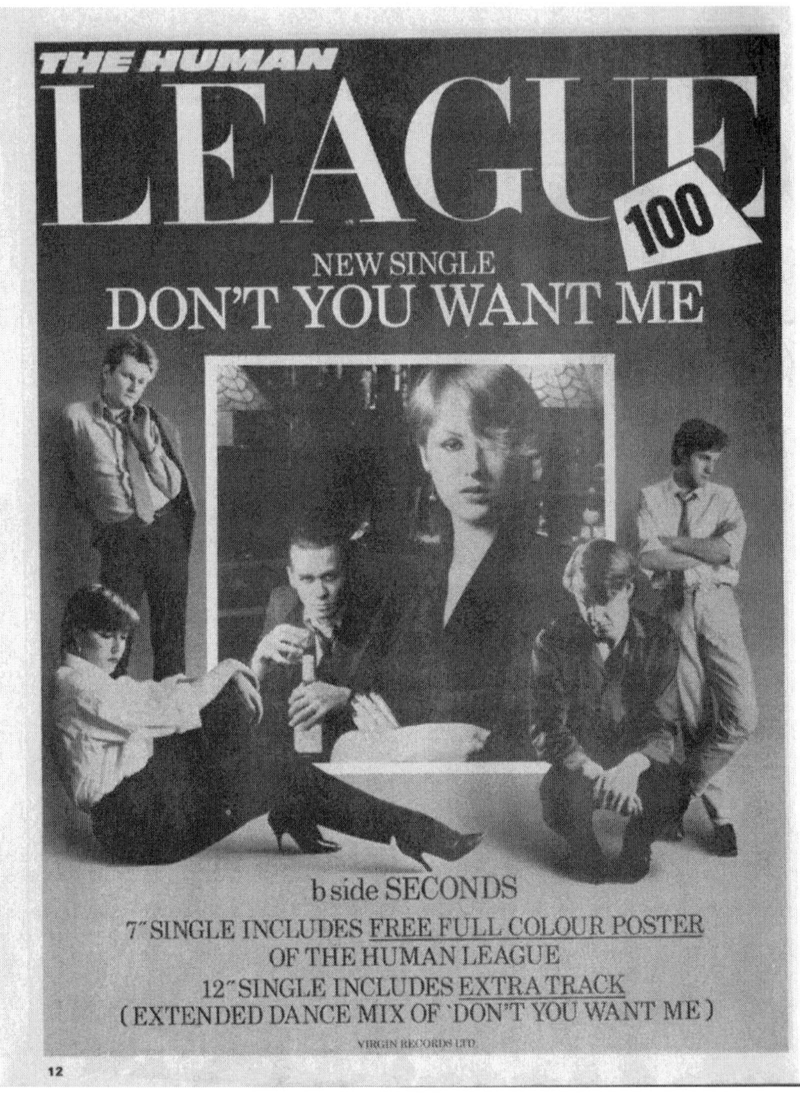

Synthpop was going to dominate the world. The robots had started to take over. In the recording studios, at least. Even in The **Times, the 1981 Man of The Year was THE COMPUTER. What the Bleep?**

Those bands dominated the charts. Punk had not brushed away the old guard, although it had started the ball rolling. After outbreaks of amazing music studding the charts in 1978-1981, and especially at the close of 1981, there was a sense of anticipation and excitement. Even in America, the newly minted MTV was letting these glamorous Brits in, sneaking past the walls that US Radio had built specifically to keep this sort of thing out.

Once those brave souls had staked out the ground for a new colourful pop music that was not going to be reliant on anything from the past, the floodgates were opened and the Seventies were finally shrugged off like the tawdry grey skin they were.

In a manner not unlike that bit in *The Wizard Of Oz;* when we came back to school after a white Christmas in 1981, and thought *Don't You Want Me?* was probably going to be at #1 forever, the whole Pop world just burst into colour. And it stayed that way.

04. TOO STIFF: FUNK GETS SERIOUS. DISCO IS EXHUMED.

How Funk and Disco freshened up the pot after Punk

ORANGE JUICE NEW ORDER GANG OF FOUR

As an antidote to boredom and two fingers up the nose of studied, empty cool, Stiff Records' parallel history of Post Punk is responsible for many joyful things. **Ian Dury** is one of them. **The Blockheads** are six more. At the dark end of the Seventies, sleepy old Pop music was in dire need of a brutal kick up the arse. Punk had burned brightly and had invigorated many but, truth be told, the Top Forty was not really that much different afterwards. More than any other independent label, Stiff cheerfully booted its acts into the charts with uncanny accuracy and regularity. Ignoring the rules on appearances, fashion, cool and common sense, they found band after band that played with real passion, soul and, crucially, a duty of entertainment, that had roots in cabaret as much as Punk.

The footage of The Blockheads on Youtube and on BBC4's vibrating documentaries shows a remarkable group; a sweaty, chaotic and scrupulously tight band. A funk band. Albeit a funk band that seemed to have more in common with the bar fight boogies and 3am epiphanies of Bruce's **E Street Band** than the legions of paper thin **Earth Wind And Fire** facsimiles that smugged up the cocktail circuit. And that was the thing, wasn't it? The Blockheads were the kind of Funk that was not supposed to be sweet and smooth. Instead it was ragged, urgent and dripping beer sweat in your face. A new crop of mainly white bands were squeezing funk into different, darker places. At least the ones we will ponder here were.

At the same time that **Ian Dury** was kicking off a string of brilliant Punk, if you really must, Funk hit singles which, in 1977 alone, included *Sweet Gene Vincent, What A Waste* and the colossal *Sex & Drugs & Rock & Roll;* things were bending their bass strings, deep down in the West Country. In Bristol, Mark Stewart formed **The Pop Group**, a flickering, Punk-informed, extremely political funk/dub band. Mark said in Rolling Stone in 2014, "At age 11 or 12 I got into Alice Cooper, Mick Ronson and David Bowie through children's telly like *Top of the Pops*. Bowie was more of a teacher than anything I learned at school. I heard about Jean Genet through "Gene Genie," which led me to [William] Burroughs, Lou Reed and weird French poetry like Lautréamont. Bowie was a teen pop star but he was also a portal. It was bizarre". Yep, He was the gateway drug to a great many things for a great many people.

A year or two later, members of The Pop Group spawned the jazzier, brighter feeling international musical mashup that was **Rip, Rig And Panic** (featuring a very youthful **Neneh Cherry**), and, up the road in Cheltenham, the remarkably durable **Pigbag**, who did THAT single and scored a Top Twenty album off the back of it. Except, being principled citizens of Punkytown, the ensuing hit instrumental album, *Dr Heckle & Mr Jive*, didn't have *Papa's Got A Brand New Bag* on it. Life was tough in the underground, or it was until the CD Bonus track reissue industry got going. I was listening to it just now and it's not aged massively well, or maybe never was a massively strong collection. However the horny parade ground Funk of *Papa's Got A Brand New Bag* is now a modern classic, kept alive in playgrounds and football grounds all around the country. You know it, even if you don't know its name. It had already sold thousands of copies as the single released ahead of the album in 1981, but Stiff re-released it and took it to #3 in the UK charts. PUB FACT: Their *Top Of The Pops* performances in 1982, include future uber-producer Nellie Hooper, even though he wasn't in the band.

These mainly white bands' records were produced by the likes of reggae head, Dennis Bovell and On-U maestro, **Adrian Sherwood,** who has been playing his own brand of slightly earnest, dark dub since the late Seventies. All these people with backgrounds in bands and soundsystems, began mixing disparate genres of party starters with Punk attitudes. Many of these committed bassheads, helped along by lashings of weed, formed the nebulous basis of what would become known much later as The Bristol Sound of **The Wild Bunch, Tricky** and **Massive Attack. Portishead** too but I always thought their music came from different, less traditionally joyous, sources like **Public Enemy, Morricone, Nico** and **Aretha** at her most heartbroken.

There is another, murkier yet, swimming lane that can be demarcated in this complex gene pool of Bass DNA. One that starts with the primal rumblings of **Iggy**'s exorcism as *The Idiot,* extends through the first couple of bass driven and slightly psychotic albums by **Public Image Limited** and on into the dark symphonies of desolation that comprise **Joy Division**'s songbook. Grinding depression, spiralling anguish, drug paranoia and relentless bass go hand in hand here, with jagged, needle-sharp guitars continually ripping open the mental wounds. No-one's going to call any of those records funky, but they all share a similar deconstruction of bass led music and they each shut out all light and colour. These are neither communal anthems, nor songs meant to be shared at all. This is a personal, contemplative and isolated art, which draws a chalk outline around its psyche and offers no optimism, no solution, save the consolation that you are not the first to be surrounded and enslaved by your own dark thoughts. I think they are each among the greatest pieces of art ever made and cannot recommend these records strongly enough. If you are game for a crack at the dark stuff, then these are songs that will stay with you for life. The chalk circle is closed firmly here, knowing that Ian Curtis chose *The Idiot* to soundtrack his own suicide.

Joy Division were not the household name they are now, back in 1980, even in the wake of Ian Curtis's suicide. Three films in recent years and the early-death-of-a-talent-plus-time equation have justifiably elevated them to the level of an iconic band now but it took Curtis' death to get them anywhere near the charts. They were and are a large cult band but, very much like The Velvets, their music has been a huge influence on every subsequent generation of bands (thus far), who have been drawn to the dark side. Their two albums are key Goth texts now and have inspired hundreds of cover versions. The list of bands that have covered the frankly uncoverable Joy Division is endless; just the ones beginning with A runs to over 40 on this fansite http://www.joydiv.org/covers.htm.

Curtis' beautiful, heartbreaking confessional poetry stands as the gold standard for bands as diverse as **Manic Street Preachers** and **Bright Eyes**. His deep explorations into his own selfishness, weakness and insecurity were merciless and beautiful. Their requiem album *Closer* inches precariously across the frail bridge from visceral art to suicide note.

It took the public a little longer to cotton on to the importance of their music but it still continues to reach new listeners every year, bands from **OMD** to **Tears For Fears** then, to **How To Dress Well** and **Nine Inch Nails** now just wouldn't exist without Ian Curtis. Joy Division are one of those bands that inspire people to pour their pain into art and to form bands, in the same way that The Velvet Underground did. Ian is another singer who was not technically gifted but his emotionally electric delivery inspired hundreds of singers to not let a lack of traditionally recognisable talent stop them getting behind the microphone, for better or, quite often, for much worse. The bleakly minimal yet immersive and hypnotic nature of Joy Division's music is even more influential and the modern electronic producers of the 21st century, from **Burial** to **Arca,** carry the flame with their harsh, inner-city soundscapes and unflashy monochrome minimalism, which is now even extending into Hip Hop in a way that would not have seemed likely a few years back. In 1979, Martin Hannet described Joy Division as "dancing music, with Gothic overtones". Damn straight.

Having much in common with Krautrock's endless metronomics and the blank stare, rolling basslines and manic twitches of **Iggy Pop**'s Berlin albums with Bowie; New York's No Wave scene in the late Seventies brought together a lot of vaguely like-minded bands, artists and DJs. Their art, although it had no real commercial impact, triggered repercussions that are still inspiring new bands to form and mutate today. It was a sarcastic, ugly stepchild of disco, with most of the frivolity, fun and key changes carved out. Bands like **DNA, Lydia Lunch's Teenage Jesus And The Jerks, James Chance & The Contortions** and **Liquid Liquid** (whose song *Cavern* was used as the backing track to **Grandmaster Flash & Melle Mel**'s *White Lines (Don't Do it)*), played a brand of dead-eyed, slightly atonal funk, which stretches the definition of Pop music a bit, being defended against casual listeners by its own grating barbed wire attitudes. In the wrong environment, the songs can oscillate fractiously between boring and oppressive, depending on the volume, but they definitely work as body music, as insistent physical instruction. Dancing is inevitable. Listen to Brian Eno's 1978 compilation *No New York*, or the brilliant, and more welcoming, Soul Jazz Records three part compilation series *New York Noise*. It's music as an incessant itch. If you don't scratch that itch and dance, it is going to drive you to distraction. That is a very Punk Rock idea, isn't it? Music as frustration. A relentless sense of tension without release and yet fusing ever more complex emotions into the tunes. It's also Proper Art, as the medium becomes the message. It's an outburst, an expression, something not intended for mass consumption.

Aside from the No Wave artists, the band that seemed the key influence in the slightly underwhelming Second Summer of Punk Funk, as it hopefully isn't known, in 2005 was Leeds' **Gang Of Four**. Just as everyone started pretending they'd always been listening to the not entirely unfunky **Wire** during Britpop, it seemed that all of a sudden bands were listening to, and ripping off, **Gang Of Four** en masse. **The Rapture, Bloc Party, LCD Soundsystem, Yeah Yeah Yeahs, Liars** and a lot of less memorable London bands, that failed to fulfil early promise, all went to or played at Erol Alkan's Monday night Trash club (1997-2007). That club night's influence among the music media had already helped propel the Garage Rock Revival in 2001 (White Stripes, Strokes etc) and would go on to incubate Punk Funk's boggle-eyed and surely adopted son, Nu-Rave (Klaxons, um, etc) and went some way to helping keep **James Murphy**'s slightly erratic but never boring DFA Records afloat. Incidentally James chose **Liquid Liquid** as the support to LCD's farewell show at Madison Square Gardens in 2012.

Gang Of Four were based around guitarist/polemicist/lyricist Andy Gill and singer/lyricist Jon King, along with Dave Allen (who later left to form the inscrutably dark disco subversives, **Shriekback**) and Hugo Burnham. They debuted on Fast Product (Human League, Mekons etc) in 1978 with the single *Damaged Goods,* which itself went on to inspire the excellent and very long running punk rock label of the same name, run by the inimitable Ian Damaged. The debut single set out their stall. Stark and minimal, scratchy and pummelling. Angry but controlled, persuasive and reasoned. The minimal songs are self-recorded live and it's all mixed very democratically. Each instrument shoulders an equal share of the weight and the band are unbelievably tight. There is no fat, no soloing, and, emblematically, no harmony. The tension is palpable and they rock really really hard.

They were Marxist leaning, deeply anti-Capitalist and clearly Punk's even more cynical and focussed children but the inclusion of Dub and Funk DNA placed them at the fore of Post Punk and their colossal influence, musically and didactically, as a free thinking band, has been felt ever since. Kurt Cobain has described the idea behind **Nirvana** as *"basically a rip-off of Gang Of Four and Scratch Acid"*. Flea from the **Chilli Peppers** says they *"were the first to make me go crazy and dance and fuck and feel like I was part of something really cool…it was really fucking art"*. **Michael Stipe** said of their debut album, *"Entertainment shredded everything that came before it. Gang Of Four know how to swing. I stole a lot from them"*. Not that **REM** are known as swingers particularly, nor Flea as a totemic Marxist (although, a totem pole perhaps…) but the Funk ripples from this commercially underwhelming British band have powered many of the titans of American rock music in the last thirty years. There are those that will trace funk metal's DNA back through the Chilli Peppers and lay it at Andy Gill's feet; but that seems a little harsh. And ungrateful.

On the *Green* Tour in 1989, introducing the new album's centrepiece, *World Leader Pretend*, Michael Stipe sings the title line from *We Live, As We Dream, Alone,* the closing song on Gang of Four's third album, *Songs Of The Free,* which is in itself a quote from Joseph Conrad's *Heart Of Darkness.* That tour represented REM at the peak of their powers, by the way. Go look at the arty and muscular *Tourfilm* DVD of that tour, if you haven't. I have little patience for live DVDs but that monochrome wonder is in a class of its own. It's a beautifully shot chiaroscuro masterpiece that works well with the music off but, y'know, I do recommend you have the sound up nonetheless, especially if you are in a new band.

Is it possible for a band's legacy to be to encourage free thinking? Without wishing to invoke the scene that greets Brian's mum as she opens the curtains in *Life of Brian*, I think so. **Gang of Four**'s principles came first and foremost and the music was not perhaps secondary but on an equal footing. The medium was still the message but their message was explicit and paramount. Not to be compromised. They walked off *Top Of The Pops* for an early potentially career making performance of the twitchy brilliance that is *At Home, He's A Tourist*, refusing to sanitise the word "rubbers" to "rubbish", to avoid a nation's blushes, or somesuch. The first two albums are gaining critical momentum with each passing season but, while I think they are brilliant, I do find their albums a little hectoring sometimes, if taken whole. The debut, *Entertainment* is more abrasive, urgent and exciting. The second, *Solid Gold,* is a little warmer and has some of the spikes softened, or at least countered by a bigger, phatter bottom end, but for that reason it pokes a slightly less effective laserwire into your cerebellum. They are not supposed to be an easy ride, either of them; and yet this is still very much pop music. If you've not checked in for a while, *I Found That Essence Rare* is still a visceral kick, a surgical strike on indolence. It's funny, isn't it; just as with films, there are records that blow you away with their fierce genius, technical prowess and/or eye-opening sucker-punches but they are not ones you necessarily want to go back to on a Saturday night, or ever. Looking at you, *City Of God*.

The third album, 1982's punsomely titled, *Songs For The Free* is almost a different band. It's almost like they skipped an awkward intermediary album and arrived, dressed to impress, at Pop's own house party. It's produced by Mike Howlett (who also produced **OMD, Tears For Fears** and **Blancmange**, played in **Gong** and PUB FACT, was the singer/bassist in The embryonic **Police** before parting company with them) and is the first that features the voice and bass of Sara Lee (replacing Allen). It houses their most famous, or least obscure, single, *I Love A Man In Uniform*. Alas despite being groomed for the top, it only reached #65 in the charts, having been banned by the BBC for mentioning uniforms (and the allure of shooting guns), which were deemed politically sensitive during the Falklands fiasco. It sounds fantastic in a club today and would have sat very comfortably in the Top Ten then, were it not for the BBC's foibles. Hearing it now, it just doesn't compute that it wasn't a worldwide hit. **Gang Of Four** were undoubtedly an influence on many of the bands in this chapter, and many in the book but by 1982 they were beginning to sound like the bands that had followed their lead. Is that a bad thing? Maybe hair shirted critics' loss was pop music's gain? And maybe they were still leading the pack; just not commercially?

Looming above all of these bands, and the only one that all your friends will have heard of, is **Talking Heads.** I think I may have been a bit harsh in leaving this band out of my opening chapter. Considered a New Wave band, they came up on the artier edges of New York's, CBGBs Punk scene, along with Blondie and The Ramones, whom they supported in 1975 at their first gig as Talking Heads. They really are no-one's idea of a punk band though. The songs are all jams, built on solid rhythmic grooves with melodic touches daubed and scratched on top. There is a strong, and over the course of the albums, incrementally increasing, North African influence to David Byrne's spidery yet fluid guitar (accentuated by the hand drums and percussion), set atop taut (is there any kind?) and jittery funk grooves supplied by the rhythm section, Chris Frantz and Tina Weymouth (who had a parallel career as the more carefree **Tom Tom Club**) and finally Jerry Harrison's bouncy and propulsive keyboards and vocals.

Their first two albums *Talking Heads: 77* in 1977 and *More Songs About Buildings And Food* in 1978 are a little cold, tense and bumpy, although the truly wonderful hit single, *Psycho Killer*, set inside a serial killer's mind, is on the debut, and turns all of the things I don't care for about the band, the studied and slightly bloodless dislocation, into a virtue for that one song. Third album, *Fear Or Music* is one of those records in the Canon of Critically Bulletproof albums, that I just never warmed to, even though, or just possibly because a lot of my friends have always sworn by it. It feels warmer, rounder and more produced. The band were another group who have maintained a long term collaboration with Eno, like Roxy, Bowie, U2 and Coldplay. He is not credited as producer on *Fear Of Music*, as is his wont, but as providing Treatments. Eno sees himself as a catalyst not a boss in the studio and while this is undoubtedly a well-produced album, try as I might, I remain pretty much unmoved by the songs. *Life During Wartime* is kind of fun(ky), I suppose, but not up with their best. Again the songs sound like they evolved from jams, rather than melodies. I will admit to having a soft spot for *Air*, with Tina's beautiful backing vocals and the Roxy-ish *Heaven*, which has A Proper Tune. So there. I am more than happy to walk away with a handful of useful burgers from sacking sacred cows. Thus far, Talking Heads' records sounds good but most of the songs leave me untouched. They seem overly intellectual (and I am truly a bit of a snob for that in the right circumstances) but lacking in entertainment for me, which has to be there too, doesn't it? Maybe I just never warmed to David Byrne. You probably love Talking Heads. Good for you; we needn't fall out over this.

Their next record, 1980's *Remain In Light*, their third in a row helmed by Eno, gave them a worldwide hit in the unforgettable *Once In A Lifetime*. I remember buying that single and I remember, a few months later, getting this album taped for me. Sorry to continue a theme but this album has seven of-a-par tracks based on jams, that seem to unravel until the last and slowest one, which sounds a lot like Joy Division...and one song, one perfect moment, bursting with life and questions and genius and fun that was obviously laser-beamed in from outer space. *Once In A Lifetime* sounds, as its title seems to admit, like a fluke. All four members of the band aligning in the perfect combination, unlocking a gem. It hogs all of the ideas on the record. My expectations for *Remain In Light* were sky high; I'd been drawn to its brilliantly weird cover, looming out of record shop windows, and I was so very disappointed when I heard it. Not, of course, the first or last time that that has happened.

I am not sure why exactly it was that *Lifetime* hit home so hard with me at the time but it did. It was like a door opening in my mind, unsettling me yet compelling me through it – into a world where things were broadly similar but tempered at enough of a psychological slant to let me know that I was surely dreaming, or at least tip-toeing merrily through someone else's dream. Doncha just love it when the memory of first hearing a song remains so vivid and visceral? I have always bracketed it mentally with **Peter Gabriel**'s *Games Without Frontiers*, released a year earlier. There is a certain disquieting, what-the-hell-is-going-on-please aspect to both songs and both dangle their exact meaning just out of reach, allowing you to sense their intentions and feelings but requiring a leap of faith, a common assumption, filling in your own gaps and details. That is about the highest compliment I can pay a pop song, really. Poetry and motion, that's all I ask.

By and large, and with the exception of Talking Heads, most of this fluid Funk music was still sloshing around in the underground in the early Eighties, but ever since **David Bowie** had made people, who'd not previously considered it relevant or possible, think twice about funk in 1975 and 1976, more and more bands were experimenting with it; usually to raggedly cacophonous effect. John Peel's sessions were the safe haven for this white funk rabble with **The Higsons** and **Maximum Joy** among many bands that flowered there but never troubled the public at large. Sweaty, shouty Big Band Funk, clipped electro-dubby Funk, the never ending disco craze, Giorgio and **Kraftwerk**'s Mechanifunk were all shouting their corners and it was getting quite hard to resist for a lot of bands.

New, young groups that were Punk survivors, or were inspired by Post Punk or New Wave or any combination thereof, who would naturally become Rock'n'Roll bands, Punk bands, can't-sing-but-have-something-to-say Peelbound bands, were slowly becoming overpowered by funk. It is arguable that, perhaps inspired by The Clash, first among the punks to blend wildly disparate genres into their tunes, and all the bands mentioned above, the new crop of groups did indeed set out to combat rockism and, more and more, they allowed a little swing into their step. I dare say that, after seeing audiences bouncing the crap out of each other, or spitting at the stage with joyous abandon, it was quite nice to see a room dancing happily and doubly nice to see the additional women that tend to come along with that sensibility.

Orange Juice, along with **Joseph K** and **Aztec Camera** emerged on Alan Horne's Postcard label in Glasgow at the tail end of the Seventies. Those bands releases pretty much set the bar for jangly independent guitar music, up until the Smiths' arrival. The Rickenbackers are fast and furious on Orange Juice's Postcard releases. Resplendent in one of the Eighties' greatest and most vibrant sleeves, their debut album, the wonderful *You Can't Hide Your Love Forever,* came out on Polydor and the songs were a little less urgent now, more spacious, relaxed and soulful. Their love of old soul records was made explicit by a cover of **Al Green**'s *L.O.V.E Love*, which was released as a single, followed wrongheadedly by *Felicity*, which sounds more like the Postcard incarnation of the band, albeit a bit more competently produced.

Despite great reviews and coverage in the music press, and beginning to find a foothold in pop world via Smash Hits, the singles weren't hits, but the album peaked at #21 in the UK and still justifiably gets critics hot under the collar. Indeed it is being re-released as I type this. You can hear and feel the potential bursting out of the band. Their tempos are a little less urgent now but the scope and vision that Edwyn Collins and Malcolm Ross had for the band is clearly evident. Non-album single *Two Hearts Together,* was allegedly a sarcastically reflexive nod to **Haircut 100**, who seemed to have taken a sanitised and organised variety of Orange Juice's ideas straight into the Top Ten ahead of them. It also stalled short of the Top Forty. These days, of course, the band would be dropped unceremoniously at this point, if not a good while before, but Polydor gave it another go. Just like **The Four Tops** perfectly executed Motown single *I Can't Help Myself,* Orange Juice's next single was also called *I Can't Help Myself* and its horns, handclaps and clever metapunnery, namechecking The Four Tops (*"it probably sounds trite")* picked up a lot radio play and the whole unlikely wheeze almost worked, ditching at sea at a very frustrating

#42. I remember seeing the cute and smart cut and paste adverts in Smash Hits for single after single that didn't quite hit home. The band seemed destined not to connect despite a big push from the label.

I Can't Help Myself was the first salvo from the new album and it was followed by *Flesh Of My Flesh,* which also fell short of being a hit. It's a Bontempi organ and lounge horns festooned easy listening track, that hints at Sinatra. Although Sinatra never opened a song with the cutting sentiment "*A penny for your thoughts, Incidentally*

you may keep the change". Zinnng. The album would come, and largely go in November 1982, before its monumental title track, *Rip It Up* was released in early 1983. You know this song. It has slipped into the national consciousness and was a massive crossover Top Ten hit. That song alone would justify any bands' existence. That liquid, almost squishy, initial bassline, reminiscent of Tom Tom Club and the synthesized droplet sounds that play off it, is a totally inspired opening and this song instantly sounded like a standard. The *"Rip it up and start again"* chorus is maddeningly catchy. This record coincides with the departure of original members James Kirk and Steven Daly and the arrival of Zimabwean Zeke Manyika on drums and more. *Rip It Up* is a meticulously produced, balanced and arranged song and must have taken a good bit of time to put together. It was surely conceived as a hit single and represents the ripping up of the old band and a bid for the Big Time. Edwyn seems a little sceptical about the mass audience judging by the lyric in the song's second chorus (which is a very Motown bonus, isn't it?), *"I hope to God you're not as dumb as you make out".* After that gobsmacking opening song, the album is packed full of surprises. The second track, *A Million Pleading Faces*, is one of Zeke's compositions and is a soulful, very African sounding and bongolicious dance track, full of hi-life guitars and Masakela horns. Steven and Malcolm had both grown up in Africa, so this is less of a red herring than it might at first appear but it most definitely does not sound like the band whose previous album was only released barely six months previously, in the Spring of 1982. 1982 had that effect on a lot of people.

Necessity was the mother of invention here because Polydor had demanded "more product", so some older songs were recast for this record, including an old Postcard B-Side, *Breakfast Time*, which sees the band neatly subsume reggae into their sound, with a little Eastern European Cossack-y sounding guitar. As you do. It works though. Malcolm Ross even reheats a **Josef K** track, *Turn Away* for the album. Something borrowed, a few things blue, somethings old and new ought to make for a very wonky record but *Rip It Up* is amazing. One is supposed to defer to the classic line up but this was always my favourite album of theirs. So the band had a proper hit. Fame and stardom finally beckoning. Just as **Haircut 100** would have never ever dreamed of doing, the band unfortunately made a bit of a dog's dinner of *their Top Of The Pops* performance, being drunk and falling off the stage and inviting a fiend called Foetus to join them. He fell off the stage too. Orange Juice were banned from the rigidly straight-laced but colossally influential program. *Top Of The Pops* was about the disciplined Business of Pop, not the unreliable human soul of Punk or Rock. What noble and heroic nonsense. It didn't matter. *Rip It Up* had crossed over and continued to climb the charts.

I remember turning up for an Album Signing by the band at an indie record shop in Cardiff. I'd have been fourteen and I brought my eleven year old sister. I think we were virtually the only ones there. The band were absolute sweethearts and gave us signed photos and all sorts of promo nonsense from their van. Sadly, I have lost most of it now, except for the photo. Oh, and the memories.

So funk was recast by Post Punk as quite a serious and worthy additional string to a band's bow. Disco, and gay disco only more so, was a different matter. I have always thought of **Buzzcocks** as more of a noisy Pop band than Punks, but nonetheless *Homosapien*, the first solo single by singer **Pete Shelley** raised a great many eyebrows. It's a pretty explicit gay Synthpop love song (*"Homo Superior, In my interior"* indeed) and duly picked up a BBC ban but the attendant publicity brought it a lot of love from the gay clubs across Europe and it peaked at #14 in the US Dance Charts. There are no guitars in sight and Pete brings his love of electronic music back out into the spotlight. He had recorded an electronic-ish, Krautish instrumental one track album called *Sky Yen* in 1974, prior to being in the band, but this single was a bold move, whichever you look at it. One that was going to attract a lot of trouble and, along with that, a lot of trouble's twin sister; attention.

It sounds like **Fad Gadget** or very early **Depeche Mode** and is a typically beautifully arranged Shelleyan pop song, topped off with his trademark fey vocals. The best **Buzzcocks** singles are like Motown symphonies of fuzz, drenched in hooks and harmony and a huge (acknowledged) influence on Nirvana. If you don't own *Singles Going Steady*, the compilation of their 45s, then you are a muppet. A MUPPET. The CD has a wealth of bonus singles and B Sides, costs less than a pint on Amazon and explains Indie music, if you ever were confused about it. Buy it now. *Homosapien* was produced by the very 1981 Martin Rushent, himself moving on from producing punks like **The Stranglers** and Buzzcocks, brushing up the synthpop magic he had used on JJ Burnel's excellent coldwave(ish) album, *The Euroman Cometh*, and was about to unleash to spectacular effect, on *Dare*. [PUB FACT: Rushent also engineered the Jesus Christ Superstar soundtrack]. Pete even looks a little like one of Kraftwerk in the *Homosapien* video, all Lego hair and neat white suit. So not Punk. And thus, of course, none more Punk.

One of the most inspiring musical transitions of the early Eighties was shot through with serious and conflicting emotions, smothered by a weight of authenticity that could be neither ignored nor faked. **Joy Division** were more than a favourite band for many. Ian Curtis' brutal poetry and untimely death left a lot of people, to whom he had offered some hope that they were not alone in pain, with emotional scarring. Joy Division's music coils itself around your heart and it stays there. If you've loved Joy Division once, it's forever. It might get buried but it won't diminish, no matter how many decades pass in between.

Joy Division had decided among themselves that they could never continue to be Joy Division if any one member left. There could be no more **Joy Division** without all four of them, so the idea of the other three continuing was seen as a betrayal by some. The notion of the first single being something that Ian had had a hand in writing, although it was not completed before he died, doubly so. It was rejected by many and thus **New Order**'s stumbling and ultimately stunning rebirth out of the ashes of **Joy Division** was rendered even more awkward.

Joy Division were already one of the most revered bands in the world, by those that knew of them. Curtis' death at 23 sealed that reputation and its potential forever in amber. Twenty Three, FFS. Like **Nirvana**, which they are in so many ways, they will never make a bad record, never blot their copybook, never let you down. For Purists, this is the perfect end. Purists though, are no fucking fun at all though, hamstrung by their own rules, and choked by their own arbitrarily high standards. Like their Puritan forebears, they are destined for a life of self-regulated disappointment. It seems obvious now, of course, but Bernard Sumner, Peter Hook and Stephen Morris had a huge amount more to give.

If I might be permitted a bold statement here; **New Order**'s debut, *Ceremony* is the greatest single ever made.

Yep. **New Order**'s March 1981 single, ten months after Ian passed, was the final song written and demo'd by **Joy Division**, and has a tireless majesty and is a constant source of inspiration to me. Tragedy can lead to triumph, if you will it so. I have played it once a week for thirty (very) odd years and I know now that I will never tire of it. The tumbling fragile melody feels on the verge of collapse and for a song that opens with the lyric *"this is why events unnerve me"*, that seems entirely fitting. The bassline keeps the song coming up for air and feeds it until the guitars rise up and swarm at your ears. So beautiful. So uplifting.

So magnificently human. It was produced by the other production genius of the time named Martin, Martin Hannett, who had produced all of Joy Division's music. As ever, his production is a little counter intuitive and certainly non-traditional but he pulls the brittle heart and warrior soul of this song out so skilfully. Perfectly executed.

The band had been due to leave for their first tour of America, when Ian killed himself and the other three ended up making the trip five weeks later, determined to keep playing, sometimes instrumentally, sharing vocals, feeling their way, while they decided which of them would be the new singer. Their manager Rob Gretton even had a go at it. Visiting New York gave the band their first taste of American clubs, and they heard Italo-disco, the No Wave bands and felt the impact that **Giorgio Moroder** and **Kraftwerk** were having on the cool new music at a grass roots level. This gave the nascent band a focus and something to strive for, seeing a future where Post Punk and Disco could conjoin and lead the remnants of Joy Division to something exciting, new and within their grasp, more or less. Barney says in the *Closer* sleevenotes, "*we went to American to get away from it all…the music in the clubs was harder and stranger. I thought 'Wouldn't it be great to have our music played [here]?'*"

The next single, *Procession*, was written by Morris, although credited to the band, as were all the songs. Synthesizers open and lead the track. Joy Division had used synths but New Order pushed them further to the front and Gillian Morris, then Stephen's girlfriend, joined the band to play keyboards full time. Some of the synthesizers the band used were made or modified by Sumner, fighting insomnia in the studio, "up all night with a soldering iron", experimenting with combining whatever technology he could get his hands on, to make new sounds. *Procession* scraped into the Top Forty, as had *Ceremony*, but neither single delivered commercially on the expectations of New Order. At the same time as *Procession*, in September 1981, a new version of *Ceremony*, with Gillian playing on it arrived. The new band had settled, without any "outside" help, as had been their plan.

The debut **New Order** album, *Movement*, followed quickly in November 1981, just a few weeks after Joy Division's thunderously titled posthumous live/oddments album, *Still*, which had made #5 in the UK album chart. At the time, *Movement* was quite poorly received, and only made #30 in the charts but really, it is remarkable that it exists at all. Curtis' shadow hangs heavy over it and titles like *The Him, Denial* and *Doubts Even Here* speak volumes. The strident and beautiful opener *Dreams Never End* is sung by Hook and the guitar and bass feel already a little brighter than before. There are more drum machines and synths used here and Hannett's screwy production prioritises smaller details in the mix over, say the guitars or vocals. The band fought bitterly with their producer during the recording. Since Curtis' death, Hannett's drug consumption had increased and, while working with him had never been simple or stress-free, the relationship had finally broken down. It was to be last time they worked together.

New Order needed to stand up on their own from then on. The record does what it says on the tin, which is pretty unusual for this band. It's movement. It's not called *Arrival* and, thanks to ABBA, couldn't be. It's a snapshot of a band in progress, growing, changing and moving forward. If the album is lacking in anything, it is to be expected. One quarter of the band was gone, including the main lyricist and, despite Gillian's arrival, they had not yet found their new momentum. There is caution, uncertainty, and although a lack of confidence is also evident, the album, even by its own existence, feels hopeful and ever so slightly uplifting. Allowing any light at all into the music that the three of them made was a hesitant and unnatural process and the album reflects that. Hindsight, divorced from the contemporary expectation for the record, has accorded *Movement* its due.

The band had indeed moved on by the time the album came out and, a month later, they released *Everything's Gone Green,* which sounds much more like **New Order** as we know them now. It had been the B-side of *Procession* but, influenced by the club music they had heard in New York, this new 12" version of the song, overhauled by the band, without Hannett, was a complete dancefloor refit, running a Moroder synth-pulse all the way through for the first time, based on their experiences at clubs like the Danceteria in New York, listening to the new Electro, Disco and proto Hip Hop tunes.

Imagine *hearing I Feel Love* followed by **Sylvester**'s *You Make Me Feel (Mighty Real)* mixed in with **Grandmaster Flash, Chic**, **Tom Tom Club** and the Italodisco of **Bobby O** (who later inspired and produced the Pet Shop Boys) and the new robotic electro records cut with **Kraftwerk** for the first time. Mindblowing. For context, it's important to remember that in rainy old Britain, Disco was not only uncool by 1981, it was old hat and a pretty cheesy, played-out relic from the Seventies.

The first single, produced and written solely by **New Order**, *Temptation*, is a revelation. Again it leads with drums and a sequenced Moroder keyboard pulse. This holds the song together and allows the band to paint guitars and bass around the song as they see fit and is strong enough to leave it awhile to carry the song, as required. Barney is attacking the vocals, leading the song, clearly enunciating the lyrics and not lurking around, behind the bike sheds at the bottom of the mix, as before. It's hard not to read this new confidence and optimism, as the band coming to terms with Curtis' death and being ready to move on, *"Heaven, a gateway, a hope, Just like a feeling I need, it's no joke*". There are unprecedentedly frivolous (for New Order) and almost Spectoresque "Ooooh-oooh-ooooh" backing vocals and the guitars are high and bright in the mix, on equal footing with Hook's emblematic bass playing. There is also an actual chorus, or two, or none; **New Order** are not conventional songmongers, and the sections are not clearly defined. Whichever way you look at it, the song is filled with hooks which lift it up again and again, in the way that choruses do and New Order don't; or didn't up until then. The nine minute 12" version of *Temptation* is something of a disco masterpiece and I'd hear it in clubs for the following ten years without its shine diminishing one jot. It would be much too much for New Order to have called it Celebration but that is what it was. A new and brilliant life as a Pop band was strong temptation indeed. Albeit a wonky, unconventional and idiosyncratic pop group. I am not sure if it is in the guitar and bass playing that still carry Joy Division's DNA, or knowing the story, or all in my head but, while all New Order's songs have a more than a hint of melancholy, they never released another sad or slow single. So Pop had found another form.

Nearly a year later, after an allegedly experimental session with a new drum machine, they released the colossal, world-beating *Blue Monday*. It became a Top Ten hit in the UK, a worldwide club hit and propelled New Order to being an influential new artist in the clubs they visited and had been inspired by, just 18 months previously. They'd managed it with their dignity and wit intact too. What a beautiful thing Pop music can be.

And what a beautiful thing the new Electro-Disco music can be too. Two of the biggest and most-groundbreaking albums of 1981 were *Dare* and *Non-Stop Erotic Cabaret*. Synthesizers, disco, gender-blurring and a healthy frisson of danger powered both of these records into the Top Ten and the nation's living rooms. Marc Almond and Phil Oakey were a new kind of pop star. They were oddballs both and your dad was not sure about either of them. This delving into the make-up box and nodding toward the darkside was classic teenage (give or take) rebellion, in the same shocking mode as Brando and Dean's leather jackets and sneers in the Fifties, the Beatles getting high and growing their hair in the Sixties, or the Sex Pistols swearing up teatime Telly in the Seventies.

As synthesizers had breathed new life into disco, and we were all going mad for 12" dance versions of our pop songs, both Soft Cell and Human League rebooted their albums, much to their labels' delight, with new Dance Versions. **The League Unlimited Orchestra**'s *Love And Dancing* was a nod to **Barry White**'s Unlimited Orchestra, while **Soft Cell**'s naturally seamier nod was to the Ecstasy pills they'd tried in New York, leading to *Non Stop Ecstatic Dancing*. Collecting 12" remixes, B sides and whatnot gave both bands a brand new and very successful new album with no effort (or recording costs). The dance remix album had not been seen here before, at least not in the mainstream, and the kids lapped it up. **The Human League**'s effort actually seems more like actual remixes, viewed now. Or dubs, perhaps more accurately. There are hardly any vocals and the songs are chopped and, yes, screwed into new shapes, rather than just extended. Indeed, three of the new tracks are under three minutes. Most odd. It wins over **Soft Cell**'s effort by having the lyrically limited but enduringly brilliant electro floor-filler, *Hard Times* on it. The art of the Extended Version or Remix was not adopted equally successfully by all at first. Some, like Duran Duran just re-recorded new, longer versions from scratch, which is the long way around, and involves the band being in a studio, rather than having someone open up a mix in the studio, to loop and re-jig the elements. Many Eighties remixes sound like the work of a bored engineer, charged with adding an extra ninety seconds of who-really-cares-what to the next single so the label could make another format for fans to buy. They would often just pad out an instrumental section by stutteringly re-pe-pe-pe-repeating drum breaks and vo-vo-vocal parts with unintentionally comedic results. The recent *12" 80s* Triple CD compilations are frustrating yet semi-essential purchases and wonderful nostalgia fests. I'd say each is about 50% incredible but, oh my, they are all essential!

Duran Duran had led the way here from the off and released Night Versions of the singles on 12" singles but chose not to gather them together for some reason (You can buy them bundled on a CD now, if you so choose, by the way. I have so chosen and they sound fantastic, back to back). Disco, funk and club culture was now freely mixing with our new wave of New Pop groups and it was no longer cheesy, non-serious music "for girls", as it had felt previously but an exciting new artform that our coolest bands were all over like flies. In 1980, the cool bands had been guitar based, be they Two-Tone or Punks, New Wave or just plain old Rock but now we had all got rid of the black clothes and embraced Synthpop and Disco – slightly camp and absolutely proud of it.

Orange Juice Rip It Up

PETE SHELLEY · HOMOSAPIEN

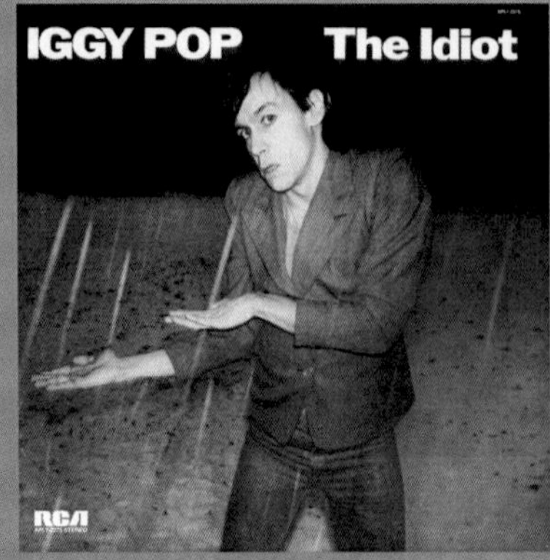

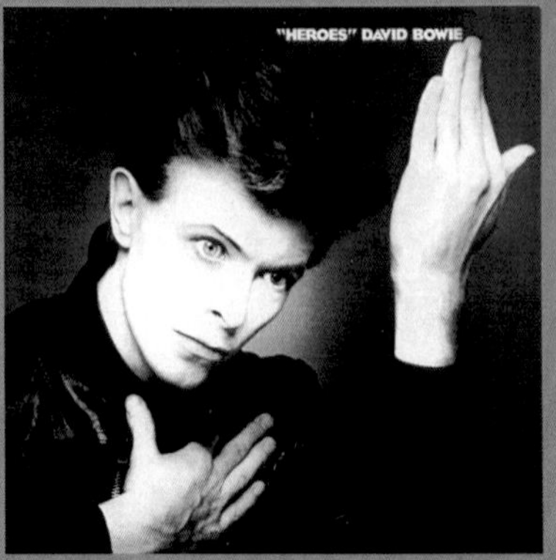

PUBLIC IMAGE LTD.
SECOND EDITION.

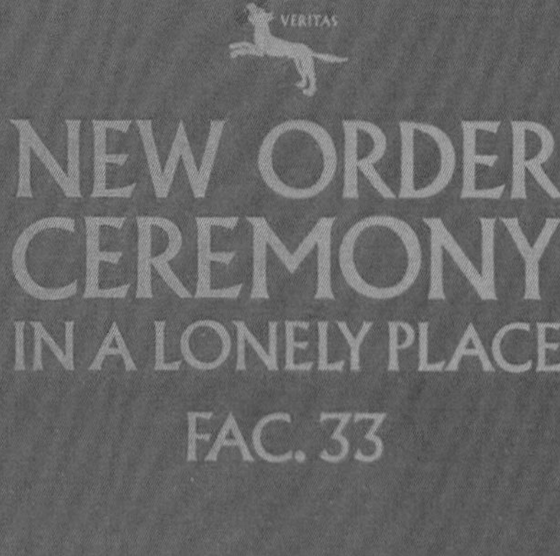

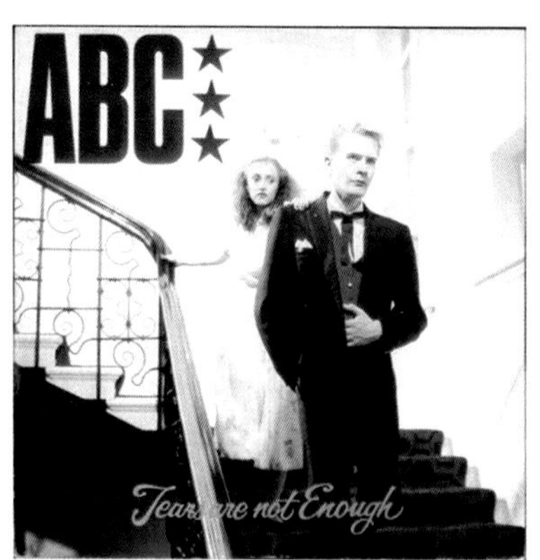

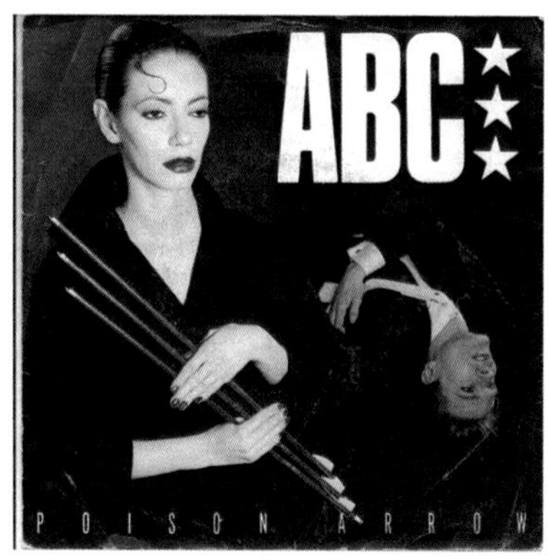

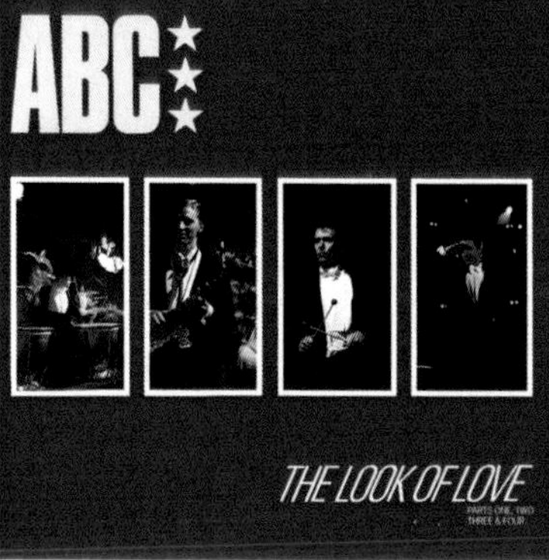

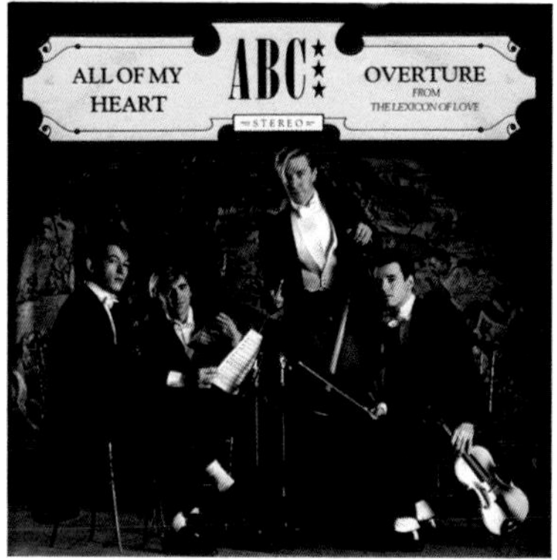

ABC
Tears are not Enough

ABC
POISON ARROW

ABC
THE LOOK OF LOVE

ALL OF MY HEART
ABC
STEREO
OVERTURE
FROM
THE LEXICON OF LOVE

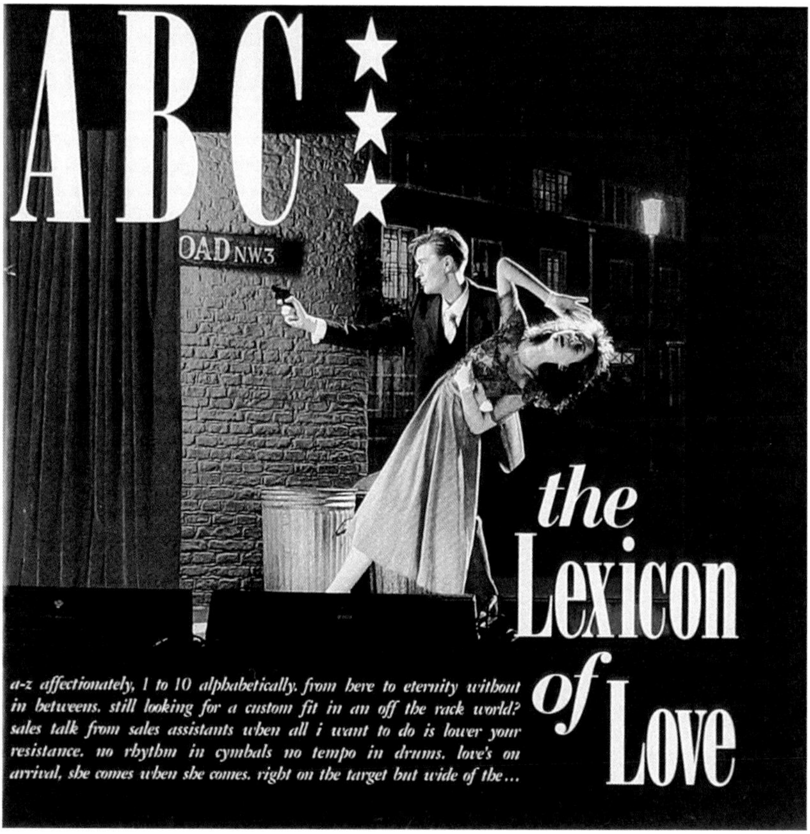
ABC
OAD N.W.3
the Lexicon of Love
a-z affectionately, 1 to 10 alphabetically. from here to eternity without in betweens. still looking for a custom fit in an off the rack world? sales talk from sales assistants when all i want to do is lower your resistance. no rhythm in cymbals no tempo in drums. love's on arrival, she comes when she comes. right on the target but wide of the…

perfect

I remember this as though it were yesterday.

Associates

18 Carat Love Affair
Love Hangover

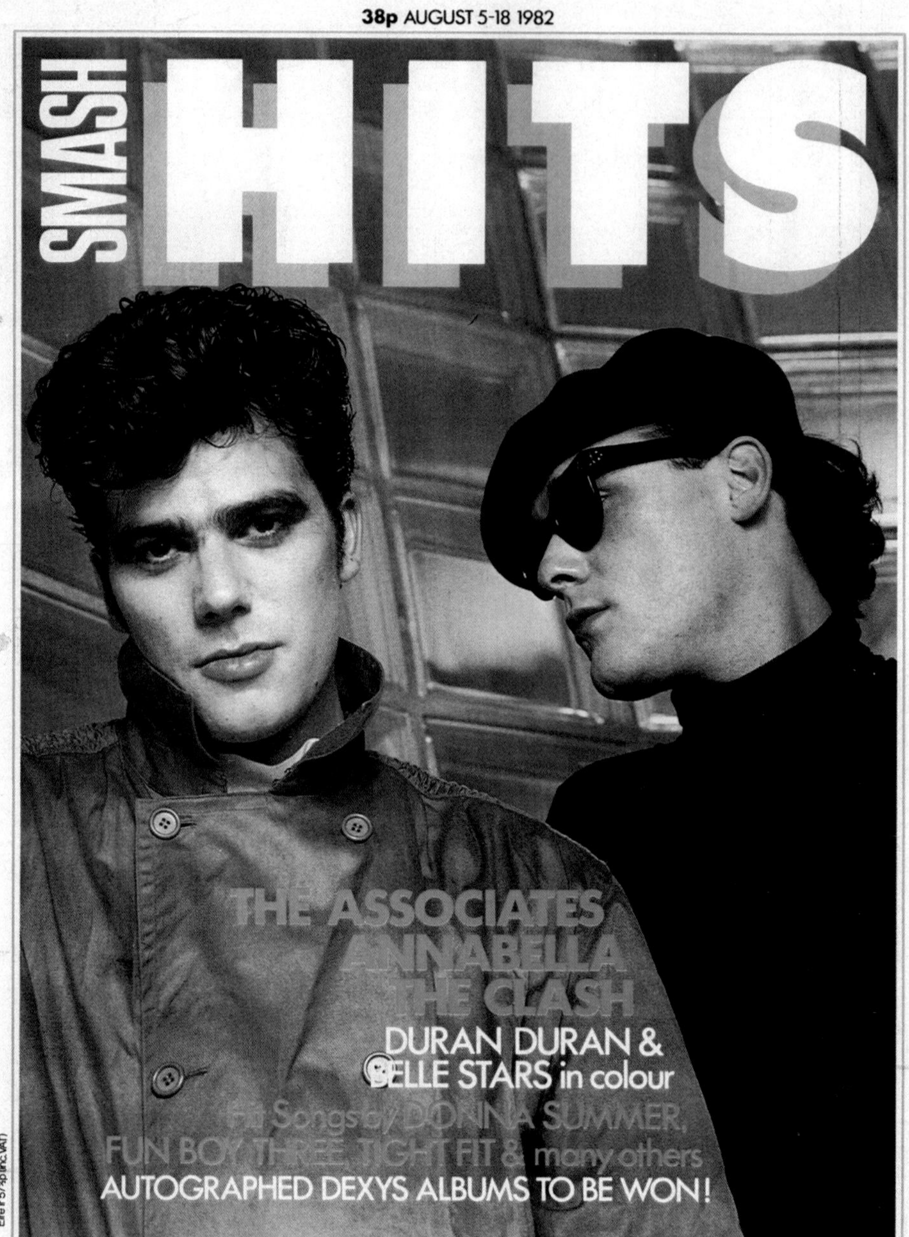

This was a good day.

BLANCMANGE
Happy Families

aztec camera
high land, hard rain

T A L K · T A L K

THE PARTY'S OVER

Tears For Fears

the hurting

05. MAD WORLD: BRILLIANT NEW BRITISH BANDS SPRING UP ALL OVER

1982: The floodgates: Smash Hits Bounces Bands Into The Top Twenty

ABC ASSOCIATES TEARS FOR FEARS BLANCMANGE YAZOO

By early 1982, however, there was something magical afoot. Not just one thing but a host of dazzling new things and they all had trousers and haircuts that were most definitely "not available on the High Street". For years, Post Punk and New Wave bands had shuffled into view via the well-trodden route of self-released, poorly-selling 7" singles, NME live reviews and Peel Sessions. Not that bands today wouldn't gape at those single sales in awe. In 1982, an agreeable-sounding NME Single Of The Week might sell five thousand copies and still bask in obscurity. You could snaffle a Hit and a major label deal with those sales now. Each week NME would document the national live scene, reviewing thirty-plus live bands (as did Sounds/Melody Maker). These groups were skinny, sickly looking and kitted out exclusively in black clothes and shades, accessorised with brown suede and cigarettes; boasting sullen expressions and serious paperbacks that seemed to take a very long time to complete.

Smash Hits had been covering New Wave and the more interesting end of Pop (Elvis Costello, Madness, Blondie, Donna, Adam, Police) since 1978 but by 1982, it was marching confidently into its Imperial Phase (© Neil Tennant) and it seemed as though opening each new issue detonated a confetti cannon of colour and fun into the boiled pea monotony of a wet school lunch hour. The new trousers were anything but black and hair was sprayed and teased and painted into all manner of alien and avian arrangements. Looking like a new kind of fun Pop group was, completely excitingly, paired with *sounding* like a new kind of fun Pop group too.

ABC! Associates! Blancmange! Eurythmics! Depeche Mode! Altered Images!! Yazoo! Talk Talk! Cocteau Twins! New Order! Scritti Politti! Aztec Camera! The The! Blue Nile! Tears For Fears! Culture Club! Southern Death Cult! Kid Creole! Thomas Dolby! Bananarama! Sisters of Mercy! Fun Boy Three! China Crisis! The Mighty Wah! Wham! Orange Juice! Heaven 17! Dollar! Birthday Party! Echo & The Bunnymen! The Thompson Twins! And, of course, **Blue Zoo.** Now with the exception of dear old Blue Zoo all of these groups had some things in common.

Firstly, you couldn't quite imagine any of them being in the Top Twenty, or even existing, a few years previously. Some of them had been skulking about for a few years – but in more bashful trousers and in no way focussed on, or suitable for, mass consumption.

Secondly, most of the groups became absolutely massive international pop stars, lasted for years and indeed most are still active right now. Pop tarts with attitude they may have been (OK, were) but these were defiantly not flashes in the pan.

Thirdly, and I must confess to a bijou smidgeon of fanboy bias here, but they did not sound alike at all. Cold doomy synths here, flamenco prodigies there, Socialist Agit-Funk (was A Thing), sci-fi boffin Synthpop, Moroder Eurodisco, gay Reggae (imagine!), Punk Funk, Sitar Electro, British rapping (British! It seems wrong saying it out loud but Wham! were somewhat unprecedented on arrival, rap being in its novelty stage), Baroque Orchestral Funk…OK, there was quite a bit of Chic-y bass playing. But all of this was not "a genre". It didn't rely on a handful of sacred texts like Britpop's template of **Wire, Kinks, Beatles** and **Buzzcocks**. It was a Year Zero free-for-all.

Fourthly, and most importantly, they were mostly British, pretty much all completely amazing and because they all arrived at the same time, on top of 1981's bumper crop of Pop, the charts were tremendously exciting and music was everyone's very favourite thing and one could confidently turn on *Top Of The Pops*, expecting to be amazed by new things.

This is the key thing about 1982. Diversity. Music in those times was a very tribal thing, with many distinct and isolated, frequently warring, factions. The wrong T-shirt could get you a smack in the mouth. There were Billowing Soul Boys, blousy New Romantics, scary Punks (lots of Punks), Mods (lots and lots of Mods), Pop Kids, Ska Kids (lots and lots and lots of Harrington jackets), skinny-tied New Wavers, acres of denim-shrouded Metallers, shadowy and slightly smelly Goths, even scarier Psychobillys with no body fat, lycra-clad Disco Girls with giant smiles, the twitchy Post-Punk holy-jumper-and-ratty-jeans brigade, committed Antpeople and tiresome Cocktail JazzFunkateers. I may have made that last one up but it was quite common and, in some circles, "acceptable" to profess to being "into jazz funk" in those days. Those **Shakatak, Shalamar** and **Imagination** records didn't buy themselves. I am sure these wine bar doyens had a collective name but I have no recollection of it and the name I gave them is frankly unkind. In later life I would realise that I liked **Imagination**'s smartly produced records. Indeed they are quite a hip name to drop these days. **Shakatak –** not so much.

You could make some pretty accurate assessments of people's musical tastes from seeing a single photograph of them. Haircuts, trousers and jackets all could speak volumes about your musical vices before you even got to the more obvious clues from band T shirts and the many, many badges that you were legally obliged to wear, often cunningly concealed from teachers/parents/employers on the undersides of lapels and the reverse of ties.

Long, greasy hair, a smart Harrington jacket and mail order "Bowie trousers" just weren't going to coexist in one wardrobe. Those were three very different people's clothes and it was inconceivable that they could be worn together. Likewise, your choice of reading material followed suit. You were either reading Smash Hits and Flexipop (girls and boys) or devoted to the more studious teachings of John Peel and the *NME/Sounds/MelodyMaker* axis (boys mainly). There were no grown-up monthlies like Q, Uncut and MOJO because Pop music was, y'know, for kids.

In the free-for-all of 1982, however, the barriers came down and all of these genres overlapped, coincided and grew stronger together. Pop music relaxed. It got cooler and smarter and decided to take on the world. The likes of **Blancmange, Tears For Fears** and **Associates** finished the year in Peel's Festive Fifty, atop both the NME's *and* Smash Hits Readers' Polls AND woke your dad up from his afternoon doze/stupor on the *Christmas Top Of The Pops*. The elusive double prize of blanket critical acclaim and huge commercial success was achieved again and again. These were truly unprecedented scenes that have never been seen again; except, arguably, maybe a little bit during Britpop but not as much as this and definitely not again since.

Indeed, of the twenty three* acts to adorn Smash Hits' cover in 1982, almost half (eleven) were also NME cover stars that year; and most of the rest had been so at some point just before or just after 1982.

Additionally, fifteen out of twenty three of those groops have released records in the last few years; three whole decades later. Amazing longevity.

*(*OMD, DEPECHE MODE, JAPAN, HEAVEN 17, ABC, ALTERED IMAGES, DURAN DURAN, BANANARAMA, HAIRCUT 100, YAZOO, TOYAH, BELLE STARS, FUN BOY THREE, SOFT CELL, MADNESS, ASSOCIATES, DURAN DURAN, ABC, MARI WILSON)*

It wasn't just brand new groups. Behold the class of 1981, who continued to rise all through 1982! Except **The Police** who took a year off to act in bad films, spend their winnings and turn to crap.

SMASH HITS Poll Winners (Best Group, Christmas 1981)

1. **Adam & The Ants**
2. **Human League**
3. **Duran Duran**
4. **The Police**
5. **Madness**
6. **Ultravox**
7. **OMD**
8. **The Jam**
9. **Japan**
10. **The Teardrop Explodes.**

Amazing! What a list. Coupled with the fact that **The Stranglers, Bowie, The Clash, Kraftwerk, Simple Minds, The Cure, Dexys Midnight Runners** (et very much cetera) were all on peak form, this year saw the Top Forty being colonised by good records. Out went (most of the) endless MOR ballads, peddled by OLD humans with big moustaches, pencil-thin mikes and vast billowing dresses....and in came situations like this...

Feb 20th chart

1. The Jam	*A Town Called Malice / Precious*
2. The Stranglers	*Golden Brown*
3. Soft Cell	*Say Hello Wave Goodbye*
4. OMD	*Maid Of Orleans*
5. Kraftwerk	*The Model*

Yep, young artists with pencil thin moustaches and billowing trousers. What a Top Five though... At the risk of coming over a bit grumpy old man, comparing this with the Top Fives of today's conveyor belt of disposable gurnpop DJ/Rapper collaborations makes me a little sad.

Such scenes as this in the charts were not uncommon throughout 1982. Let us also not forget that hoary old Classic Rock was in its NWOBHM pomp and at least two of **AC/DC, Iron Maiden, Black Sabbath, Deep Purple, Status Quo, Motorhead, The Who, Queen, Judas Priest, Pink Floyd, Whitesnake, Gillan** et al had Top Forty hits at any given moment this year, it seemed like boring Pop had been squeezed out. The charts had changed forever, and very much for the better.

The other thing that jumps out now is the fact that the **Duran** or **Clash** or **Stranglers** or **Soft Cell** or **Jam** of 1982 was different from the previous year's model, and different again from the 1983 version. The Clash had absorbed New York's embryonic hip hop street culture, Soft Cell has moved from Pervdisco to torch ballads, The Stranglers, of all people, had embraced JJ Burnel's beloved Eurosynthpop for *La Folie*, The Jam had added Fun(k) in the shapes of **Curtis Mayfield** horns and Motown grooves, and **Duran** were leaving the alleged Chic Pistols aesthetic of their debut to slither out like **Roxy Music** lounge lizards.

Not only did every new crop of bands seem to want to stand out and do something new but also, more crucially, they wanted to reinvent themselves each time with every album and, if possible with every single. The freedom! The confidence! The open-mindedness. And, of course, the technology.

Fairlights, for those had access to them, were a revelation. Contrary to the Luddite opposition view at the time, the machines did not play themselves. They were powered by ideas. If an electronic band felt that French sounding waltz, or great slabs of Music Concrete were the way forward for the new song, and many (OK, maybe just OMD) did, then that is how the records ended up.

Most bands did not have access to the criminally expensive Fairlights but they had heard the variety and possibility of the new sounds and improvised. Increasingly affordable keyboards and the same Heath Robinson-esque imagination that had driven post punk bands to innovate were applied to big Pop songs. Some of the more dour, experimental make-a-song-to-fit-the-new-noise antics of pre 1981 bands such as **Cabaret Voltaire, Ultravox** and **The Human League,** were coupled with the earnest but insular jazz-and-beret leanings of Geoff Travis' acts like **Young Marble Giants** and **Scritti Politti.** Bands did not stick to their own patch any more and swiped little bit of anything that they fancied from the breadth of music to create this New Pop.

Inspired by the Top Forty' welcoming of some of the more oddball records in recent years; from **Laurie Anderson's** gobsmacking *O Superman* to **Flying Lizards**' *Money*, along with the breakouts by **The Human League**, **Soft Cell**, **OMD** and **Japan;** there was a sense that if you believed, you could have a hit. Young bands in rehearsal rooms could go on to enthral a mass audience if they were prepared to have the odd key change, a misty middle eight and could face singing both in tune *and* with the vocals sitting at the top of your song, rather than burying them in the mix. You too could make it happen, especially if you had some new, or nearly-new, ideas.

Together this meant that the whole vocabulary of pop music had changed. All of these records boasted new sounds, new recording techniques, new ideas and were borne out of a completely Blank Page attitude from the artists to get something catchy and new onto vinyl. There was a mass breakout from the prison of guitar, bass and drums and it was FUN.

Fun had not been something for serious musicians to indulge in. Serious Musicians were, as the proudly boasted term implies, very serious. Albums were made without the slightest consideration for including singles. Singles were for girls as far as many of the Seventies generation were concerned. And Fun was, well, not just for girls exactly but definitely neither a priority for serious and proper musicians, nor anything that they would like to see mentioned in a review. This was music as hard work. Graft. But by 1982 you need not be serious nor indeed a musician to make a hit record. Blasphemy. The professional musical excesses of the earnest Prog Rock gentlemen of **Pink Floyd, Yes** and **Genesis** are often cited as The Thing to which Punk was a reaction. I am not sure that is true. Mr John Lydon is quite the fan of **Faust** and **Van Der Graf Generator** among others. The problem with the likes of Prog Rock, along with the Seventies' Top Forty staples such as **The Three Degrees, Showaddywaddy** and **Brotherhood Of Man** was that they were really fucking boring and tame. THAT is what the Punks were rebelling against.

The records of Punk and then Post Punk were made by artfully rebellious kids to tease out the rebellion of their less rebellious peers. All this rebellion was taken quite seriously. Post Punk records were often very serious, albeit in an interesting and cool way; not remotely intended for mass consumption nor parental approval and, for the most part, quite low on Fun, except in a stern, ironic fashion. The problem with serious is it tends to lead to boring. And that, as the **Pistols** appropriated from **the Stooges**, is *No Fun* at all, whatsoever.

Joy Division made two of the least Fun; most beautiful and desolate albums ever and were very serious, if not traditionally gifted, musicians but they played by Punk Rock rules and would never for one moment consider, for example, smiling in photographs. That would be admitting to having Fun. I think very few bands are genuinely started as emotionally cathartic pressure valves. Getting drunk with your friends, getting laid and avoiding working in the local frozen pea factory remain the top three motivations for getting on stage. That, and being a secret show-off. Let's not overlook that one. No show-off, no singer, no band. That is a rule.

Candid Joy Division footage from the time reveals the same japery and piss-taking that you get in all bands and, while Curtis' suicide is not going to make my argument that they had a lot of fun being in that band, a particularly easy one to pin on them, it's true of all bands. **New Order's** move into disco (aka Fun) was initially regarded as heresy among the raincoated, nicotine fingered masses. Fun was simply not on. Smiling too could do one. These were the old rules. The new rules were much less...rigid. Indie bands pulled the stick out their collective arse.

Take **Billy Mackenzie**, who entered my life for the first time via *Top Of The Pops* and the cinematically demented glam disco of *Party Fears Two* in February 1982. **Associates**, (Billy and Alan Rankine from Dundee and a variety of other contributors) had made a couple of very good but not hugely successful albums in *The Affectionate Punch* (Fiction, 1980) and *Fourth Drawer Down* (Situation 2, 1981, a collection of the many singles they had released in the year preceding).

Their affection for Fun, mischief and **Bowie** was laid out from the beginning by their debut single, a cover of His *Boys Keep Swinging*, released just six weeks after **Bowie'**s single came out. They gave great copy in interviews, such as *"I was just listening to the combination of Rankine's guitar and my voice and I had an orgasm...it just shows how music can get me in a froth"* (Melody Maker 1981). Associates worked with some very innovative producers, like Flood and Mike Hedges, who went on to be massively successful and continue to be so to this day. Having subsequently dug into those early releases, I like much about them but they skewed toward weird over Fun.

I wasn't alone. None of them sold too well and Billy is quoted as saying of them *"I thought it was the going to be the year of singles. And it was. The thing...was that they got peeled off the turntable halfway through. We want to keep our singles on the turntable this year"* (Melody Maker 1982).

Nothing, but nothing, prepared my teenage mind for *Party Fears Two* though. Swathed in the cotton wool of TOTP's standard dry ice for weirdos; Billy, smirking continually (at his own image in the monitors, it transpires), and dressed in a buttoned up trench coat and beret, fronting a band that included vampy Martha Ladley (the other Martha in **Martha and The Muffins**) playing lace fingered one-handed piano, Michael Dempsey, cool in standard issue Scottish band Byrdsian bowlcut'n'Rickenbacker and the movie star (almost Vulcan) looks of Alan Rankine in a white fencing suit, wearing chopstick antennae (obviously) and strumming a banjo that he was holding onto tightly in the way that I know now is caused by hallucinogens. Or nervousness. Or both.

As it turns out, the appearance nearly didn't happen as Billy tried, with typical heroic self-sabotage, to back out as he had had a new haircut, which he was *"too embarrassed to reveal on the street, never mind on national television"* (c Tom Doyle The Glamour Chase). Hence, presumably the beret.

Eye-spinning Wagnerian Space Disco was new to me and Billy's colossal voice gradually builds and builds throughout the song only going into interstellar overdrive at the end. There was none of that indie band can't-hear-the-words going on here. Billy's words were blasted through your ears and eyeballs to the back of your brain with diamond accuracy. What he was going on about exactly was not completely clear then and no clearer now. I didn't understand it and I liked that a lot. Confusion stretches you if you let it.

Years later, I asked Billy what the song was about and ended up more confused than when I started. All I got really was that it was *"about being young"*. Confusion notwithstanding, the song spoke very clearly to me on an emotional level. There was dissatisfaction, there was identity crisis, there was stubbornness and there was, or seemed to be, a happy ending, or at least an opportunity for moving forward, up and away from anything and everything I didn't quite understand. I have read elsewhere that it might be about an inability to commit. Perhaps it is. I think it is just fine for different people to have different takes on these things. Explaining and dissecting art is a bit of a fool's errand, for the most part.

I was used to **Simon Le Bon**'s non-sequiturs and Burroughs/Bowie stylee cut-up lyrics but I suspected that they meant as little to him as they did to me. Not that that mattered overly. It's Pop music. It doesn't HAVE to mean anything. I liked **Duran Duran** a great deal from the first single onward and, while they have had suboptimal years (OK, decades), their last album (2010's **Mark Ronson** *produced All You Need Is Now*) is pretty great. But Billy's delivery was all feeling and whatever the hell the song was about, it was obviously personal and he meant every word, smirk or no.

It turns out that almost no-one else was au fait with Wagnerian Space Disco either; until that night. It was one of *the* legendary *Top Of The Pops* debuts, that catapulted an act from obscurity to being household names (at least for a time) and it wouldn't be the last one that year. Associates had been signed by Warner Brothers, and no doubt were being given the big leveraged push by the label, but whoever thought that people were going to lap up that single was both very clearly mad and, of course, completely correct.

It only took a couple of months from that night, to take them from the relative backwaters of the Peel Session to the cover of Smash Hits and a proper, hit album in *Sulk* and many more TV appearances.

To my young eyes, the cover of *Sulk* looked exotically lush and sexily sci-fi. I can see now that it's an undoubtedly very expensive, Peter Ashworth shoot with thirty metres of cotton, some smart underlighting and a giant pot plant from a hotel foyer* (*actually the conservatory of a Surrey Mansion) but that matters not. The lush sci-fi sleeve perfectly mirrored the records contents.

The first half of the album is as weird as successful Pop music gets. Doomy to the point of covering suicidal **Billie Holiday** "hits", adrift on swirling horror soundtrack drones, nightmarish lyrics and murky, alien instrumentation. The second side is much more fun, breezier and skippier, and houses the singles and the choruses.

This is of course against the rules of major label albums. The Singles are the first few tracks of the album and any chorus-free portentous, snail's pace recollections of bad acid dreams (*No*), swathed in choirs of angry angels are best kept on the cutting room floor or, if "necessary", hidden at the end of the record.

But where is the Fun in that, right?

Made in one of Camden's non-exotic warehousey districts by the band and producer Mike Hedges, I can only imagine that Warners were not playing too close attention to the sessions. Acid crazed experimentation was the way forward. Obsessive re-re-re-recording and re-re-re-mixing each track to the point where the specific instrumentation is often hard to discern was the order of the day.

They discovered the answer to questions such as "What do drums sound like filled with water?" (Answer: they are made of pulp, so they turn to drum soup and don't make any sounds that porridge can't match); and "What happens if you piss in a guitar?" (Answer: not much of note but its resale value is not what it was); and "What do iron canisters sound like, when thrown down a stone staircase?" (Answer: quite cool actually).

At the end of it they came up with an album that sounded like nothing I'd heard before (and not much since). Any "sensible" major label A&R would have made them scrap side one and demand "more songs like on side 2". Thankfully that did not happen and instead of a cool Eighties pop record, what we have is a masterpiece: naked and shameless ravings set to music that befits such derangements. The album was pretty much universally praised (NME: *"Associates are an elusive butterfly"*; Sounds: *"a kitchen sink album with gold, enamelled taps"*)

Another thing that you might have expected across *Sulk* is a bit more of the raw, soaring voice that swaggers insouciantly though *Party Fears Two*. Never less than stunning, it doesn't really get to sail into space for most of the time. But that would have been too easy. And no Fun. Perversity is the abiding theme of **Associates'** and Billy's career. That and self-sabotage.

Of course the band fractured almost instantly and Alan left on the verge of the victory lap that was the *Sulk* Tour. The usual reasons abide; madness brought on by seeing piles of cash for the first time, a taste for drugs and the luxurious indulgence of "creative types" that major labels do so well. Billy kept and bred whippets for all of his life and naturally, when the label brought him down to London for TV appearances, then, in addition to his suite at some pricey hotel, he would need an adjoining suite for the dogs. Naturally.

Associates never toured or played much after that record, which is something of a shame. In 1996, I signed Billy MacKenzie to Nude records for a comeback record. Prior to signing him, I went with my boss to Billy's flat near Earls Court for a private show. Fourteen years on from 1982, I had never seen Billy perform live and was aware that disappointment might be looming. Ha.

Billy and his collaborator, Steve Aungle, on piano and an audience of two during which Billy sang many of the breathtaking songs he had *"lying around"* and took requests, including songs from Sulk, kicking off with a blistering, soul-swivelling rendition of *Breakfast* from *Perhaps,* which is, ahem, perhaps my favourite song of his and really and truly ought to be a standard by now.

Effortlessly cantering up and down his still pristine multi-octave range and very obviously happy to be showing off, I am surprised that he didn't shatter every window in the neighbourhood. It was what older persons would recognise as a Maxell Moment. Billy performed as though he were headlining the Palladium. Comparison with the bands I'd have to go and see night after night as an A&R is just not appropriate. Or relevant. Not even close. His voice was operatic and would rise up to the sky and swoop down to the most intimate whisper in the space of a single word. **Aretha Franklin** is about the only Pop singer that bears mention in the same misty breath. Without doubt the best "concert" I have ever been to, or ever will and, even typing this, brings tears to my eyes.

What was clear to me on that day was the same thought I had on seeing *Party Fears Two* on the telly way back: Billy Mackenzie is a totally natural fucking star.

Party Fears Two took them to the cover of NME; *Sulk* hit the Top Ten in May, in tandem with the second single, *Club Country* (telling lyric *"If we stick around, we're sure to be looked down upon"*), which flew up to Number 13 and brought another brace of striking TOTP appearances, including one with Martha gamely attempting to do the duet bit of the song with Billy grinning impishly at her, while hiding both the microphones and making her chase him about the stage to try and get a look in or make the miming look remotely convincing. You can see in his face, as he dances with one mike in each hand, that he thought these are both MY microphones.

The third single, *18 Carat Love Affair,* was the final instrumental track from *Sulk, Nothing In Something Particular,* with added vocals and was so brilliant and straight-up poppy, that the band graduated to the cover of Smash Hits. I couldn't say what most of its readers made of his responses to questions like "*What is worse than going to the laundrette?*" with *"Giving into temptation"*; or *"How do you relax?" with "I usually try to intimidate people"* coupled with completely candid answers about posing with a hairbrush and trying to be a pop star as a kid, but I was sold. The man was taking the piss and loving it. What a pop star.

The follow up to *Sulk,* 1985's *Perhaps,* was effectively a **Billy MacKenzie** solo record and was recorded, rejected, re-recorded and took four producers (including Martyn "**Heaven 17**" Ware and Martin *"Dare"*

Rushent), three years and a quarter of a million quid. It flopped but had two beautiful singles in *Those First Impressions* and *Breakfast*.

Billy's legend grew and grew however with each of several unreleased albums and by the time he signed the deal with Nude, the list of people who wanted to work with him included **Bono, Massive Attack** and the **Cocteau Twins.** The wonderful torch ballads, chosen from his impressive pile of unreleased tracks, including several tributes to Morrissey by the way, were to showcase Billy's stratospheric voice and Steve's piano. I felt they would cement his reputation up there with Bowie and Scott Walker, but as the thing came together, Billy decided with typical contrariness and disregard for, well, everything, that he'd prefer to make *"songs like **The Prodigy**, those guys have really got something"*. And right about then, I could see why his career had never run either smoothly or in the way anyone might have expected.

Tragically Billy's mother died at that time. That hit him very, very hard and, I think, the spectre of Billy returning from the wilderness and actually making the record that everyone had always wanted him to, the career redemption, proved all too much and he took his own life in January of 1997. I'll always be grateful to Simon Raymonde from the **Cocteau Twins** (and now MD of Bella Union records) and others, including Bono, who helped finish some of the songs, released as *Beyond The Sun* in 1997 to universal acclaim, if slightly disappointing sales. It was nonetheless a pleasure and a boyhood dream realised to spend time and work with Billy. I have a photo of him from his last session up in the hall in my home and so I think about Billy MaKenzine most days still now, even if just for a moment.

Do yourself a favour though and go listen to one of the live versions of *Breakfast* on Youtube. Words are not going to cover it and tears are not enough.

The other big band for me in February 1982 was **ABC**. I was aware of them because they'd had a self-released Top Twenty hit with *Tears are Not Enough* in 1981. Prior to that, they'd done time as a quite good synthpop band called Vice Versa. Based in Sheffield, they shared ideas and stages with the earlier incarnations of The Human League, along with gigs with **Soft Cell** and **Depeche Mode**. Fanzine writer Martin Fry was the last member to join and pulled the band in a newer direction. Perky funk, lively horn stabs and a strong falsetto was the way forward along with a love of black 70s soul and disco from America, along with, and as a result of, **Roxy Music** and **David Bowie**.

White boy indie bands doing slightly ironic and none too slick funk was A Thing back then, from **ACR** to **Haircut 100, The Higsons** to **Pigbag.** I thought *Tears...* was pretty damn great and, while my falsetto version at home was not popular at all, I was so inspired by the Hollywood glamour that the *Tears Are Not Enough* sleeve made so inviting, that I didn't care. Martin descending a swooping staircase, dressed to the nines, or possibly tens, with some starlet vainly chasing after him, was heady stuff in Cardiff. As, to be fair, I imagine it was in Sheffield. Just as **Associates** created, and then inhabited, a fantasy world and lifestyle, so did **ABC**.

After their hit single, they signed to Phonogram and hooked up with producer **Trevor Horn**, having failed to ensnare **Grace Jones'** producer, Alex Sadkin. Trevor had been one half of **Buggles** and had written the timeless wonder that is 1979's Number One single Video *Killed The Radio Star.* He had also just produced a string of brilliant fantasy pop singles for **Dollar** in 1981 like *Give Me Back My Heart* and *Hand Held In Black And White*. It seems obvious in retrospect and Trevor was clearly in the business of Pop that Martin had set **ABC**'s sights on, but regardless it was a truly inspired pairing. Especially when you consider Trevor had *"no idea who their audience was"* and thought the music was *"disco, but in a **Bob Dylan** way"* (c Lexicon sleevenotes).

Looking back, I think the sleeve for *Tears....* was as much an indication of **ABC**'s new sound as the record itself. This was to be full-on luxurious glamour and the fantasy Hollywood life, albeit done with a knowing Northern wit, that is captured and detailed in the Gered Mankowitz sleeve for their debut album *The Lexicon Of Love*. The front displays Martin determinedly escaping to the red curtains and lights of the stage from the dustbins of (for some reason) London's NW3, pistol in one hand, damsel in the other.

Meanwhile the back sleeve, a tad disingenuously, has the rest of the band as stage hands, behind the scenes making Martin's fantasy happen. So it must be with all singers in bands, to some degree though, eh?

The Lexicon of Love is a concept album. The concept was making a world-beating record that would make the band superstars. *"We'll have to compete with **Smokey Robinson, Michael Jackson** and **Kim Wilde**...we'll take any blame but we will go for the prizes. We are committed and if we succeed, we'll succeed magnificently; and if we fail, we'll fail magnificently. The magnificence is important"*, Fry told Paul Morley in 1981. And so it is.

And so it was. The fearless ambition, droll wit (and the occasional cheesy pun), mixed with open heart diary extracts that make up the songs on the record are paired with a super sumptuous mixture of funk bass, Burt Bacharach strings'n'bongos, Stax Horns and Fairlight artifice, all astride astutely elegant melodies make this one of the key albums of the Eighties. At no point does it sound like four men playing instruments in a room.

The tongue was just about detectable in the cheek, if you were checking, the eyebrow arched just so and the package was completed with the none-more-Vegas gold Lame suits. Let's not forget that Sheffield under Thatcher in 1982 was not like Las Vegas in 1982 in any way at all. It was still in the grip of the Industrial Revolution.

Those suits were to become the bane of the bands' life, and subsequent albums saw them shake them off with a succession of challenging image reboots, culminating in the band actually turning into a cartoon. Martin even ceremonially flushed his suit down a toilet in a Japanese hotel at the end of the Lexicon tour. They are however indelibly date-stamped with the record and have inevitably made a resurgence in recent shows. **ABC**, among most of the other big acts from 1982, are still making a good living out of 1982. Indeed Martin's contact email on the **ABC** website is GoldSuit@xxxxxx.

Lexicon's songs were smart. And wordy. I am not totally convinced that most people I know use the word Lexicon unless referring to this album, which is an irony that is sweetly perfect. And, my word, the songs were popular. The album went on to sell three million copies and it was absolutely inescapable that year. You didn't have to buy it to know the songs. Not just the singles but all of the tunes blared out of shops, cars and radios all year long.

February 1982 brought the first finished fruit of the album in *Poison Arrow,* which I bought on its release and played every day until the album came out. It rose to Number Six and the band graduated from one hit wonders to the covers of Smash Hits and NME in the same month, both publications equally in thrall to Martin's manifestos, birthed as a politically and stylistically minded fanzine writer, and the sublime brass balls of the music. The band had conjured a fully realised world around them that bore no obvious connection to their background and experience and they had done it PERFECTLY. As with so many of the album's songs, *Poison Arrow* was so perfect that many were convinced that it was a cover version.

Perfection was the idea and all blemishes and human errors were happily airbrushed out by the band and Horn (along with his future **Art Of Noise** and ZTT sidekicks). Many bands at the time were scared of samplers replacing humans but Martin said *"he wanted to hear his voice coming out of a Fairlight"* (c Lexicon sleevenotes*)*.

After perhaps the **Human League**'s *Dare*, this was the first record that really encapsulated the sound and aspirations of the 80s. *Lexicon*'s deep-pile luxury, rose-tinted windows and blissful escape from real life became signifiers for more than just bands. It rode a wave that had a huge cultural impact. This machine tooled finish became the grail for so many. Bands quested after this perfection. Some came to realise it but most failed; lacking the purity of vision, the strength of personality and, most obviously, the quality of songs.

It's a record that contains no filler at all. When moved by reverie and a second bottle of wine I can still sing the whole record, front to back, word for word. Lacking the funds at first, I had it on a C90 (with Scary Monsters on the other side) and I played the album daily for months.

By the end of 1982, **Michael Jackson** had released *Thriller* and CBS followed Michael's orders and released almost every song as a single. I felt a little sad when they stopped pulling singles from Lexicon because the swelling strings and sexy Glammy stamp of opener *Show Me*, the bittersweet disappointment of the **Smokey Robinson**-esque gumshoe (that is how I saw it, OK?) in *Many Happy Returns,* which features some of the most outrageous rhymes ever committed, and the twinkling bossa nova disco of *Valentine's Day* would surely have all flown into the Top Ten. I would have done my part, for sure. But as I will go on to try and convince you in later chapters, while the seeds of the Eighties are undoubtedly in the ground and nicely watered this year, and are ALL contained in this record, there were still proud punk rock principles behind the music and actual notion of conspicuous consumption left a nasty taste in the mouth.

And anyway, Martin flushing the lamé suit was perhaps a sign that they had had enough of the album after eighteen months. Or perhaps they were convinced that, like the Beatles, they were about to graduate to the silver screen. Alas, the **ABC** film, *Mantrap*, was to all intents and purposes, and by their own admission, a massive pile of crap.

Still, ambition is ambition and ridicule is nothing to be scared of, right kids?

If **ABC** came to Cardiff, I don't recall but I was way too young to get into shows at the time anyway. I had to wait fifteen years, until the unfairly maligned Phoenix Festival of 1997 to fulfil that dream. It was a beautiful day and a perfect, *Lexicon*-heavy set and I still have a photo on the wall at home of one the country's leading indie label A&Rs and myself singing our hearts out, possibly drunk, certainly being given a wide berth by the rest of the audience, and definitely having the time of our lives; living the dream.

Living the dream really was the case for the band back when the album was being recorded, on the hoof, while touring and promoting *Poison Arrow*. The spoken word section in the Bacharach-aping *The Look Of Love ("one day Martin, you'll find true love")* was inspired by **Iggy Pop's** "*Jesus, this is Iggy*" monologue in *Turn Blue* from *Lust For Life*. While ABC were recording the track, Bowie popped in to see **Tony Visconti** in the studio next door and heard the track and suggested they leave an answering machine message in that bit of the song, little suspecting He'n'Iggy were the inspiration in the first place. **Bowie** also watched the band from the wings at their triumphant show at Hammersmith Odeon. Many of the list of names that the band had scattered ambitiously across their manifestos, from **Stevie Wonder** to **Warhol**, from **Bowie** to **Roxy**, were all fans of the band by the end of 1982. And *Lexicon* was only beaten in sales that year in the UK by the **Kids From Fame** and a couple of compilations. Dreams do come true.

I was not then aware of **ABC**'s history prior to *Tears...* I got my new bands from Radio 1's Peter Powell and Kid Jensen and of course from Smash Hits. So while many of the crop of 1982 had murky or indeed quite respectable pasts, a great many of them just seemed to appear out of the blue, fully formed.

Aztec Camera's Roddy Frame certainly had no previous because he was only 16. *Pillar To Post* came out in August and was and is a completely perfect song in every respect. There was provenance and history in his singles for the Postcard label, home to many of the cool Scottish bands of the time but Roddy was something else. Deft, natural, complex flamenco inspired guitar playing with simple, playful and honest lyrics about heartbreak that defy the truth that a young teenager had written them. Or maybe I have forgotten the chasms of despair and romantic disaster that sixteen year olds face. Probably I have, although I am pretty certain nobody I knew at that age was as handy with a metaphor as he.

I just opened the inlay booklet from my CD of **Aztec Camera**'s debut album, *High Land Hard Rain* to quote from this masterpiece but alas the lyrics are all in Spanish. And not by Roddy Frame, so cheers for that, WEA.

Fortunately, my memories and the internet can help;

"The salted taste of all your tears and woes
Sent me in haste, my melancholy rose
Those tasteless lips were closed
You watched me come, you see me go"

High Land Hard Rain didn't emerge until 1983 but these songs were written in 1982 by an actual child prodigy. I've seen Roddy play lots of times over the years, including a particularly blistering set in 2012 and that song has the same emotionally surgical impact now as it ever did. And hearing it live means you don't have to endure the very unpleasant and pingy 80s Linn Drums that did make the album very slightly less than totally perfect. It's another album that I have not stopped playing for any length of time in the last thirty years.

From the sublime to the very much ridiculous...

....In, I might add, a good way. From appearing with **Iggy Pop** and **The Jam**, seeing **Springsteen** checking them out at an early show, to recording their first demo with Steve Jones and Paul Cook from the **Sex Pistols;** a cover version, in Swahili obviously, called *Aie A Mwana*, I absolutely loved **Bananarama**.

Keren Woodwood, Siobhan Fahey and Sara Dallin made a string of completely brilliant singles that somehow mixed a very British take on The **Shangri Las,** along with a bit of doo wop, some classic Spectresque girl group sass and perhaps a teeny bit of **Bow Wow Wow** in there. Indeed **Malcolm McLaren** sniffed around the band for a time trying to sex them up, but this band was not going to be a controversy baiting cypher. What stood out about Bananarama was that they were Fun. Lots of Fun. Girls-night-out Fun not "showing out for boys" Fun. Very much aware of the criticism likely to come their way, it was a case of What You See Is What You Get.

They were also, prior to the tiresome **Spice Girls** machine, the most successful British Girl Group ever. For a group whose only time in the studio previously was to record backing vocals for the B side of *Is Vic There?* By **Department S**, their debut, *Aie A Mwana* was a triumph. They also recorded a brilliant and very Bananarama version of **Sex Pistols**' *No Feelings,* which is one of the bonus tracks on the re-release on the debut album, *Deep Sea Skiving* and is hugely recommended.

As a teenage arbiter of pop's motivation and tactics, I was able to dispassionately note that they were all completely hot too. I made a bit of a study of this hotness/aceness ratio via the medium of listening to the tunes while putting posters of them on my wall in the gaps that weren't already occupied with the ongoing **Clare Grogan** Investigation.

Bananrama's next move was to team up with **Terry Hall,** who was responsible for the biggest case of national mourning in pop music since *Ziggy Stardust* resigned eight years previously, for breaking up **The Specials** at their *Ghost Town* peak (until **Paul Weller** took that title from him later in 1982) to form **Fun Boy Three.**

One can easily make the case that **The Specials** and **The Jam** were Pop groups anyway. And so I will: they were. But they were bound by certain musical and political conventions and there was only so much wriggle room around each band. The magic of 1982 is that all those shackles came off. If intelligent angry young iconoclasts wanted to slip off the yolk and make a **Shangri Las** record or a **Curtis Mayfield** track, for Fun, y'know, then they just took the risk and did so.

Bananarama exuded fun and they just looked like they were having the time of their lives. *Shy Boy* followed a brace of singles with Fun Boy Three straight into the Top Five. The following single *Cheers Then*, had a little too much bitter and not enough sweet and faltered but they carried on with the Top Forty hits for another ten years straight.

Another bright spark this year, who popped up, after a couple of singles in 1981, including the almost hit *Europa And The Pirate Twins,* was **Thomas Dolby**. Born in Cairo, he claimed at the time, which was presumably the same Cairo that **Madness** got the Night Boat to, Thomas was a Londoner and as much a muso boffin as his name and reputation implies.

Raised on jazz, he said in a recent interview *"I got my hands on a kit built synthesizer in the mid 70s and never looked back"* (© wikipedia). As all new bands were obsessed with **Kraftwerk** and **David Bowie**, it was very common, and virtually mandatory, by 1981 to get modern and forsake the boy meets girl themes of pop music, to write instead songs about machines, technology or even Power Stations, sometimes metaphorically, sometimes just about the actual technology.

Europa was very much a 1981 record, all monotones and stasis, but the singles that followed, *Windpower* and of course *She Blinded Me*

With Science, with its iconic video featuring science boffin de jour Magnus Pike, showed that even science can be a source of Fun for Pop songs and were set among lush and glistening productions.

In the case of *Science*, an absolute party's worth of Fun that took Mr Dolby into the US Top Five, where 1983's massive hit *Hyperactive* cemented him as a proper star, who went on to be a successful producer and session musician, playing for **Belinda Carlisle, David Bowie, Stevie Wonder, Herbie Hancock, George Clinton** and on another of 1982's key records, **Malcolm Mclaren**'s *Duck Rock* and, as befits his reputation, has soundtracked films and video games and invented more ringtones than I can be moved to list here. Also, he is the musical director of the brilliant TED conferences. Smart.

Smart was quite happy to be seen out and about with Fun in 1982 and this pairing made some of the greatest pop music ever heard. Ever. **Talk Talk, Blancmange** and **Tears For Fears** were among lots of bands that came over as being pretty clever men, having a dabble in Pop and making it all look very easy.

The 1982 Synthpop bandwagon was endless. Some great singles failed (looking at you **Vicious Pink**), others should have (looking at you **Blue Zoo** with your Number Thirteen hit that was in no way hyped/bought into the charts) and still others gave bands their sought after hit. Included here must be **The Mobiles**, whose *Drowning In Berlin* has elevated them to one of the great One Hit Wonders, along with **Icehouse**, who have had a long career elsewhere but are only known here in the UK for *Hey Little Girl* which filled a **Japan**-shaped gap in the market that year. More on Japan in chapter six. Much more.

February also brought the first single by **Tears For Fears,** whose teen angsty OMD-ish synthy tales of doomed romance and insanity were intriguing from the off. Relatively conventional of haircut and swathed in very un-1982 black clothes, Smash Hits took to them right away as did night time Radio One. They entered the game as an NME/John Peel Championed band and did not fully enter their Pop pomp until the world conquering second album *Songs From The Big Chair*.

They were serious. Even grave. Despite the psychoanalysis derived name, the sullen photos and the gloomy subject matter of their songs; they knocked out a succession of poppy singles. *Pale Shelter* came my way first via Smash Hits and the radio but it barely sold anything. Research has shown me that *Suffer the Children* was actually their debut in 1981 but that was very much under my radar. Both singles were subsequently hits after the career making *Mad World* had struck gold and the Top Ten. It's had a life of its own since and hit Number One decades later, covered by **Gary Jules** from the *Donnie Darko* soundtrack, repositioning the band as quite cool again having subsequently succumbed to the studio excesses, crap albums and splittings-up of later, huge American success. *The Hurting* seemed to be a key album for a lot of people at the time with its psychobabble tales of growing pains and slight sniff of something darker and unspecified, which allowed a lot of humans to project their own angst and problems onto. Damon Albarn's 2014 solo, *Everyday Robots'* sleeve is a nod to that of The Hurting. It's also a brilliant pop album and I can sing along word for word to it now.

Side note: the first time I realised that Tears For Fears were getting off pop's Naughty Step was when I witnessed American Hip Hop DJ, **RJD2** mix together four different copies of the *Head Over Heels* 12" into something quite mind-bendingly spectacular in a London club in about 2002. It went on for about ten minutes and has really, really stuck in my mind. Not strictly relevant, but there you go.

There was no shortage of hot, new, or nearly new synth pop duos around. I was quite surprised to find out recently that **Blancmange** had a past as a slightly more painful post punk noisenik outfit. Their run of singles leading up to the breakthrough classic *Living On The Ceiling*, included *God's Kitchen*, and *Feel Me*. Their debut album *Happy Families* is packed with brilliant songs and their big hard basslines, wonky percussion, sitars and general odd unpopstarry demeanour make it a favourite to this day. It also contains *Waves*, which is one of the great ballads of the Eighties and sounds like something **Frank Sinatra** might have sung.

It should also be noted that they called their second album *Mange Tout*, which is a joke title so ought to be a bad idea but it really is a great joke so passes muster.

Out of **The Tourists**, who put out two of my favourite New Wave hits in *I Only Wanna Be With You* and *So Good To Be Back Home Again* around 1979, came the **Eurythmics**. Now it is about as fashionable to admit to liking the Eurythmics, as it is to liking **Ultravox** these days and that is just the way things go. Both groups have themselves to blame for this. But let's delve back beyond their future c-c-c-crimes, and remember that Annie Lennox with her smart suit, pointy cheekbones and golden skinhead haircut looked completely amazing and was a brilliant pop star for a few years from 1982 on. Full of quotes and desperate for attention, as a good pop star should be, her self-described *"gay ginger skinhead in a suit"* look guaranteed them front covers and if you were around then, you probably liked them too. Their first album, *In The Garden*, was not very good and a flop. It does however feature Holger Czukay and Jaki Liebeziet of **Can**, the drummer from **Blondie**, the songwriter from **DAF**, and was produced by Conny Plank. Any record with that cast these days, and I do mean any, would be about the hippest thing music journalism could cope with. But, whatever, that was then and it was crap.

After two further flop singles in 1982, *This Is the House* and *The Walk*, they struck gold with the sleazy throb of *Love Is A Stranger* and kicked off an enormous run of progressively worse singles. *Love Is A Stranger* remains a brilliant, brilliant pop song though.

A further legendary synth duo that emerged from another band this year was **Yazoo**. Vince Clarke left **Depeche Mode** the minute they started getting famous in 1981 and set up camp with the Aretha-esque punk soul powerhouse that is Alison Moyet. Taking a ballad he'd written for Depeche, their debut single *Only You* was an instant smash and rose to Number Two in March. It has become a classic and hit Number One when covered a capella **by The Flying Pickets** a few years later. *Only You* was a hit in America and the next single, July's *Don't Go*, took on an even longer life as a much sampled proto electro classic. The parent album, *Upstairs At Eric's* took up residency in the charts and stayed there until and after the band's next record. **Depeche Mode's** first few albums passed me by a little and those singles sound horribly dated and thin now. They got more interesting when Clarke left and pervy old Martin Gore started writing S&M and Industrial sounding hits, which took the band to America, who welcomed them in a way that no-one could have predicted and where they remain a stadium sized draw, that hardly anyone sniggers at.

Trevor Horn was the mastermind behind Theresa Bazar and David Van Day aka **Dollar**'s run of rather brilliant hit singles that sat somewhere between disco and synthpop, but still had a vein of quintessential British end-of-the-pier crapness, that betrayed their past in the successful cabaret act, Guys & Dolls. Before Horn got involved, they had enjoyed a first flush of fame, had four big hits, traded up labels to WEA, gone rock, flopped, pretended to get engaged and had run completely aground by 1980. Horn came on board and wrote/produced the brilliant and, yes timeless, sequence of hits; *Mirror Mirror, Give Me Back My Heart, Videotheque* and *Handheld In Black And White*. Perfect pop songs each and much beloved of 2009's Chillwave groups (or should be) and also, it seems **ABC**.

Another lost band from 1982, much beloved by no-one, pretty much, expect me was **Fashion**. They had a past in Birmingham as an experimental Gothy Post-punk band, **Fashion Music** with a different singer. They ended up splitting, getting Troy Tate from Teardrop Explodes as singer and disappearing into the ether. I'd love to tell you they burned brightly for a time but they didn't really. However their super stylish monochrome look that combined Bauhaus with Milli Vanilli, and Zeus B Held produced album *Fabrique* was much championed by Arista for a while. They looked fantastic and so Smash Hits came on board and they even scraped into the Top Forty, OK Fifty, although that feat does seem a little suspicious now. *Fabrique* was super clean future funk, not unlike Rick James or Prince even and a lot of it sounds pretty contemporary now that new hipster bands are taking their influence from Eighites and Nineties R'n'B. Go on, humour me, go listen to *Move On* on Youtube.

Bands came and went quite fast and there were some stunning one hit wonders in 1982; king (and queen) of which were **Hayzi Fantayzee,** whose loopy and elasticated (and brilliant) cowboy electro hymn to John Wayne's cock, *John Wayne is Big Leggy* is the most jaw dropping. They were mates of Boy George and Jeremy Healy went on to be a very successful DJ. It seemed that anything could be mined to make a hit. **Musical Youth** took Seventies reggae to #1 with *Pass The Dutchie*, Sixties veteran **Toni Basil** scored a #1 with *Hey Mickey's* cheerleader pop and **Mari Wilson** mined the Fifties for her sole hit, with the brilliant, and mainly evergreen Radio 2 staple, *Wanted*. **The Damned**'s cheeky old English eccentric/nutcase bass player, **Captain Sensible**, dipped yet further back to the Forties for something of a surprise #1 with *Happy Talk* from the Rogers And Hammerstein musical, South Pacific. The Forties also contributed to the otherwise pretty inexplicable **Kid Creole And The Coconuts** whose Doo Wop slash Tropicalia was launched from No Wave label, Ze, to international acclaim and many scratched heads. There seemed to be no rules anymore. It was confusing but it was fun.

The biggest WTF *Top Of The Pops* moment ever happened in the autumn of 1982 when Boy George caused the national jaw to drop when he sauntered onto the show to sing **Culture Club**'s absolutely fantastic reggae ballad, *Do You Really Want To Hurt Me* in September. His life had been changed by **David Bowie's** *Starman* TOTP appearance in 1973. Along with so very many of the groups mentioned here, George idolised Bowie. Emboldened with Bowiepower, he emerged from London's New Romantic Blitz Club along with Visage and Spandau, looking like no-one else before or since. To say he was a six foot dreadlocked, be-kaftanned and bejewelled drag queen does little justice to George's look. He set out to turn heads and did so, on a colossal scale. When he turned to music, it helped that he has one of the UK's finest ever Soul voices and is as smart as a whip. It was probably hindered just a little bit by the fact that **Culture Club** chose a sort of gay white Reggae as the medium for their brilliant song-writing but George was and is a contrary fellow, to say the least and....Goddam, if it didn't work. Eventually.

The band's look guaranteed them coverage and George was very much a player on the scene in London long before the band. Virgin signed them and pushed the first few singles, *White Boy* and *I'm Afraid Of Me,* pretty hard in spring and summer. A hit in The Face and ever ready with a shocking quote, George pitched his schtick exactly perfectly. He resisted being overtly gaysexual but mixed theatrically camp acid wit, with a **Bowie** style character role. I say "resisted" but to the world outside London, his inversion of the Seventies longhair "is it a girl" conundrum by appearing as an technicolour Amazonian Geisha Rastafarian with a Smokey Robinson voice was never going to go over with dads and was without question going to bring George the notoriety he craved.

He was out to shock, but was so damned funny and cute and, once the tabloids had calmed themselves down, not that threatening at all. The nation's girls and gays went out and bought *Do You Really Want To Hurt Me* the very next day and it started motoring from Number Thirty Three toward Number One. It took four weeks to reach the top *but Top Of The Pops* had the power to turn a minor hit into a smash.

The record it displaced was *Pass The Dutchie* by the (again, recently reformed) **Musical Youth** whose *but Top Of The Pops* performance made their single leap from Twenty Six to the summit in just one week, making it the only time Britain had two consecutive Number One reggae singles.

Do You Really Want To Hurt Me? remains a wonderful, wonderful single and went on to sell a million copies, be a hit in the US and set up **Culture Club** to be a massive worldwide band who, along with **Duran Duran**, will never see a Best Of The 80s compilation released without one of their songs.

A funny thing about these bands: almost all of them made their best albums in 1982, sometimes debuts, sometimes not. Almost all of them were very, very successfully internationally. And almost all of them went very rapidly downhill in 1983. The reasons for this are going to be something I will be coming back to in later chapters.

06. GHOSTS: NEW POP'S MISFITS HAUNT THE CHARTS

Bold, beautiful and unprecedented music flowers in Britain and the Top Ten welcomes even the weirdest songs.

JAPAN MONSOON GRACE JONES PiL LAURIE ANDERSON

Radiohead are often cited as the band with the most adventurous career arc and a tendency to taunt/stretch their fans, as they push their music into unfamiliar territory. They refuse to rest on the tried-and-tested, kicking away their own crutches, and learning to walk afresh each time. A slightly pedantic qualification to such allegations is to cite **Talk Talk**'s revenge on Pop and ascendance to a higher Jazz plain, but that really is doing **David Sylvian** and Japan a disservice. Japan have slipped from the Accepted Critical Canon a little in recent years. Unjustly so. And they have a very weird backstory indeed.

At their inception, **Japan** were an averagely grim glam rock troupe, with a few good tunes. Except that story is barely true at all, despite photographic evidence such as the above. They may have *looked* a bit like Hanoi Rocks on their way to Court but they were a strange and unique band from the off. I don't recall **Motley Crue** writing reggae songs about *Rhodesia*. If they did, then I am truly sorry, Tommy Lee – I have misjudged you. Before it opens out into a weirdly anthemic and uplifting Broadway show tune, *Suburban Berlin* from *Obscure Alternatives* starts like a Middle Eastern refugee from Bowie's woefully under-appreciated *Lodger*, which is particularly impressive given that *Lodger* came out a year later. *Adolescent Sex's* title track takes **Lennon**'s *Whatever Gets You Through The Night*, loses the celebrity status and turns up the heat, making something sweatier and way more fun. Japan could be fun too. At times.

The first two albums, both released in 1978 are, broadly speaking, New Wave and, with the exception of **XTC**, most New Wave albums have a couple or three rubbish songs on them. Generic might be a more accurate word for those misfires but let's be uncharitable and stick to rubbish. Japan might have been very broadly New Wave, and *Communist China* IS quite reminiscent of **The Only Ones**, but they were never generic ANYTHING. So the lesser songs on the first couple of albums are perhaps more accurately described as indulgent or experimental. Or deranged and misguided. New Wave is supposedly Punk's housebroken puppy but there is little here that was born of anarchy.

More obvious on *Adolescent Sex* is a disco and funk undercurrent; which deep disco scholars may detect evidence of in *Suburban Love*'s chorus of, ahem, "*Earth, wind and fire*". Following the one-two of the ambitiously titled *I Wish You Were Black* and the lithe, handclapping cod **Herbie Hancock** grooves' of *Performance,* comes *Lovers On Main Street,* which channels the **Stones'** exile in that postcode. Such wrong footing could *only* be trumped by a Barbra Streissand cover. Obviously. Quite a howlingly bad **New York Dolls**-y style Streissand cover too.

It really is no wonder that Japan caused a lot of head-scratching on arrival. It feels as though there was a nutcase behind the wheel of the band or perhaps just several people navigating the band in completely opposing directions. I don't suppose it helped that Hansa, their label, seemed at a loss as to how to market the band either. Among their many random tactics was paying a famous Japanese wrestler called, amazingly, Kendo Nagasaki, based on a warrior with psychic powers, to bust into the NME office in full dress, brandishing albums and saki. That sort of thing is going to make the path to being taken seriously quite a bit less simple to navigate.

You know when you see an advert for a foreign music festival and wonder why The Wildhearts, Vampire Weekend and Avicii are right alongside each other on a bill? That is how the first two Japan albums feel to me. Smack rock, reggae, disco and Barbra Streissand covers. What The Flop? Oddly enough or, completely obviously, depending on your perspective, they were an instant hit in Japan and the debut rapidly sold 100,000 copies. Sylvian remains hugely popular in Japan to this day.

Japan were further separated from the pack by Mick Karn's very distinctive fretless bass playing, which is way less offensive than that sounds despite being both "fluid" and "rubbery"; and also by David Sylvian's weird strangled, vibrato Bowie/Ferry tones. It's a shame that the focus-grouped musical mainstream these days has very few properly weird Marmite voices. Sylvian, John Lydon, Robert Smith, Andrew Eldritch and Richard Butler, to mention a few, all deployed voices that were an acquired taste for most. They made few concessions for a more palatable delivery. This was part of the enduring legacy of punk – daring to be different. Being boring was the worst sin of all. Defiant and perverse, technically unruly and gratingly ugly when it was called for, their voices all followed the music to whatever odd places it fetched up, with a disregard for commerciality that served them incredibly well and gave each an instantly recognisable calling card. There's a lot to be said for artists that spend longer trying harder to be themselves, before they break cover.

It was customary, nay even obligatory, for bands to write about exotic or movie-mythologised foreign lands from Cairo to Berlin, Vienna to Tel Aviv. There were no cheap air fares back then and, aside from driving into France or taking a package break to Benidorm, most British people just did not travel abroad that much. The internet has since revealed, or at least made available, all of the secrets of the world but back then my knowledge of Vienna was defined by **Ultravox,** *The Third Man* and half-remembered associations with Classical Music's A Team. I don't suppose I was alone in this ignorance either.

Japan's detractors, and they are many, label them as dim cultural tourists, who ignorantly lumped Japan and China together in a brightly coloured oriental puzzle box. This is not entirely untrue but their twin obsessions remained and they stuck to their guns and it is perfectly possible to fascinated by both. Despite a lot of rockisms on the first two records, the arc of the band represents a gradual excision of all Rock and western musical tropes, in favour of Eastern instruments and melodies.

Their next album would lose most of the guitars in favour of disco-based pop, further exotic meditations, and, oh my, go on to invent New Romanticism. In 1979, album three's title track, *Quiet Life* was quite the inspiration for **Duran Duran**'s whole aesthetic and *Life In Tokyo* was a brilliantly unexpected collaboration with **Giorgio Moroder**. The album failed at the time, despite being rather great. It also provided my entry point to **The Velvet Underground** with their transcendent, hungry cover of *All Tomorrow's Parties*. I wonder how many other people first got into the Velvets via a cover version? Not only did everyone who bought the Velvets' debut start a band, it seems they also all recorded cover versions.

Japan's strong look, pin-up singer and extremely idiosyncratic ideas made them stand out a mile and ensured they always got press. In the po-faced grey world of the late 70s music papers, this was, alas, mainly ridicule. The thing is, all of these albums have some amazing and original tunes. Japan took a few albums to figure out and get good at being Japan but they got there. It then took them a little longer to write consistently well and ditch the musical red herrings that litter the first four albums. They were birthing something wholly unique and, looking back, you can see the various facets falling into place from the very beginning. *Deviation's* muted Japanese horn stabs are about five times more effective and appropriate when they resurface of *Tin Drum's The Art Of Parties*, for example, but you would be an exceptionally gifted seer to puzzle out the end of Japan's path from its first few steps.

It seems clear that Japan didn't really know what they had, or if people would like it but they knew it was something. For example, around this time, future hit and Japan standard *European Sun* appeared as a lowly B-side for the Japanese market. Simon Napier-Bell, Japan's impresario music manager (T Rex, Wham etc) and jolly scoundrel, first met David Sylvian in 1975, seventeen years old with an acoustic guitar and long blonde hair slung over his back (can you imagine?) and could see that he had something. Presumably, at first, that was cheekbones you could cut your fingers on, blue eyes that called across a room and a certain dignity. Not for nothing would he subsequently be voted "the world's most beautiful man". The rest of Japan were handsome and exotic too but David was a rare and beautiful creature, who appealed to boys and girls alike.

Their fourth album, and first for Virgin, was the luscious *Gentlemen Take Polaroids* (1980) and the title track gave the band their first nearly hit (#60 in the UK). Japan's first wholly convincing album picked up some good reviews and peaked at #51 in the UK. It's a really luxurious and atmospheric album, with an average track length of well over five minutes and produced strikingly and patiently by John Punter, who also helmed *Quiet Life*. After the epic and romantic sweep of the title track, *Swing*'s largely instrumental, vaguely Asian and slightly jazzy synthscape sets the tone and, in retrospect, announced where Japan were going. It features another unexpected cover in Smokey and Marvin's *Ain't That Peculiar* and the truly mesmerising and devastating seven minute *Nightporter,* which draws on **Erik Satie** and **Rachmaninov** for tone and **Cole Porter** for heart.

The tribal drums, on those songs that have drums, are loud and strong in the mix throughout and represent the final pillar in the band's sound. Eschewing rock rhythms and cherry picking musical influences from all around the world really made Japan stand out. Giant kettle drums, fretless bass, oboe, sax and banks of synthesizers set to *Traditional, Japanese* would make a band stand out today as well, I think.

All the parts of Japan are now assembled. They are finally a tight, original band with a unique song-writing style and a handsome singer with a weird emotive voice, albeit one with a fourth failed album to their credit. Time to write the classic album, right?

And so they did. *Tin Drum* was a proper hit album in November of 1981. Its cover was everywhere and Japan started having hits. Lots of hits. If you have a band on your label and they are not successful and they leave your label and become successful elsewhere, then it is tempting/obligatory to reissue the records they made for you, to ride the wave of success and recoup your investment. It's frowned upon to re-release right in the middle of a successful campaign – but it happens – and this is what Hansa did to Virgin in 1981. And 1982.

After gaining traction with the frisky *The Art Of Parties* and getting great reviews for *Tin Drum,* Japan had hits during 1981 and 1982 with Hansa tracks; *Quiet Life, Life In Tokyo, European Son* and *Smokey* **Robinson**'*s I Second That Emotion,* on top of *Tin Drum*'s *The Art Of Parties, Cantonese Boy, Visions of China* and also *Gentlemen Take Polaroids'* title track and *Night Porter.* Many hits.

This was a bit confusing at the time. In 1982, *Quiet Life* was a snip at £2.99 in the Nice Price racks and seemed completely de jour with its recent titular hit and Giorgio's New Romantic synthpads, yet was 3 years old. It took me a while to notice that *Assemblage* was not an album per se and also had *Quiet Life* on it. Boasting the pick of the first three albums, it was also completely brilliant, if bafflingly erratic stylewise. There is nothing more exciting in life than discovering a band or author or director and then finding out that they have a treasure trove of a back catalogue.

And then there is *Ghosts.*

Now these aforementioned tunes are all brilliant singles and it was amazing and exciting to see Japan feted as New Romantic pop stars and see Sylvian's face looming out from magazine covers and the fecund band produced a hit every other month, or so it seemed, for a few years. Really, it was. I had not heard the older albums at this point, so this was a barrage of brilliant singles.

But *Ghosts* was something special. It's one of the weirdest singles ever to grace the Top Five. It has no drums and is very, very quiet for the most part. Whatever the various ticks in boxes required for a hit single are, Ghosts has none of them. Except one; it is amazing. Also exotic, beguiling, unusual, impassioned, beautiful and very, very memorable. Oh and timeless. It did have a chorus too, of sorts, so let's make that two boxes ticked. It still possesses all of those singular, but not single-y, characteristics today and is something you really do need to hear, if you have not.

Japan were a band that took time to find themselves and were pushing, if not forward, then at least always away from themselves, with a view to find what they could be. *Ghosts* seems to be about that yearning and a desire to move on, hindered and held tightly by the past and, to me, always felt of-a-pair with **This Mortal Coil**'s take on *Song To The Siren*. There are parallels sonically and thematically and both singles are glorious wild cards from the artists concerned.

I had never ever heard music like *Ghosts* before; never mind massive hit singles like *Ghosts*. Hearing it for the first time, it felt like the world was whisked silently away as you were parachuted through the dark into someone else's dream. Waking, trapped in a secluded haunted house, the eerie silence interrupted only by floorboards creaking and half heard sounds that draw you into room after room and finally reveal themselves as your own thoughts. The sickening gut punch of finally realising something you've half known for ever. The dream is real and the person turning the key in the lock is you; always has been and always will be.

Ghosts also came wrapped in a particularly cool low key monochrome sleeve. A low-lit Sylvian with his head in his hand, against a background of BLACK. It was not shouting fun at all. I'd say it wasn't glamorous either but David Sylvian in 1982 was the ultimate in dour androgynous glamour and intense sophistication in my eyes.

Kudos is due to Virgin's marketing department for the singles' sleeves. Japan's early sleeves looked like they contained Japanese Heavy Metal records and somewhat miss-sold the contents. *The Art Of Parties* and *Assemblage* from 1981 had sleeves that captured the moody tones of the newer records and *Visions Of China*'s cheeky Pop Art Mao seemed very cool. Hansa's *European Son* sleeve with a Polaroid on a map of Europe was a bit reminiscent of Ultravox in trenchcoat spy mode for me but finally a beautiful visual aesthetic was enclosing Japan's music.

The single sleeves; from *Nightporter*'s multiple silhouettes by the window through *Ghosts* and particularly *Cantonese Boy*'s double pack 7" really summoned what I now recognise as the clean lines of Japanese design but sandwiched among the bright technicolour sleeves that lit up Smash Hits each fortnight, they really stood out as austere, alien and quite adult.

This view does necessitate looking at *Tin Drum*'s sleeve with charity rather than clarity. Its black and white tableau: a single bulb lights Mr Sylvian at a table in a spartan room with a peeling (yeah?) Mao poster, pausing from reading his (little red) book, eating steamed noodles (me neither), rice and something (peasanty) with chopsticks, having presumably just come in from toiling in the paddy fields, wearing the clichéd conical straw hat that's hung behind him. It's really only missing a "Me so solly" thought balloon. Not that I thought that at the time. At the time, I thought, as was presumably the idea, that Japan were actually turning Chinese. Or at least showing supreme solidarity with the Guangdong massive. On the one hand, you can sympathise; the multiple single re-releases came with sleeves that the band probably had little hand in designing but, alas, they must have signed off on *Tin Drum*. A later re-release loses this wretched sleeve, it should be noted.

The sleeves for the collaborations with former **Yellow Magic Orchestra** man and sometime member of Japan, Ryuichi Sakamoto, *Bamboo Houses* and the earth-shatteringly windswept, *Forbidden Colours* and every Sylvian album sleeve afterward, echoed his music's ascent to a higher esoteric aesthetic, away from Pop and onto Proper Art. The unintentional comedy was shelved, aside from the blip of calling a later solo album *Dead Bees On A Cake*, which made me laugh out loud when I read it for the first time. Beautiful record, though. I am sure the title references something suitably obscure and tragic.

Either way Japan never had a bad sleeve, or any other record at all, ever again. In the spirit of 1982, as with The Jam, The Specials and more, the band split at the height of their popularity. It's almost as though these massive bands thought it was not going to get better than it was in 1982. Just sayin'. *Tin Drum* was the last album from Japan. Except it wasn't, quite. In late 1982 they recorded a live album. I have almost no time for live albums unless I am deep in the throes of obsession, or feeling both extremely flush AND drunk, but this is wonderful. *Oil On Canvas* had a beautiful sleeve and the double vinyl artefact felt suitably weighty and expensive and...well....exotic. It gave the band a chance to recast songs from as far back as *Quiet Life* in the new Japan paradigm. Hearing the band glide through these songs, knowing who they are and how the music should sound is breathtaking and a pure delight.

The audience is mixed down to a polite background whisper and there are a few new studio instrumentals thrown in that don't break the flow at all. It's all very hushed, deliberate and, yes, Japanese in design and execution. It's also the Japan album I most often reach for these days. I hadn't realised until writing this that *Oil On Canvas* was a DVD also. Out of Print alas, but available on the artfully titled Very Best Of Japan DVD, which is, yes, also out of print.

Japan were not the only artists to take unusual records into the Top Twenty. Another refugee from Hansa records, who had developed her a few years previously as a pop act, **Monsoon**, fronted by **Sheila Chandra** scored a massive hit in 1982 with *Ever So Lonely*, a song that turns the tablas on the **Beatles**' Indian experiments from *Revolver.* A westernised take on traditional Indian music that shines today just as fiercely as it did thirty years ago. She was just 17 when *Ever So Lonely* hit #12 in the UK charts but had already had a career, acting in Grange Hill, which she describes as *"a sulky teenager playing a sulky teenager".*

It's not really much of a "song" per se, with only a few lines, repeated over and over but its drones, tablas, sitars and mangled guitars make it sound both dreamily ethereal and (also) akin, sonically, to **This Mortal Coil**'s *Song To The Siren*, which she later covered. It's also exceptionally danceable, especially on the 12" version. I probably had not heard *Tomorrow Never Knows* at the time and gawd knows I hadn't heard any Indian music in my life and this song felt dazzling and weird and wonderful. Still does.

It also sounded like nothing else in the charts. It's tempting to see it as a novelty hit and seeing as the follow up, *Shakti,* stalled just outside the Top Forty, it didn't exactly kick open the doors for acceptance of Indian music in the UK. That would come, to some extent, after the late Eighties fashionability of Bhangra and the rise of Bollywood in the UK in the Nineties, although many would probably be hard pushed to name more than a couple of Indian musicians even now. Even **Cornershop**, who have several classics, a number one single and a very cool catalogue to their name, are still way short of the National Treasure status that they deserve.

I really don't think *Ever So Lonely* was a novelty to those who bought it. It was just beautiful and different and mind-blowing. That, along with being infernally catchy and instantly memorable, was all it took to have a massive hit in those days. Radio One was a lot more open-minded in those days and the strangest records, from **The Flying Lizards** to **Laurie Anderson** to the appalling records mentioned at the end of this chapter, got airplay, if no-one objected too much. **Flying Lizards'** recording of **Barrett Strong**'s *Money,* whose amazingly basic recording was rumoured to have cost less than £100 and consisted of toy instruments, dustbin lid percussion, some odd sounding sax and utterly deadpan female vocals on the top. It was a massive hit and, along with their version of *Summertime Blues*, allowed the band to make three albums for Virgin. The first, a mixture of covers and originals, sold well; the second was a well–received but commercially inert album of originals by the band's mastermind, record producer David Cunningham. His studio background belies the recording budget story, which nonetheless worked a treat as a marketing trick. Stark and basic though Money's recording is, it works brilliantly. (PUB FACT: The band also featured David Toop, the writer/curator of *Oceans Of Sound*, which beautifully catalogues the infinite variety of musical sounds from **Debussy** to **Aphex Twin,** actual Howler monkeys to **Coltrane**. The album that accompanies the book is well worth seeking out, by the way). The final Flying Lizards album, *Top Ten*, is all cover versions of pop standards, from *Sex Machine* to *Suzanne*, in the same deadpan fashion. It's vanished from view but I'd love to hear it now. Their version of *Money* is now a staple of film soundtracks and documentaries about finance. Barrett must be very pleased.

Laurie Anderson is a multi-media performance artist from New York and now, sadly, the widow of **Lou Reed**. She is best known for her really rather amazingly odd album *Big Science,* which sold very well given its esoteric contents, on the back of the single, *O Superman*. To call it unusual does it a disservice. It's based on little more than a simple, clipped and infinitely looped *huh huh huh huh* vocal sample, with a very heavily Vocodered Anderson delivering deadpan flat intonations, like the transcript of an answerphone message, which might be a greeting from an alien, or a parent – none of which concerns Superman – (obviously) over the top, topped with a little birdsong and not much else. For eight minutes. Amazing. A Top Five hit, of course.

It was normal then to hear **Genesis, Shakin Stevens** and the extremely out there *O Superman* nestling alongside **Adam & The Ants, Visage, Elvis Costello, XTC** and **Dollar** during the day on Radio 1. Amazing. Radio 1 was for young people and current music, Radio 2 for old people and old music. Simple. The variety was quite breathtaking compared to now, where things are compartmentalised more and 6 Music, Radio2, Kiss, Xfm and the ILR stations take things that the more narrowly focussed Radio One won't touch. Pop music was a much broader and more challenging church in the early Eighties and people were exposed to more interesting types of music. And its unofficial and unconventional pope was David Bowie. The local boy made god.

David Bowie and his reputation for being "a bit odd" loomed large over music at that time. He sparkled with proper Pop star weirdness and inhabited a buzzing cloud of rumours and active disinformation. The beautiful starman who fell to Earth: commercially successful and critically bulletproof. Untouchable, a level above mortals. It's very much like now really, except it isn't; because in 1982 he was in the eye of his own hurricane. He hadn't put a foot wrong in 12 years and was white hot and breathing fire after his triumphant Seventies and he walked among us. Kind of. He had not yet changed gear to being the Superstar working on a five year album/tour/massive-holiday/disappear cycle. So when he took his foot off the pedal for the first time in a decade, his momentum carried him along.

Bowie had released *Scary Monsters* in 1980 to blanket acclaim and His currency was sky high. Depending on where you sit on *Let's Dance, Scary Monsters* is regarded as His last completely successful album, before He went off the boil a bit. I think it's the last album of His golden years and after that He stopped trying quite so hard for quite a while. *Let's Dance* has only 5 songs that are credited to him, and let's face it, can you recall *Shake it, Without You* or *Riccochet* right now? OK, fine, *Riccochet* is quite good, but you know what I mean. Massive props for *Let's Dance* and upper-medium sized props for *Modern Love* notwithstanding. His next album, *Tonight* was mostly covers too. So, yes, in fact, anyone who disagrees that *Scary Monsters* is the end of his unblemished romp is wrong.

Despite two whole years without a Bowie album after getting two a year for so long, it didn't exactly feel like he was away. *Scary Monsters'* singles continued into the summer of 1981 and November saw the small matter of his second #1 single, the chest-beating Queen collaboration (and future sample bonanza) *Under Pressure*. Also in November, RCA issued *ChangesTwoBowie*, a second iconic hits collection, and with it, another Top Thirty hit with his breathtaking cover of *Wild Is The Wind*, drawn from *StationToStation*. The two *Changes* compilations were heavily promoted well into 1982 and every home seemed to have one or both.

Bowie managed a further three hits in 1982, despite not being "active". A Christmas collaboration with **Bing Crosby** *Little Drummer Boy*, an EP of **Jaques Brel** covers *Baal's Hymn* and *Cat People* with **Georgio Moroder.**

So, then as now, you just cannot escape David Bowie, even when he is not really there. In 2013, He, or His legend, was omnipresent once more, and hearing His music, perhaps for the first time, will have influenced a new generation of musicians. He Himself was absent and has yet to make a public statement beyond a few words, even on the occasion of the death of his old friend and inspiration, **Lou Reed**. He did not give one interview in support of His actually-rather-good new record, *The Next Day*. Such are His still mysterious ways.

Another devotee of David Bowie was **Grace Jones**. Born in Jamaica, her parents moved to New York when she was a teenager, where she became a model. She was very successful, working with Helmut Newton and others, subsequently moved to Paris and graced the covers of Elle and Vogue. During her time in Paris she shared an apartment with Jerry Hall and Jessica Lange. Can you imagine the scenes? Or indeed the queue for the bathroom?

It's really not hard to discern how she succeeded once you've seen her. She is a living sculpture. Flipping Bowie's androgyny on itself she came across as part Amazon warrior and part mahogany statue, fierce and proud. Camp as Christmas, mad as a mongoose and wholly sexual, with a temper and ego that saw many reduced to tears, she is a true one-off. I'd LOVE to be stuck in a lift with her, but probably not overnight.
Chris Blackwell cannily signed her to Island in 1977 and she made a trio of disco records with Tom Moulton (**Three Degrees, Gloria Gaynor** and, oh my, *Disco Inferno*), littered with covers of show tunes and originals, including a magnificently demented version of *Tomorrow* from the musical *Annie*.

In 1980 she put disco aside and embraced New Wave, albeit from an odd angle. Recording with Blackwell's Compass Point Allstars, a Jamaican equivalent of the Muscle Shoals studio and houseband – it featured Sly and Robbie, Wally Badarou and a revolving cast of talented players. Subsequent albums *Warm Leatherette* and *Night Clubbing* saw her own inimitable takes on songs by **Iggy Pop, The Normal, Roxy Music, The Police, Pretenders** and **Smokey Robinson** and **Joy Division.** How to describe these records? Well, for a start, you haven't lived until you've heard her eight minute, heroically unhinged, dubby take on Joy Division's *She's Lost Control*. Not so much about epilepsy any more, it is, as all her covers are, about Grace now. She is the Papa Lazarou of cover artists, stealing songs for herself.

These albums have roots in reggae, rhythms stretched tight over simple synthpop drum machines, spacey keyboards and twitches. The backing tracks are all there to service Grace's prowling reinterpretations of the songs. Choruses are maintained but sung into new shapes, and verses become angry internal monologues. She pulls the songs apart and reassembles them to suit her own needs. They are often quite unrecognisable from the originals. Not all of them are successful but *Love Is The Drug* is stunning and *I've Seen That Face Before (Libertango)* is a quite beautiful and unique record, combining her strange ways with traditional French chanson-ery to stunning effect. It's pure liquid genius and it sounds like nothing else.

Her third album at Compass Point, 1982's *Living My Life* was mostly original songs, written by Grace and her collaborators, including *My Jamaican Guy* and *Nipple To The Bottle* which were big international hits and remain fantastic songs. Having learned tricks from disco and then found developed her own deranged way of delivering a song, there was no-one and nothing like Grace now. And of course the benefit of sounding like no-one and nothing is that the records still sound fantastically timeless thirty years later.

Later in the 80s Grace signed to ZTT and recorded *Slave To The Rhythm* (which was originally intended for and recorded by **Frankie Goes To Hollywood**) with Trevor Horn and had another career renaissance. And again in 2008 she released the pretty fine record, *Hurricane*. For a window into Grace's mind, do yourself a favour and read Miranda Sawyer's Guardian interview with Grace from 2008. It's online. An OAP she might be but dayum, it sounds like a fun night out. I finally got to see her play a few years back and it was all I could have wanted. It was as much about her impossible, geometric outfits as the songs. She's not just a pop star really or even that much of a gifted singer; not just a Bond villain, not just a supermodel; she's wayyy more than that; she's Grace Jones, Living Art, terrifying voodoo disco queen. Her presence is electric, her records brilliant and she makes the charts a better place. I only wonder why she never covered Bowie? Why, Grace, why?

Another artist that took a sharp left turn into the charts was John Lydon. **Public Image Limited,** Lydon's post-Pistols band with Steve Levine and Jah Wobble had a run of hit singles and albums from 1978 with records that fleshed out a whole new sound, a harsh, metallic, industrial dub, topped with Lydon's penetrating, taunting voice. It really was nothing that anyone had previously heard on record but its perverse hectoring served as a key inspiration to a lot of Post Punk bands. It certainly was far from Pop music and yet the legions of Pistols fans took these grating and angry songs into the charts again and again, starting with a Top Ten appearance for the debut single *Public Image* in 1978, which, somewhat misleadingly, is actually a fantastic pop single. It is surely the most searing, fully-formed, steamroller of a debut single ever, with the exception of **New Order**'s *Ceremony*, which also saw a new butterfly emerge from the wreckage of a previous band's um, wreckage, if I might refry some metaphors for you.

PiL's singles and albums carried the Pistols confrontational attitude and finally matched Lydon's always-brilliant, angry lyrics (he doesn't get enough credit for those, does he?) with coruscating, jarring new sounds that left *Never Mind The Bollocks* sounding like souped-up pub rock'n'roll, which it is. Absolutely stunning, feral, anthemic, ground-shaking souped-up pub rock'n'roll, mind you.

Do yourself a further favour and watch PiL's *Top Of The Pops* appearances for *Flowers Of Romance* and *Death Disco*. *Death Disco's* flapping dread dub is 95% rigorous, venting anger and 5% Swan Lake. *Flowers* sees Lydon draaagging the song along by its ears, dressed as half-vicar-half-clown, playing a violin, matched with tub-thumping drums and chaotic cello. I would give anything to have attended that taping, if only to see the look on the audience's faces. *Top Of The Pops* was watched by the whole family and would bring all kinds of thrilling and demented freaks and weirdos into people's homes, if only fleetingly.

Another completely unprecedented and affecting band that arrived in 1982 was **Cocteau Twins**. They emerged from Grangemouth in the misty gut of Scotland, a formerly bustling port dominated by a colossal oil refinery of steel and grime. Debut album *Garlands* on 4AD sounded like nothing anyone had heard before. I first heard them in session on John Peel in the summer of 1982. The gossamer of the later records' production had yet to be applied and the band sounded raw. Really exciting and throbbing with a sense of the Banshees early albums' ragged metal scrapes.

A clattering drum machine and Will Heggie's bass doing Cure-esque runs, was overshadowed by Robin Guthrie's weird, FX-laden, guitar. He'd obviously heard a few Cure and PiL records too but this felt like something different. It would be wrong to call it wild but it was not bound much by structure and its fluid folds and rapturous waves, rolled all over the songs in a freeform jazzy way, dipping into feedback, spiralling through riffs and mini-melodies but almost never stopping as though each song was his own suffocating guitar solo. That sounds unkind but the freewheeling shapes and textures were stunning to behold. He was not the star of the show though. That honour fell to Elizabeth Fraser. A small and super shy woman, whose songs ebbed, with similarly loose structure and flew skyward, coiled around Guthrie's guitar, commanding your attention but keeping their clearly personal meaning obscured.

Garlands' songs have little sections where she sings a line or so in which one can make out the words but mostly her elastic meter makes the lyrics hard to make out. Liz was the soul of the band, singing with passion, urgency and sometimes anger; that much was clear. Such was the unprecedented noise of the **Cocteau Twins** that they intrigued and inspired a huge section of Peel's audience right away. Everyone wanted to know more about them and find out what on Earth she was so fired up about.

On subsequent records, and perhaps tired of people trying to decipher her personal lyrics, she decided to retreat, just as Michael Stipe did at much the same time in America, into glossolalia. A brilliant looking word, I hope you'll agree. It means speaking in tongues. So from then on, she avoided English almost altogether and let her mouth follow Guthrie's guitar wherever it went and, freed of the need to make any sense. This path led to a wealth of weird and wonderful places and songs. My favourite album of theirs is *Blue Bell Knoll*, which pops and pings a little more firmly than the increasingly dreamy and beautiful albums inbetween and shows a tantalising electronic direction that the band could have pursued. Later still they left 4AD and signed with Fontana and the *Four Calender Café* album features whole chunks of intelligible words and sadly lifts the veil in a way that felt unnecessary, and clumsily intrusive, like colouring a Chaplin film or um, Kiss touring without their make-up. The music lost a little of its spark.

I still get those shivers from electrifying new music. An attack of idleness drove me to the Rough Trade shop at the weekend. That and the knowledge that they had put aside a copy of a limited (aren't they all?) edition vinyl release I had my eye on. Also, I had two notional albums burning a hole in my iPod from two new bands that I was interested in working with. One for the way there and one for the way back; and all on the first hottish day of the year. Perfect. And as usual I ended up being talked into buying a few more albums and singles while I was there, which also turned out to be excellent. Unexpected pleasures are the best. 1982 was unique in that people bought all sorts of amazingly brilliant, weird, and experimental sounding records in great numbers, making the Top Five a very odd place. It is a bit sad that there are not that many jaw-droppingly weird records in the charts any more.

In the interest of balance, it should be noted that, thanks to enthusiastic radio support, 1982 has some, if not all, of the worst one-off Novelty #1 singles of all time; including **Tight Fit**'s face-palmingly pointless *The Lion Sleeps Tonight*, **Charlene**'s whimsically vile *I've Never Been To Me*, **Nicole**'s knuckle-bitingly pathetic Eurovision winner, *A Little Peace*, The fucking **Goombay Dance Band**'s unforgivable Kumbaya-slash-Boney-M atrocity, *Seven Tears* (that I had to buy, to my shame, at a record shop, in public, for my sister's birthday present), **Shakin Stevens**' vacuum-packed *Oh Julie*, TWO fucking **Bucks Fizz** singles, **Renee and Renata**'s operatically inexplicable *Save Your Love* and the borderline calls of The Damned's **Captain Sensible**'s geezerish reading of *South Pacific*'s *Happy Talk* and **Musical Youth**'s admittedly infectious junior Junior Murvin-ish *Pass The Dutchie* and....worst of all, Macca and Jacko's arse-clenchingly, ear-slicingly awful and heinous, *Ebony And Ivory*. I think many of these records were originally championed by Terry Wogan on his hugely powerful Radio 2 show and you must admit that it does add up, along with his patronage of Eurovision, and THAT *Floral Dance* record, to incontrovertible evidence that he either has the worst taste in music of anyone ever or he hates us all. Or Both.

07. FLOORSHOW: ARTPOP'S DARK UNDECURRENT STEPS INTO THE LIGHT

The gloomy, leather jacketed hordes finally hit the charts.

BAUHAUS SISTERS OF MERCY SIOUXSIE AND THE BANSHEES

We are talking Goth. **The Sisters Of Mercy, Bauhaus, Siouxsie & The Banshees, The Cure** et al. It's a particularly divisive term, even for a music genre. As such, the term is one giant intellectual snub if you have no time for this kind of music and the start of an intense debate as to who is or isn't Goth, if you do. Whatever was (or wasn't) Goth in the early Eighties, it most certainly is something quite different now. It is unrecognisable today, after a reshuffle of the basic DNA, with added facial furniture, toweringly appalling shoes and all to often, totemic self-harming. Its blackened bedroom gloom spills into the diverse fanbases of **The xx, Skrillex** and **Paramore.** The original Goth strain is now subdivided into Gloom, Horror Metal, Darkcore, Ethereal Wave (snigger) and weird Gaia Goths; none of which sound like any sort of Satanic picnic. It's enough to make you pine for this "bench" of Goths.

No bands, well, no-one of "significance", openly called themselves Goth and rightly so: genres tags are for followers, not leaders (Except Peter Murphy quite recently, just before he was linked to that alleged "meth'd up hit and run" incident, so he might not have been on completely top form).

It is quite unusual as a genre, in that the less-than-brilliant bands huddled under its banner are not only not brilliant but also magnificently terrible, without exception. There was no middle ground at all. There were no quite good Goth bands. You either instinctively distanced your band from the tag, regarding it as a waste product of your own genius and acted as a scornful puppet master, dismissing events haughtily from afar, or you were caught in Goth's contemptuous, dark headlights, and exposed as slightly silly individuals, who didn't read the invite to the party properly. It is, of course, completely apt and correct that Goth has this dark and empty heart.

The birth of Goth is hard to pinpoint. Possibly because there was no such event. Perhaps Goth was summoned into existence to fulfil a need by a group of fans of certain events, films, bands, records and trends in usage of adjectives in the weekly music press. Lots of quite disparate bands over the years, from **The Doors, The Velvet Underground, Diamond Dogs-era Bowie, Suicide** to **Joy Division** had been described in the media as having Gothic aspects, meaning mainly maudlin and dark. The music press being what it is, such labels are subject to a Darwin-esque struggle for lasting power amid a maelstrom of adjectives and pejoratives. One convincing argument for the label gaining traction is that Ian Astbury from the **(Southern Death) Cult,** used the terms Gothic hordes to describe fans of **Sex Gang Children.** So perhaps the Goths were the followers, more than the bands; at least at first. Mick Mercer, erstwhile Melody Maker journalist and Goth historian, points to certain fans of Adam's original Ants, pre-Midge Ultravox and **Gloria Mundi** (me neither) as forming a group that showed up en masse at early shows by **Bauhaus** and the **Banshees** as being OGs – the, um, Original Goths.

Is Goth then less a type of music, and more a giant, billowing, black cape? There are, of course, musical tropes that connect quite a lot of Goth records: thundering, tribal (ie big ones only) drums, guitars twinkling with aqueous minor chords, downscale bass lines and longish, slowish dirges, topped with a rich baritone.

The darker sides of *Low* and *"Heroes"*, and particularly, Iggy's "Berlin" albums were key texts in the embryonic Goth culture. The deep booming voices and slow, grinding rhythm tracks of *Nightclubbing* and *Breaking Glass* contain much of the DNA found in future **Sisters Of Mercy** reels. Surely **Moroder** and **Bowie**'s *Cat People* is the ultimate Goth floorfiller, being both a moody slowburner at first and then adding gasoline half way through to give clubbers a chance to throw shapes and start jostling when Moroder pushes his big GO button.

It took me several years to discover that dirge is not necessarily a pejorative term in the way that NME and Smash Hits used to use it and that quite a lot of songs that I liked were, in fact, dirges; including most things that the Gothfather, Leonard Cohen wrote. Similarly, it took me a long time to get around to listening to Laughing Len because Neil from **The Young Ones** made him out to be deathly dull. True story. He's not dull; he's a funny, poignant and beautiful man. Len should probably sue the writer, Ben Elton over this for lost royalties. Or just for being disappointing.

Like so many music tribes, Goth is just as importantly an act of rebellion, – a secession from the mainstream, from your family and your peers. And this is where the giant black cape comes in; figuratively or, sadly all too often, literally. It's all very much concerned with introspection and tightly bound to that nobody-understands-me teenage alienation "phase". The records are to be played while alone in your bedroom, rather than the communal hive mind of Rave or even the cracking heads catharsis of Punk. Goth is spiky and unfriendly, warding off the casual listener. It's not something that "everyone" is supposed to be able to understand. "I am not a Goth, I am an Individual", a (recovering Goth) friend of mine always used to whisper in my ear, if we passed a gang of completely identically dressed and coiffured kids. Never gets old, that one.

One's intent and commitment in the Goth Arena is clearly demarcated by one's appearance. Entry Level, or Weekend, Goth was easily achievable by purging all colours from your wardrobe. Obviously this look could, and should, be upscaled to skinny jeans, pointy shoes and a cheap second hand dress shirt from the local antique market for that Three Musketeers flourish, with a back T-shirt underneath and a black leather jacket and/or frock coat to finish. The layered, wafty look is always in for Goths.

Now go grow, crimp, spike, dye and backcomb your hair. Just look at these cute little guys....aren't they just awesome?

After that are the dark alley options of "pretending to be an actual vampire" with phials of unpleasant liquid around your (and your BFF's) neck; "looking like a Victorian corpse/doll" amid make-up so caked that smiling was not feasible, even if required, which of course it never was. And finally of course, there was the final nail in the coffin that was ...intentionally smelling of noted insect (and human) repellent, Patchouli oil. Patchouli oil is a weird one. That something-from-the-back-of-the-shed smell is unequivocally vile and serves no purpose (insect repelling notwithstanding) and yet, from Whitby to Camden, Berlin to Osaka, you'd catch a whiff of it in a pub or supermarket and know there was a Goth lurking in a corner nearby.

Grand Wizard Goths are ridiculous individuals and rank among Jehovah's Witnesses and twitchy 24 year old City Traders, as people you'd make some effort to avoid contact with; but the Mid-Level Goth look was a strong one in the 80s. A romantic and mysterious outsider was basically what we were shooting for, I think.

Yes, "we". I was young and I did want to be a romantic and mysterious and, ahem, slightly dangerous sort. It was supposed to be a bit sexy. Goths always did quite well for sex. Being mysterious and aloof will cut out the need for chit chat and thus the chance of screwing things up by saying something dumb. You could assume a lot from the way people dressed in those days and frankly, a nice **Sisters** T shirt and upstanding hair often broke the ice by themselves.

As a group, Goths were very hospitable to those unwelcome elsewhere: outsiders, square pegs and the perennial teenage outcasts; fat kids, who were drawn in by the security offered by a multi-layered outfit that, say, deploying **The Kids From Fame** exposed-midriff-and-legwarmers look lacked.

Dear reader, I can't insist that the Pop garden was unrelenting genius because **The Kids From Fame** were fucking everywhere in 1982 – a genuine international craze. The original, slightly forgettable Alan Parker (he DOES love musicals, doesn't he?) film begat the genius that is the immortal party anthem *Theme From Fame* by **Irene Cara,** for which I am grateful. I too want to live forever, Irene. It's probably in my Top "Ten" most played 12" singles, along with, since you asked, **New Order**'s *True Faith* and *Ceremony,* **Bauhaus'** *Bela Lugosi's Dead,* **The Sisters Of Mercy**'s *Reptile House* and *This Corrosion,* **InDeep**'s *Last Night a DJ Saved my Life,* **Stone Roses'** *Fool's Gold,* **Happy Mondays'** *Wrote For Luck,* **The Chemical Brothers'** *Setting Sun,* **Snoop**'s *Drop It Like it's Hot* and **LCD Soundsystem**'s *Losing My Edge*. That list is not too up to date, is it? Well, it takes several decades to get in there, so well done, Calvin'n'Jim.

But, oh my, the infernal, unstoppable spawn that was The Kids From Fame. Total media domination. The TV show, the posters (Coco! Leroy! The sadfaced girl! The other ones!), the albums, the massive gigs, the live albums, the infernal *Starmaker* but mainly…legwarmers. Legwarmers were an odd thing really; they didn't make much sense to me, especially worn in a combo with Deely Bobbers, 1982's other "fashion" craze. Nor should they make sense, I suppose, in retrospect. Girls in general didn't make all that much sense to me in a great many ways back then. I am guessing that if you wanted to survive the grim Welsh summer, and rock a miniskirt (and you so did, thankfully), it was a godsend. **The Kids From Fame** was the 2nd biggest selling album of 1982 (behind a Barbra Streissand Best Of) and 90% of young ladies were seduced by the dance side. No men though. Not in South Wales in the Eighties. OK, a few. But not many. And not me.

Anyway, where was I? Hair. Goth hair was where the real commitment started. Goth hairstyles covered a lot of ground from short spiked hair (for weekend or school Goths), to ever-longer, sculpted, partially-shaved and endlessly, endlessly backcombed, haystacked, face-obscuring creations that required a good can and a half of Ellenet, or Boots ownbrand equivalent, to withstand the not insignificant average rainfall of a night out in Cardiff.

The level of commitment to the look was also linked to the degree to which you became a target for abuse, while out in public. Cardiff's

Goths would mainly go to the one exclusively Goth pub and one of two possible basement clubs in the city centre. Wall-to-wall eyeliner, leather and hairspray; a community of brave outsiders. It was kind of fun to run, OK skulk, with a gang sometimes. A gang of individuals, obviously.

One night a bunch of about half a dozen of Cardiff's finest open-collared-stripy-pastel-shirts-and-chinos gentlemen came to the pub on a Saturday night; their malevolent intent immediately clear. All eyes looking sideways at them, tension skyrocketing, spider senses all at maximum tingle. They presumably thought that seven against fifty were odds in their favour. Within seconds they'd knocked enough pints over, all at once, to light the fuse. The whole pub erupted as one angry, scared, caged animal – limbs everywhere, fists and boots pounding. I can still see the blood and glass arcing across the room. The screaming and chaos was intense. Things moved very fast but played out in that fight-or-flight split-second slow-motion that you only usually experience in car accidents. The Intruders didn't get their easy win and it was all over in minutes but there were a lot of people needing needlework at the Infirmary that night. It was unbelievably scary. I looked after the womenfolk – that is to say, I hid. I am a lover, not a fighter.

The dress code was one thing but the one idea that linked all Goth bands was that they set out to make serious music, not so much important, with a capital I, but music of worth; a marginalised, dark art for marginalised, dark times. It was a reaction against the perceived frivolity and optimistic party music of the charts; and of course, an extension of the Punk period's anger and energy. Goth groups realised that "harder and faster" had run its course but "darker and slower" might be cool. Punk's ideas of rebellion, separation and reinvention were still important. Assimilation into mainstream society was very much seen as selling out, failing and something to be viewed with shame. Punks did grow up but they often didn't want to give up. And starting to look like a Punk or a Goth was still pretty shocking to parents in those simpler times and was an emphatic two fingers to The Man.

Preceding and subsequently sidestepping the Goth tag (which dates back to a 1967 review of **The Doors**), some Goth bands were initially labelled Positive Punk, after an NME article made mention of the phrase. The NME's whims slipped easily into the lexicon of music in those days. I think its power and influence was at its peak in the early Eighties. A Single Of The Week would sell you a good few thousand singles and possibly a small profit. Imagine that, youth of today.

After Punk, the System remained unsmashed and, realising that, there was some new level of underdog unity manifesting itself. Positive Punk wasn't so much smiles-and-thumbs-up, Macca-esque positivity as something (very) slightly educational, rather than nihilist, politically speaking; empowering and vaguely Tribal. It had romantic aspirations to being an Outsider Art movement, and was relatively mutually supportive after punk's anarchy. This mutual support often didn't extend much beyond pulling injured or dazed parties out of the elbows-akimbo bruise factories that were the ferocious and occasionally cathartic moshpits, which you'd find at every show but that was still quite a nice thing.

The early incarnations of **The Cult**, namely **(Southern) / Death Cult** were prime examples of Positive Punk, along with the jagged Artrock of **Bauhaus,** punk stalwarts **Siouxsie And The Banshees,** post punks **The Sisters of Mercy** and the hollering and chanting of **Theatre Of Hate.** These bands took Post Punk's scratchy guitars and set them amid loud, thumping bass drum rhythms. The most important addition, however, was a little old fashioned star quality.

Ian Astbury, Pete Murphy and Kirk Brandon were all Rock Stars, cut messily from the classic template. All cheekbones, untamed hair and leather jackets, working the mike stand and throwing silhouettes in the spotlight. Post Punk had been light on showbiz and dynamic frontmen – this was a step away from that shyness and/or disaffection with the trappings of the spotlight. Fun might have still been on the Naughty Step but feral glamour was very much valued.

Theatre Of Hate's single, *(Do You Believe In The) Westworld*, which had reached the Top Forty and revealed the band that I'd read about and had assumed were just a shouty mess were not so at all. Theatre Of Hate's ever-so-slightly confused Aztec slash Eastern European symbology, tattooing drums, twangy guitars and Stax-y horns were actually wonderful and very accessible and the songs were quite the inspiring rabble rousing thing, even if it was never all that clear (to me) what they were getting at. They seemed to embody the camaraderie of revolution in a general, and, to be fair, very enjoyable way.

Theatre Of Hate were a Goth hothouse, staffed variously by Billy Duffy and Nigel Preston from **the Cult** and Craig Adams from the Sisters, uber-sessioner Mark Thwaite (Tricky Ministry, PJ Harvey). They later morphed into the Kirk Brandon dominated Spear Of Destiny, whose slightly naïve but convincingly romantic outlook was very compelling, when they steered clear of details or such dimly political musings as *"there's a lot being done against youth"* in *Smash Hits*. The first three Spear albums are quite weird to listen to now. And I do listen to them, quite a lot still. I used to be a massive SOD fan. Like The Cult, they dipped at random into history and various rebellious causes and iconography. Unlike The Cult, their musical palette was all over the shop. Tender ballads, driving Folk songs (kinda), actual Reggae and soaring anthemic'n'epic rock mini-operas are bent to their will and yet their second album, *One Eyed Jacks* gave Punk and Goth clubs two of the finest and most aggressive "dance yourself to a pulp" anthems in *Rainmaker* and particularly the slam-dancing slow-fast-slow-VERYFAST wonder that is *Liberator*. How very rum.

Siouxsie And The Banshees have been included in so many scenes and genres now that labelling them does them a disservice. Although I have put them in the Goth chapter, you'll notice. Siouxsie was a punk rocker. She was right there at the epicentre as part of the famed Bromley Contingent (see also Billy Idol, Philip Salon and Jordan (not that one)), and can be seen sniggering in the background on the Bill Grundy Show as The Pistols unleash the proverbial Filth and the alleged Fury. Siouxsie's style is so obviously Goth that it's easy to forget that there was no Goth just yet. Her look influenced Vivien Westwood's clothes, the whole punk look and then endured to become the template for a generation of Gothettes. Strong work!

Early Banshees shows at The Roxy saw the band playing a set consisting of just a lengthy version of *The Lord's Prayer,* with **Marco Pirroni** and **Sid Vicious** accompanying Sioux and Steve Severin, which you might argue was a semiotic shredding akin to Jimi's demolishing deconstruction of *The Star Spangled Banner* at Woodstock, although it might just be a band looking for something controversial and, um, Pistolian with which to bait the press. The band were huge favourites of Peel and when they got around to writing some songs, the versions on his show of early songs like *Metal Postcard* and *Love In A Void* were the very best. Harsh, minimal and jagged guitars and drums tattoo out intense jerky rhythms while Siouxsie howls and shrieks on top. It is not friendly and welcoming music. Its spikiness is EXACTLY what you'd expect from someone who looked as fierce and brilliant as Siouxsie. It's taunting and challenging and, like Siouxise herself, it's looking for a reaction from you.

Rapidly turning into a real band, as opposed a stunt one, they shopped around for a deal and Polydor obliged. Their debut single *Hong Kong Garden* sounds like it was written about a Chinese Takeaway. And it was. Originally called *People Phobia*, it had changed and softened a touch and fetched up at #7 in the UK charts in 1978. It was an early success for one of the many (ex-)Punks knocking around in bands and looking for something that Punk might evolve into. Calling these quite varied bands Post Punk was a masterstroke of vagueness, don't you think? Anyway, it's regarded as one of the earliest and finest Post Punk singles. It's also a LOT more poppy than anything else they were playing at the time which confused some of the fans, of whom Siouxsie said, *"Those basing their presence here tonight solely on 'Hong Kong Garden' were very confused. The single, with that devastatingly simple hookline, must be one of the surprise successes of the year, but the rest of the set was hugely different; dark, ponderous, black aura music issuing forth."*

Their debut album followed in November 1978 and was hailed By Nick Kent in NME as sounding like a mixture of Can and The Velvet Underground. I am not sure that is true but it is certainly justifiably high praise. The second record, *Join Hands*, saw another more minor hit in *Playground Twist*, which became one of those mid tempo Goth club staples that would see the dancefloor filled with capes and hair and expert arm-waving and even the odd dark mime of the chorus' chirpy hook, *"Hanginnnnnng"*. It also sparked an argument that left the band reduced to Siouxsie and Steve Severin, after which they recruited Budgie (ex-Slits) and, on a temporary touring basis, Robert Smith from their support band and label mates, **The Cure**. Side 2 of

Join Hands includes a fourteen minute recording of *The Lord's Prayer.* Rather you than me on that one, though. Probably best kept as a legend.

For a band that had started out so discordant and bitey, a major label deal and an early hit single saw the band change quite rapidly over a few albums and then settle into their own groove. Barked and haranguing vocals, huge drums, rolling basslines and some sneaky, snakey guitars are not everyone's idea of Pop music; however The Banshees were regulars on *Top Of The Pops* for the next few years with *Christine, Happy House, Arabian Knights, Israel, Fireworks* and the truly wonderful *Spellbound*, whose performance to camera I can remember vividly as though it were not thirty odd years ago. Gulp. *Spellbound*'s parent album *JuJu* remains my favourite of the early Banshees records, joint with the more lushly produced successor, *A Kiss In The Dreamhouse*, only equalled or perhaps topped only by *Peepshow* in 1988. I should point out that their 1983 live album, *Nocturne*, is absolutely astonishing, in exactly the way that most live albums are not. The band sound huge, super intense and focussed. It also boasts the slightly darker and heavier live version of **The Beatles**' *Helter Skelter,* which the band had released as a studio single a few months previously. Their intro music was **Stravinski**'s *The Rites Of Spring* and the way it crashes into a cataclysmically heavy take on *Israel* is one of my favourite album transitions ever. Their regular output and touring in the Eighties, along with Siouxsie's iconic look saw the band adopted by all Goths ever. They were quite the rarity too having a female singer and, being proper Goths, they would slit your throat if you ever accused them of being Goths. They have a point. They don't look like Goths; Goths look like them. Fealty from Team Goth was ensured when Siouxsie offered up quote like this, "*My earliest memory is pretending to be dead. My mum used to keep stepping over me while I was laying on the kitchen floor. I was five. I once took a bottle of pills to make it more realistic*"(The Face 1980).

Siouxsie and Budgie's on-off side project, **The Creatures** is also worth mentioning here. It's an outlet for non-Goth leanings and the Showband Doo Wop of *Right Now* and the Disney soundtrack (a good one, like perhaps *The Jungle Book*) bamboo banging of *Miss The Girl* are two of the best and Poppiest singles of the Eighties and must not be overlooked. Their slow, breathy undoing of **The Troggs**' *Wild Thing,* not so much however. It's just wrong.

Bauhaus were another rum bunch; devilishly handsome and spiky of hair and cheekbone. Fierce, taut, punky guitars, rolling drums with

Pete Murphy's abrasive, careering voice unleashing streams of consciousness lyrics over the top. Even more so than the Sisters Of Mercy, this was a band that dealt mainly in foreboding, unwelcoming "songs", peppered and alleviated by some very poppy singles. Northamptoners, Daniel Ash, Kevin and David Haskins recruited Murphy because he looked the part (and he so did) and their first show was New Year's Eve 1978.

Within six weeks of forming, they recorded a demo that featured their signature tune, the nine and a bit minute *Bela Lugosi's Dead*. This stark, twitchy, dubby and very slow song was often played in full at clubs, allowing for lengthy expressive shuffling/dancing and mocking thereof. It's still the first Bauhaus song people will call to mind and I still absolutely love its sketchy, scratchy genius. Despite its protracted length, it has a kinda verse chorus structure that Bauhaus soon disposed with. *Bela* was released on Small Wonder (Cure, Crass, Cockney Rejects) records in 1979, immediately sold out its 5000 white vinyl pressing and many, many repressings. Despite its length, it received play on Radio 1, including Peel, who invited them for a session that went out January 1980.

Further singles in 1980, including a cover of **T Rex**'s *Telegram Sam*, led up to the release in October of the self-produced debut album, *In The Flat Field* on the fledgling 4AD label. It went to #1 on the Indie Album charts and even grazed the Top 75 of the actual charts, despite mixed reviews and little support from the media. 1981's *Mask* album, again self-produced and engineered in part by Mike Hedges, on 4AD parent label, Beggars Banquet yielded the brilliant, angsty singles *Passion Of Lovers* and the perky, almost disco, *Kick In The Eye*, which both got to 50-odd in the charts.

For a long long time, *Mask* was the only Bauhaus album I owned. I bought it from a boy in school for £2. I'd heard the singles on the radio and was excited to get the album. I can see now why he was willing to part with it. Bauhaus are committed to their art to a commendable degree but the consistent press accusation, at the time, of them not really having any songs is not wholly without foundation. That said, *Mask* sounded like a mixture of **David Bowie** and *Dirk Wears White Sox*-era **Adam & The Ants**, two things I was firmly in favour of, and I persisted with the record's weird, dense grooves and breathless, free-wheeling vocals. Word for word you get great VFM from Mr Murphy. I wouldn't say I've ever loved it, but I was in thrall to its miasmic charms and dark entries and, damn, it seems I still know all the words to *Mask*, listening to it as I am today.

Persuaded to work with producer Hugh Jones next, the band turned in *Spirit*, which is a wonderful, deft, subtle, arty melodic gem that any group would be proud to have in their catalogue. Obviously the band hated it. Despite more radio play it too stalled outside the Top 40. They re-recorded it in typical obtuse fashion for their third self-produced album *The Sky's Gone Out*, which contained another glam cover in *Ziggy Stardust*. Released as a single in October of 1982, *Ziggy* saw a number of weird things happen to Bauhaus.

1. It gained them even more savage reviews than ever, citing sacrilege and furthering the "lack of songs" theme.
2. They appeared on the cover of Smash Hits.
3. The single went Top 20, peaking at #15.
4. It sparked a rumour that Murphy was David Bowie's illegitimate son. This was given some credence at my school, either because Murphy was lying about his age back then or because no-one thought to check. It turns out Peter is just 8 years younger than Bowie, so that is the end of that.
5. People who had found Bauhaus difficult or "wankers" started to like them and The Sky's Gone Out hit #4 in the Album Charts, aided smartly by a free copy of the rather brilliant live album *Press The Eject*.
6. Bauhaus appeared in the new, and quite bad, David Bowie film, *The Hunger*, performing *Bela Lugosi's Dead*.
7. Murphy got the job as the dude in the wind tunnel chair in the long-running Maxell Tape campaign and thus further accusations of being a sellout.

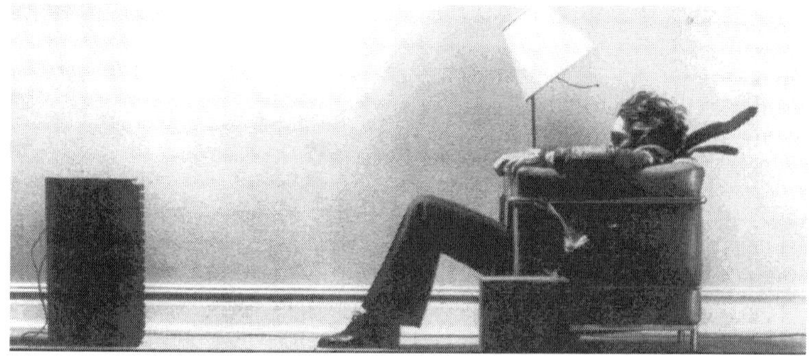

Murphy's looks subsequently saw him as the blueprint for Neil Gaiman's supernatural character, Dream, in the brilliant and somewhat gothic, as distinct from Goth, *Sandman* graphic novels.

Bauhaus managed one further album, *Burning From The Inside*, and a further TOTP appearance with the brilliant and uplifting, Goth "date single", *She's In Parties*, before splitting in 1983. Atypically, both Pete Murphy and the others, as **Tones On Tail** and particularly as **Love & Rockets** went on to have huge success in America.

Bauhaus have reformed a few times since. I finally saw them play at the Brixton Academy in 2006, and they were fantastically exciting, weird, wired and, for them, quite crowd-pleasing. They also recorded an album at that time but I am not keen to hear it; fearing the worst. I am not a Bauhaus purist, as you may have surmised, and I can't really urge you to buy their albums but get a copy of *Crackle*, the Best Of, which is a damn fine introduction to a very artful singles band, that succeeded on their own terms but committed many sins of indulgence along the way.

The Sisters Of Mercy from Leeds also broke through (a bit) in 1982, taking cues from the mixed bag that is **Cabaret Voltaire, The Velvet Underground, Motorhead** and **Suicide** and their name from a particularly brilliant **Leonard Cohen** song. Their initial no-fi recordings are quite Punk Rock in their way – a basic drum pattern, distant tinny guitars and mumbled, guttural vocals being pretty much all of it. 1980's Neil-Young-and-smack referencing *Damage Done* single was released on their own, archly titled, Merciful Release label and, when I finally got to hear it, revealed itself to be a fairly rubbish attempt at recording an OK song. And I say this as a massive fan of the band. A shame really because, in those pre-YouTube days, it was something I had lusted after hearing for years and years and was one of the Eighties' more rare 7"singles, selling for over £100 and attaining sacred relic status in the Goth world.

It is a bit counter-intuitive, I know, but I miss the questing necessary to complete your collection or hear that elusive song that you only know through word-of-mouth descriptions. The missed chances to hear it on the radio, the twentieth generation cassette copy, with the beginning and end missing; it was a game played with enthusiasm by enthusiasts.

In this case, those that had heard *Damage Done,* painted it as the ultimate Sisters song, their own legendary *Teenage Kicks*-y debut 7" single. I can see now that they were either deaf, mad or trying to be difficult. But given what followed, it had all seemed very plausible. Alas it's more of a sketchy prototype than a definitive statement.

The effort put in to hear all of a new favourite bands' tunes seems very quaint these days, where a search for "Sisters Mercy discography mp3" will bring the whole thing and more direct to your ears in minutes. Perhaps it would be better to say: direct to your hard drive. My own pet theory is that most of these colossal song dumps go largely unlistened to.

Back then, underground meant underground – concealed. An underground band or subculture wasn't something you could just decide to be into on a whim. It took time and many levels of increasingly hard-to-attain success. It really did take determination to discover all the music and that meant that you only got to it if you REALLY wanted to put the effort in; casual whims remained unfulfilled.

It did lead to snobbery and elitism, of course, but that has always gone hand-in-hand with music fandom – it just takes different forms for different generations. Squat gigs and Xeroxed fanzines still exist today for those wanting to stay under the radar. Cassette releases are enjoying a very low key resurgence in 2015 and that is something surely designed to veer away from being inclusive.

It's hard to argue this point against the Instant Gratification streaming generaton of today but, as with many good things, delayed gratification is often the most intense and focussed pleasure. Bringing home a record that you had to choose ahead of others, according to the paucity of funds, represented a choice and that album was going to be played and played until it revealed its charms or unmasked itself as a dud. I remember the first time I bought three new albums in one day as being the very height of decadence. And it's fair to say that one of those lost out on my attention. Today's music fans acquire music at such an unchecked rate, that great swathes of it must get little more than a cursory passing glance, at best.

Anyway, **The Sisters Of Mercy**. I was a latecomer to this party, I must confess. It was a few years later and only after being subjected to *Temple Of Love* repeatedly by a girlfriend and sundry club DJs that I got past the deep, rumbling baritone of Andrew Eldritch that had put me off. One day it all clicked...permanently. True what they say about Goth bands not making themselves welcoming. That back-of-the-throat singing style is a choice and I found it all a bit overly-mannered and a little perverse at first but I was eventually seduced by it, along with all the heavy mannered intrigue and perverse romance of The Sisters.

Intrigue was a key part of The Sisters mythology. Andrew Eldritch was a puzzling, compulsive frontman – as smart (and skinny) as a whip but with an ungovernable ego, as good frontpersons should be. He studied languages at Oxford and was studying Mandarin at Leeds, when he was seduced by music's dark underbelly. The songs, when they came were literate, mysterious, passionate, romantic, oblique, cruel and soaked in narcotics. Shelley, Dante, Bacon, Bowie, Coleridge, Crowley, Brel were key figures in the Sisters mythology and gave rise to a very European sounding music, despite the **Velvets** and **Stooges** influences, which were worn proudly as B-side cover versions and live staples. (They also covered **Hot Chocolate, Kylie** and **Dylan**, so make of that what you will). No Sisters show was complete without a blisteringly intense cover of **Iggy**'s *1969*. The band very much had a cake-and-eat-it attitude to the rock star life. They both revelled in and distanced themselves from the rock cliché and this irony-surfing was all helmed, more or less successfully by Eldritch's smarts and wit.

I don't think anyone actually *saw* them play until they did a few outdoor festival slots in the UK around 1992. Previously, all anyone had ever seen was dry ice and lots (and lots) of it. Pumped out by the ton and completely obscuring the stage end of whatever venue they played, no matter how large, the smoke screen was lit like an electrical storm and, once in a while, you'd catch a glimpse of a silhouette or a shadow, amid the punishing, hypnotising strobing. A crumple-hatted Eldritch smoking furiously at the mike or the neck of a guitar, rocking up and down amid the all-consuming onslaught that was their stage show. This shadow theatre, the ominous monotone of the ever-present drum machine (dubbed Doktor Avalanche) and the pounding guitars made **The Sisters,** to the initiated, one of the most thrilling live bands ever. Never gauche, always aloof, and always, always just outside of reach, unknowable. Totally cool.

I used to watch *Wake*, their video of a farewell (to the original line-up) Albert Hall show, over and over again as a kid, much to the mockery of my friends, who couldn't see what I could on the screen. Not that I could actually see it per se but, oh my, I felt it. It really was powerful stuff and was very much about getting lost in the huge, throbbing, widescreen music. Not unlike the stageless euphoria of a rave in its internal-yet-communal experience, and also in its expressive, I-am-a-tree-in-spring arms aloft dancing.

Eldritch, alas, is a sore loser and will hold onto a grudge for decades, it seems and, as such, was at a legal impasse with his record label, WEA, for years and that means that Wake is still not available on the new fangled DVD format, never mind Blu Ray. I actually bought a DVD bootleg of it quite (OK, very) recently, and was nervous that it might not have stood the test of time. Fear not, dear reader, it has. So cool. Sooo cool.

Initially, this legal dispute (which ended in 1997) and latterly Eldritch's pigheadedness has blocked the release any music since 1993, which is a damn shame because, as a night-time trawl through Youtube will reveal, The Sisters have debuted several albums' worth of new songs onstage since then. I enquired a few years ago, what it would take to get Eldritch back in a studio. I got a three word response: One Million Pounds. It's a shame that I didn't have that money spare and, of course, that no sane person would make it available for The Sisters these days, because they really are due a Gary-Numan-esque critical re-evaluation.

Their influence on **Tricky, Big Black, NIN** and each new generation of dark music is obvious but a blotted copybook toward the end of their flirtation with fame, such as Eldritch's idea to cover (Top Gun's) **Berlin**, has put them on the critical bench for the duration. Do seek out **Lambchop**'s aching version of *The Corrosion* when you get a minute.

"It's hard being a cult band when you want to be immense" said Eldritch in 1983 but regardless The Sisters slowly became a very big cult band indeed on the back of a string of singles from 1982 to 1985, alternating slow, not immediately penetrable but ultimately magnificent dirges like the Reptile House EP (allegedly solely the work of Eldritch), which makes no concessions at all to being likable and stands, defiant and unhurried, as a hardcore Slow-Goth (Sloth?) classic; with classic Pop (relatively speaking) songs like Temple of Love, Alice (produced by John Asheton of the Psychedelic Furs), Train and Floorshow that filled dancefloors for ten years and still do at weddings and parties, if I am on the decks. These brilliant singles and EPs sold by the tens of thousands and the iconic none-more-black lino-cut sleeve images adorned the walls of a generation. The band's iconic star/man logo used to be visible on every high street, painted painstakingly onto the back of leather jackets (my own proudly included), tattooed on upper arms, and on a million T shirts. No need for mention of the bands' name – the logo was the mark of a secret society.

After *Temple Of Love* had lodged itself permanently in the Indie Charts, a deal with WEA followed and their first album, the unimpeachable Goth Classic, *First & Last & Always*, was released in 1985 and debuted in the Top 20. Ten perfect songs and a record I still play to this day. Naturally it was born out chaos; the band were on the verge of disintegration, strung out and bickering while making it. It seems that after Eldritch's dictatorial monomania on previous releases, he retreated into sundry psychoses while the rest of the band wrote the bulk of the music. Wayne Hussey (ex-Dead Or Alive) was mainly responsible for the poppier, by Goth standards, Side 1 and Gary Marx created most of Side 2's grinding, heavier, almost dubbier tunes , with Eldritch coming in adding lyrics at the last minute. "Metal Dub" was an early self-descriptor of the band's sound and it is not as mad as it sounds, at first. Not quite anyway.

Opener *Black Planet* is presumably Eldritch's drug-addled idea of a joke about the whole Goth Overlord tag, which metatextual intricacies may well have been lost on some, himself included (I am not sure they ever played it live); *Walk Away* is allegedly aimed at the soon-to-walk-away Gary Marx, *No Time To Cry* is a sarcastically vacuous attempt at hit single ("Everything will be alright, everything will turn out fine" indeed) and very nearly was. The rest of the album walks that fine line – writing about the Blues' staple, the interchangeable desolation and inevitability of problems with women and drugs, that also became Jason Pierce's stock-in-trade. There is romance evident throughout but, being Goths, it's doomed and/or soiled and always short term *("Life is short and love is always over in the morning")*. Fulfilment is not a strong Goth trait. Being always the victim, ever the bridesmaid, is the destiny of all Goths *("A Rock and a hard place, waiting for me")*.

So yes, it's doomy and gloomy but, oh my, it's brilliant pop music. I must have sung along to *Marian* and *First And Last And Always* hundreds of times over the years. The latter's introductory riff still gives me goosepumps and the song has been a popular gig opener for The Sisters for decades. The liquid jewel that is *Nine While Nine* is a stunning piece of work, that ought alone to earn the band enduring kudos. It sums up all of the tropes of the album: lost love, inchoate desperation and narcotic nights in shining leather. The title puzzled me until, years later, as a student I was imprisoned in a drug testing facility in Leeds and spotted that "while" is used instead of "until" in Yorkshire, for some reason. So it might as well have been called *All Night Long*, except both Rainbow and Lionel Richie had tarnished that one.

The epic closer *Some Kind Of Stranger* is the Goth *Total Eclipse Of The Heart*. This joke would curl in on itself and then emerge wide-eyed and beautiful from within, when Eldritch returned, virtually solo but under **The Sisters Of Mercy** banner, in 1987 with Bonnie/Meatloaf's producer Jim Steinman in tow, for the Top Ten worldwide hit, *This Corrosion*.

Before *This Corrosion*'s breakthrough, the band grew to the point where they could sell out the Albert Hall, but they remained a cult band, whose singles stalled outside the Top 40. After touring the album, Eldritch relocated, along with Wayne Hussey and Gary Marx, to Hamburg to write the follow-up. Fuelled no doubt by their legendary consumption of intoxicants, they split up almost immediately with new boy, Hussey departing to form his own band, **The Sisterhood**, taking the name of the devoted and slightly scary Sisters fanbase/streetgang, much to Eldtritch's chagrin, who felt, probably quite rightly, that that was his domain. **The Sisterhood** played shows and featured songs Hussey had written for the Sisters' second album, bootlegs of which, with Eldritch singing, are only a click away for the curious.

In a brilliant showbiz spat and with maximum spite, Eldritch himself reclaimed the name by releasing a single, the brilliant but cruel, *Giving Ground* (lines like *"what you have lost, will never be found"* are aimed squarely at Hussey) under the name **The Sisterhood**, followed by a mini-album of throwaway-ish tunes, that triggered an advance from their publisher awarded to whichever camp released a record first. One of the songs, *Jihad*, started with a woman repeating the figure he had won in a legal dispute with Hussey over the name The Sisterhood, instead of an actual lyric: 2-5-0-0-0. Excellent grown up behaviour, I am sure you will agree. As it turned out, Wayne Hussey went on to form **The Mission**, who became a semi-serious prospect, while Eldritch went to ground for two years to bring out his inner Meatloaf and pursue a life without guitarists.

It's interesting that Eldritch is vocal about his love for **Motorhead.** Anyone who likes hard and fast Rock likes Motorhead, from **Metallica** to **Queens Of The Stone Age**. Dave Grohl was thrilled as thrilled could be when Lemmy contributed to his thrash tribute band, **Probot.** They may have accidentally invented Thrash Metal and pioneered playing very fast indeed but Motorhead were/are loved just as much by many punks for their short sharp shocks and total lack of musical fat. Lean, mean and fast, Motorhead were cut from the same cloth as the punks and Lemmy has said he felt more kinship with the punks than rock fans, as a whole. He even did a stint in **The Damned**, filling in for a few shows, when they had misplaced their bass player. Motorhead may seem like a relic now to some but they have been influencing bands for four decades, showing how keeping it simple, fast and brutal can happily coexist with writing some of the best Pop singles you will ever hear. Yes. Pop singles. *Ace Of Spades*, you know of course but *Too Late Too Late, Overkill, Please Don't Touch, Stone Dead Forever* and the impossibly great, *Killed By Death* and the definitely dubious *Jailbait* are just as brilliant. Bass players from Mick Jones to Peter Hook have all lined up to praise Lemmy's constant and insistent way with a fourstring. Also Lemmy does the singing on **Hawkwind**'s eternal, psychedelic and proto-Goth floorfiller *Silver Machine*, which alone ought to make him some sort of rock royalty. Do yourself a favour, listen to the brilliantly titled, Motorhead Best Of, *No Remorse* before Lemmy dies. File it in between The Ramones and Metallica in your mind, if that helps. They wrote the rulebook on kicking ass. They really did. I used to think Lemmy would live forever. As I am sure he did. He's been sick lately. Let's hope there's a cure for what ails him.

Robert Smith, Lol Tolhurst and Michael Dempsey first performed together in April 1973 (!) under the name Obelisk. That means they have been going for over 40 years. Gulp! They became Easy Cure (via Malice) and won a recording contract with Hansa in a competition in 1977, the recordings from which never saw release. A disagreement about direction led to that deal being annulled quite quickly. By 1978 they'd signed as **The Cure** to Chris Parry's freshly minted Fiction records and had already independently released their debut single, *Killing An Arab* on the Small Wonder label. The Camus-derived title was pure press bait and the band were accused of all kinds of malfeasance, amid much coverage. There's a sense of Fall-esque tension and sullen confidence about the single and it stands up very well today, as a bitey teenage Pop song. The Middle Eastern effects on the guitars are smart and not overplayed; choppy Wire-esqe riffs and blank verses are tempered with a proper chorus, backing vocals, nice flourishes and it's all wrapped up in less than 150 seconds: a perfect debut single.

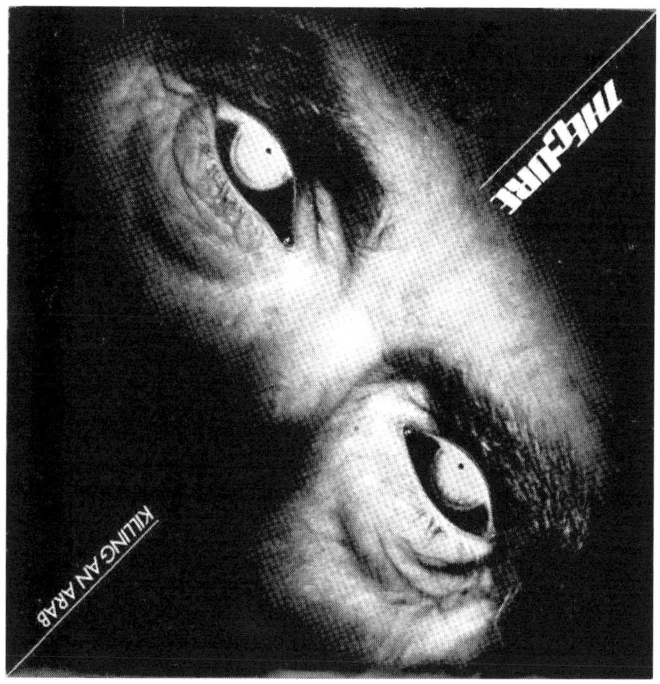

Their debut album, *Three Imaginary Boys*, produced by Parry and Mike Hedges, is a bit of a mixed bag. It opens brilliantly with longtime live favourite, *10.15 Saturday Night* – a taut tale of loneliness and social exclusion, followed by Accuracy and Grinding Halt. It sort of wanders off at this point, covers **Jimi Hendrix**'s *Foxy Lady* (very very badly) and rallies with *Fire In Cairo*. Overall it all sounds a bit indistinct to my ears, lacking power, urgency and tension. It shares a sound with the prevailing New Wave winds, and the raw, choppy chords of the Stiff Records' artists and you can see what they were aiming for but the vocals are badly recorded and the whole thing sounds like a live demo, rather than a produced record.

The record company decided which songs were put on the album, as well as the cover artwork, allegedly without Robert Smith's consent or approval. For each Cure album since, Smith has ensured he is given complete creative control over the final product. Nonetheless, after a strongish response from critics, *Three Imaginary Boys* almost hit the Top Forty.

I think the American version makes more sense – retitled *Boys Don't Cry* – which includes *Killing An Arab* and the two non-album singles that followed it. The first, *Boys Don't Cry* followed a month after *Three Imaginary Boys* and is their second classic single, an Indie disco staple to this day. Robert describes it as a *"Seventies attempt to write a Sixties Pop song"*. It very neatly sums up the perennial bumpy ride that is teen romance. I always thought it was a complementary/answer song to **Frankie Valley**'s *Big Girls Don't Cry*. Regardless, there's nothing in the lyric that doesn't apply to virtually every 16-19 year old in the country at some stage in their life, both now and in 1979 – but you already know that, right? Sure you do.

Jumping Someone Else's Train is another wired, late night ride through the city and Robert's growing paranoias. Smith is quite disparaging about the debut album now; damning it as *"lightweight and throwaway"*; and, compared to the swirling doom clouds of The Cure we know and love, it is, but those first few singles remain twitchy teenage Indiepop perfection.

The black cape of Goth – the despairing and depressant tropes – were defined retrospectively, with bands as disparate as **The Damned** and **Joy Division** being labelled gothic, gloomy and doomy. The dark political times created these negative outlooks. Perhaps Goth existed before any of the Goth bands; lurking in the shadows, waiting to draw them in. Post Punk's workmanlike no-frills attitude incubated those outlooks and, amid the dark, joyless nights, and dark, jobless days of Thatcher's Britain, it became a logical, musical rut to fall into – there not being too much to smile about for a lot of people in Britain.

Wearing all-black clothes until they were ragged was almost a statement in itself in the era of cheaper, colourful, bright and disposable Polyester and nylon clothes, imported from the Far East. A rejection of fripperies and excessive consumption in place of concentration on more important ideas was the subtext; although, looking back now, it's just another outfit/uniform, I suppose and one born out of the practicalities of living outside of The Man's grasp; that is to say, being an unemployable monochrome peacock, who scares old ladies.

Robert Smith made his true feelings and intentions evident with the second album, *Seventeen Seconds*, released less than a year later. It was co-produced by Hedges and Robert and is instantly recognisable as **The Cure** who have endured for decades now. Swathed in reverb, spacious and beautifully detailed; it defines and nails the classic Cure sound and belies the fact that the whole record was recorded in seven days. The rhythms are tight and full and Robert's greatly underrated, fluid guitar playing unhurriedly paints the songs on a big, big canvas in lengthy splashes. Songs are enhanced with keyboard flourishes, spotlights and shade and then topped with vocals that have (this time) been carefully and thoughtfully, recorded. Robert is not the most naturally gifted singer and yet, when nestled in a skimpy mist of reverb, he emits a huge and emotionally vulnerable, old soul of a voice, carrying both the weight of the world, and a flickering torch of hope. The lyrics are economically written; all about love, betrayal, existential pain, desperation and cut with just a hint of voyeurism; or perhaps just love from afar. All the major teenage food groups and worry beads are here.

The whole record sounds confident, original and perfectly formed. There really aren't any antecedents to **The Cure**, with vocals and guitar working as one to make the huge, signature sound. There are shades of **The Banshees, Joy Division, Wire** and **Television** in there but The Cure are one of those bands that you can recognise within five seconds of hearing a song. They are not songs, but Cure songs, and very hard to cover, for the most part. Similarly, it's something that you can't easily rip off or adapt, without sounding like a pale imitation; not that that stops bands from doing so, year in, year out.

The Cure now offered a complete lifestyle package and acted as a rescue service for sensitive, misunderstood teens and have done so now for two generations. Singing explicitly about love and romance sets them apart from their Goth peers' artful obfuscation and, not uncoincidentally, is one of the reasons that Robert is now seen as a cuddly National Treasure, rather than bracketed as a demented recluse, as many other Goth Lords are now. The other reason is outlined later. Clue: Pop.

I get demos every so often, from bands whose entire palette is lifted from **The Cure,** who have become so locked into their corner of the Cure-niverse that outside influences just don't have any relevance or currency. The Cure IS music for these hardy souls. They are tough ones to reply to because the bands don't account for the fact that The Cure are still going and have that "sounding like The Cure" thing down perfectly, thank you very much.

My friend had a Heavy Metal band way back in 1980 and one week their teenage guitarist went AWOL. He wouldn't answer the phone or his door. When they eventually tracked him down at his mum's, he had cut all his Rock hair off and was clutching a copy of *Seventeen Seconds*. He said he'd had a revelation, he'd listened to the album 100 times that week and it had changed him completely, mentally, permanently and he couldn't have anything to do with Rock music any more. Amazing.

Despite its age, I am sure that if a band today dropped something akin to the tightly looped, inward-looking and cataclysmic *A Forest* into the public ear, the internet would explode, and more lives would be changed. Perhaps 2013's *Husbands* by **Savages** comes close. No cigar alas because it lacks *A Forest*'s effortless, weightless grace. Five months after *Seventeen Seconds*, they were back in the studio to make their third album, *Faith*, which it would be a bit uncharitable to call more-of-the-same. A bit but not much. Anchored by the pulsing *Primary* and the lush Sloth of *All Cats Are Grey*, this continued, rather than furthered, the band's vision. It has a no frills, economic approach, which is seen through to the plain, rather (and actually) monastic grey sleeve. Most of the songs are stark, very slow and there is a quasi-ascetic anti-Pop approach evident. More of the same was just what the doctor ordered, however, and it charted at #14 (and went to #1 in New Zealand).

A few months later **The Cure** released one of my favourite singles, *Charlotte Sometimes*, which again doesn't feature on any album. For my money, this is the first time the band condensed the heavier, spacier, psychedelic sounds of their signature slower songs onto a fast, OK, midtempo Pop song; with lyrics lifted from a children's book of the same name by Penelope Farmer.

May 1982 saw the third and doomiest of this doomy trilogy, the somewhat depressing *Pornography*. A Top 10 hit and a perennial Goth favourite, this is much harder going, and offers a bigger, denser and noisier sound that has made it such a talisman to Industrial bands over the years. There are few spaces on the record and the combined feelings of oppression, depression and aggression come through clearly. Their first without Hedges, who was replaced by Phil Thornally – its gestation was messy, with the band drinking, tripping, self-sabotaging and fighting with dogged enthusiasm. According to founder member Lol Tolhurst, "*we wanted to make the ultimate, intense album. I can't remember exactly why, but we did*". They certainly did.

It felt like the banks of criticism The Cure had received for being gloomy and depressing had driven them to take these traits to new depths. Perversity is a common thread, both in their story and in the wider Goth world. Luckily the ever growing Goth Nation was ready, very willing and able to up the doomy ante and match The Cure, grimace for grimace, sulk for sulk. The family pack of self-loathing that comes through with Robert's lyrics on Pornography was a red, OK black, rag to a Goth bull. With the next level available to The Cure seemingly just recording themselves drunkenly crying over a series of cheerless, reverbed drones, it was time to change tactics – and band members – again. Perhaps seeing the fun that other Post Punkers were having in the charts, they decided to it was time to go Pop.

Much surprise was registered or feigned with the band's subsequent run of singles and albums and the Goth Nation felt a little seduced and abandoned. Subsequent singles, like the rather forward *Let's Go To Bed* and *The Walk* felt natural to me, given that the band had the likes of *Boys Don't Cry* in their oeuvre. *Primary, One Hundred Years* and *A Forest* felt like off-kilter Pop songs to me anyway. My definition of Pop has always been a broad, and often dark, church indeed. The band's last few singles had lurked around the bottom of the Top 40 but the fizzy, Electropop synths of *The Walk* took the band into the Top 20 and peaked at #12.

Previously, the Eighties' Post Punk equivalent of serious album based prog rockers, and perhaps feeling backed into a musical corner, **The Cure** were now becoming actual Pop Stars. They'd been on *Top Of The Pops,* very much as outsiders, with the likes of *Primary* and *A Forest* but it wasn't really until 1983's *The Love Cats*, by which time Robert had established the classic Cure Look of Cure Hair (a vertiginous, scrappy back-combed, collapsed beehive of conspicuously-dyed matt black), worn with smudged red lipstick and clean, white basketball boots, that the band formally arrived and Normals started singing and buying their singles. Normals – buying Cure records! Did they KNOW the title of their last album? It was absolutely unheard of, unfathomable and just plain wrong.

The Love Cats, with its perky Fifties double bass, vaudeville piano and assorted shivers and tinkles, was a tough pill to swallow for your average Goth. It sounded just a little like Madness. I recall the shocked and confused looks on some faces at school the day after

THAT completely brilliant *Top Of The Pops* performance. It was nothing short of A Betrayal. They, the fans, had gone hand-in-hand with the band deep into the forest of the subconscious, tasted the pain and been comforted that someone shared their feelings and now...Robert Smith, THE Robert Smith was prancing on *Top Of The Pops*, play-acting with his paws and singing about being a happy cat. What the actual fuck was he playing at? Hadn't the Goth Nation committed to the band, set themselves apart? Had they not bled for him? Not to make too much comment here, but the Venn Diagram of Cure fans and self harmers has a generous overlap, so that sentiment was super real for many.

Robert Smith is undoubtedly a Pop Star now but the kind of kitsch, fully formed and hermetically sealed eccentric that only England can produce. The videos for *The Love Cats*, the first from long time collaborator Tim Pope, painted a very cutesy, if still defiantly odd, picture of the band. The video for the follow up, *The Caterpillar*, with the band performing in the not ungothic Butterfly House at Kew Gardens, with bongos and SMILING, was the very definition of whimsical. This run of Pop singles continued, via otherwise quite doomy (phew) albums *The Top* and *Head On The Door* (which went Gold in the US) with the storming party-starter, *Inbetween Days* and the twitchy, claustrophobic *Close To Me*, each with brilliant videos, that swept through America, courtesy of the brand new invention that was MTV. Non stop music TV needed feeding and the brighter and more colourful the clips were, the better. MTV was aimed at the youth. Creedence and Neil Young were out and colourful American hair metal and Pop music, a very large proportion of it British, was in. It's funny to note that the gap between the clothes and appearance of **Motley Crue** and **Duran Duran** in the early Eighties was only about as wide as a tattoo at times.

MTV had launched in August 1981 as a basic cable channel in the US. By no means all American households had access to cable and MTV was highly covetable and kids would have MTV parties, round at those friends who were fortunate to have it blowing all kinds of freaky colourful new bands into their homes, all day and night. Cool Pop Music on National US TV in those days, was sporadic and very much An Event, on the rare occasions that it happened prior to MTV. Bands didn't habitually make videos, unless they were global stars, who could not be on TOTP in the UK and playing live in Tokyo at the same time; or happened to have access to film equipment. And ideas. The introduction of home Video Cameras in the early Eighties meant that this facility was suddenly cheaper and way more widely available.

The first video played on MTV was, impressively prophetically, **The Buggles'** *Video Killed The Radio Star* (followed, slightly less impressively by the inexplicably popular Pat Benetar). *"MTV's effect was immediate in areas where the new music video channel was carried. Within a couple of months, record stores in areas where MTV was available were selling music that local radio stations were not playing, such as* ***Men at Work, Bow Wow Wow*** *and* ***The Human League****".* (*Inside MTV – Google Books*).

Radio formatting in the USA was, and is, very rigid and will only play songs that fit, or can be crowbarred into, very narrow, pre-existing genres. It stifles or, more accurately, ignores new music and new types of music. The early Eighties in Britain were an absolute hotbed of creativity and the UK charts were constantly besieged with new, strange and massively varied bands. The fact that these bands either had substantial hits right away or, like Eurythmics and The Thompson Twins, underwent a rebirth to emerge, synthed up and retooled for the times, meant that labels were increasingly ready to pay for videos, seeing their massive potential as international marketing tools. MTV held the doors open for these intrepid souls. A Second British Invasion was in full flow and British bands filled the US charts and hearts like at no other time since 1965.

JAPAN · OIL ON CANVAS

JAPAN TIN DRUM

Smash
HITS
35p
USA $1.75
OCTOBER 30-NOVEMBER 12 1980
HIT LYRICS INCLUDING
FASHION
TOWERS OF LONDON
ONE MAN WOMAN
JAPAN

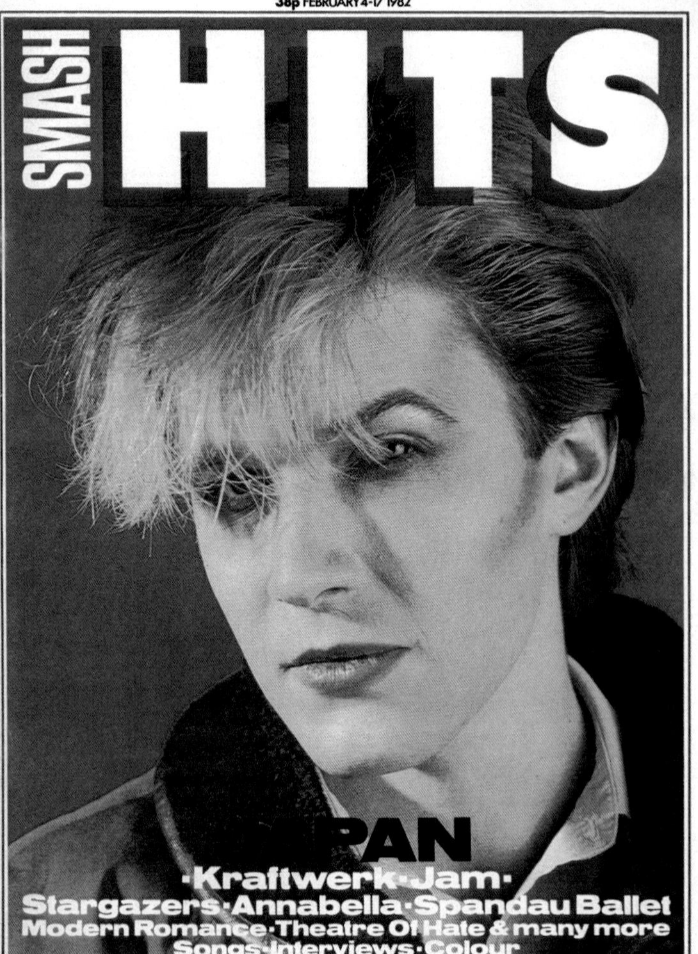
38p FEBRUARY 4-17 1982
SMASH
HITS
·Kraftwerk·Jam·
Stargazers·Annabella·Spandau Ballet
Modern Romance·Theatre Of Hate & many more
Songs·Interviews·Colour

GRACE JONES / NIGHTCLUBBING

GRACE JONES / ISLAND LIFE

40p (Eire ir 60½p inc. VAT) OCTOBER 28-NOVEMBER 10 1982

Smash

HITS

SONGS·FEATURES·COLOUR

BAUHAUS

HAYSI FANTAYZEE

WHAM!·ADAM·JAPAN

SCARLET PARTY·AC/DC

VOTE IN THE READERS' POLL

What a Pop Star looked like in 1982

Happy Christmas, 1981

Yo! Malcolm goes Hip Hop

The film that incriminates its audience
BOYDS CO. & VIRGIN FILMS LIMITED
IN ASSOCIATION WITH MATRIXBEST LIMITED
PRESENT
THE GREAT ROCK 'N' ROLL SWINDLE
X
WITH MUSIC BY
SEX PISTOLS
WRITTEN & DIRECTED BY
JULIEN TEMPLE
EXECUTIVE PRODUCERS
JEREMY THOMAS & DON BOYD
STARRING
WITH
Mary Millington
SPECIAL GUEST APPEARANCE
THE BLACK ARABS
Irene Handl
RELEASED BY VIRGIN FILMS
Sid Vicious
JOHNNY ROTTEN
Paul Cook
STEVE JONES
Malcolm McLaren
Helen of Troy

MAL
MALCOLM MCLAREN!
1059 FM

Grandmaster Clash?

08. DUCK ROCK: PUNKS IMPORT ELECTRO + HIP HOP FROM NEW YORK

Black culture freshens up British Pop music. Again.

MALCOLM MCLAREN AFRIKAA BAMBAATA THE CLASH

Malcolm McLaren is one of Pop Music's most interesting and controversial characters. He was born in the Forties, was a student fan of Situationism in the Sixties and, thusly inspired, utilised his wits and pursued controversy as an art form. And for his own amusement. Oh, and for profit – even though Scrabble players have always known you can get Cash from Chaos.

He had managed the **New York Dolls** for a time in the early Seventies before hitting paydirt with the **Sex Pistols.** McLaren had met the Dolls, the controversial and outspoken Glam monsters, in New York on a trip to promote his freaky Kings Road clothes shop, which changed its name as many times as it changed its stock, most famously being called *SEX*. Prior to Punk, *SEX* was a hip, sceney hangout, selling bondage gear and Vivienne Westwood's headline-writingly controversial clothes, and it positioned him in the eye of the Punk storm, where he oversaw the assembly of the **Sex Pistols**, including recruiting John Lydon to sing and Sid Vicious to play bass. And yes, he could play his bass serviceably enough, despite what many, principally McLaren, would have you believe instead. [Youtube: Sex Pistols Soundcheck Winterland Jan 1978, 4.40 in].

It's difficult to credit him with puppet-mastering absolutely all of the hype that enveloped and powered the Pistols. They were a ferociously talented band, after all, but he certainly encouraged their Olde English Bad Boy behaviour and knew where and when to put the media spotlight on them. However he is reported to have been mortified straight after the Swear-ageddon (Fuckgate?) of The Bill Grundy show, thinking that the band had massively overstepped the mark and invited a media blackout. It was later retrospectively dubbed as another McLaren triumph after seeing the column inches and The Mirror's front page headline the next day; *The Filth And The Fury*. *Never Mind The Bollocks* is ambling toward its 40th Anniversary now and seems to be considered much less of an essential musical text these days, which is a damn shame; whereas the totemic *"You dirty fucker"* TV footage is omnipresent clip show fodder, albeit somewhat dimmed now in its power to outrage.

Daily Mirror

BRITAIN'S BIGGEST DAILY SALE

TV's Bill Grundy in rock outrage

?!★!

Judge in 'murder' pardon shocker

THE FILTH AND THE FURY!

THE GROUP IN THE BIG TV RUMPUS

When the air turned blue..

A POP group shocked millions of viewers last night with the filthiest language heard on British television.

The Sex Pistols, leaders of the new "punk rock" cult, hurled a string of four-letter obscenities at interviewer Bill Grundy on Thames TV's family teatime programme "Today".

Uproar as viewers jam phones

By STUART GREIG, MICHAEL McCARTHY and JOHN PEACOCK

Shocker

WHO ARE THESE PUNKS? PAGE NINE

McLaren is due more of the credit and all of the blame for *The Great Rock'n'Roll Swindle* however. It was created without the input of Johnny Rotten, although it uses some of his isolated vocal tapes, seemingly edited without his permission. A second Pistols album would have been a hugely lucrative proposition. This is not that. This is an awesomely stupid attempt at such a record, wrapped up in a tawdry pantomime and seems like a couple of naughty schoolboys' drunken thrusts at upsetting as many people as possible. I am a very big fan of it.

The sprawling, and I really do mean sprawling, double album that accompanies the film has much actual treasure but is littered with all sorts of rubbish, covers and embarrassing skits; some of it extremely irritating, much of it a lot of fun. The Pistols' mythology is just not complete without *Frigging In The Rigging, Silly Thing* and Sid's unique, um, deconstructivist butchering of *My Way*, is it? A few tracks on the album and great swathes of the film are notable for putting McLaren himself in the spotlight. Allegedly a **Sex Pistols** film, it's really rather more a mainly unfunny musical sketch show about how brilliantly clever McLaren was for inventing them, in his own words with all due modesty (ie none).

It is, by any sensible estimation, a failure. Except perhaps financially. However it is such an insanely magnificent and heroic failure that you really must admire McLaren's balls, for willing it into existence. It took two years to hit the screens but an even vaguely official Sex Pistols Movie was theoretically a license to print money, regardless of quality.

Said theory was not lost on Malcolm and thus he pushed and bent it to its illogical conclusion. Its director, Julien Temple, made amends for *Swindle*'s myopic comic opera by much later making the tense and exciting documentary film, *The Filth And The Fury*, which redresses the balance of the story in favour of the band and the songs and is consequently really exciting. It's one of the best Rockumentaries ever and really must be viewed as the id to *Swindle*'s ego.

Once you've heard him gurgle and hiss, "My name….issss...Malcolm McLaren" through a gasmask, you won't forget it, nor will you be in any doubt that in front of the cameras really is where Malcolm wanted to be. That man came alive with an audience or a camera and to see him in full flow is still impressive. His background in soaraway Sensationalism meant that he simply wouldn't let facts or logic ruin his argument or stem his synaptic flow. It doesn't seem too huge a leap to assume that Malcolm himself got excited about the Punk maxim that not being "a singer" was no hindrance to being a frontman. History tries to tell us that John Lydon was not a proper singer. What bollocks! While his voice might have been rough and untutored by mid-Seventies Pop standards, that lad had a serious set of lungs on him. He wanted what he did to be grating and it *was* grating but he was a gifted and powerful singer, for sure, and an amazing frontman with a heart-stopping stare and phenomenal stage presence.

Now, if only there was a new, base and sexy artform that valued talking over singing, then that would be something that would further McLaren's own ambitions, wouldn't it?

The series of albums he made in the Eighties is pretty much unrivalled in terms of breadth and ambition, even by Bowie's standards, and he remains under-credited for them. They are not wholly successful records but they each have a couple of world-beating ideas, which have no business working at all – but do. At least for a bit. The records wear a little thin due to those ideas being stretched way beyond transparency but each album contains a magnificent conceptual triumph that reeks of the two-fingered attitude he engendered in Punk. This cannibalising of disparate, unusual or old-fashioned musical elements to create something new along with his eager acceptance of sampling culture was very prescient indeed for the early Eighties. For a long time in Britain, sampling was regarded with suspicion and branded as *cheating*, as had been the case for each of the many recent technological advancements in recording and playing music. You can only guess the levels of glee that *that* word sparked off in Malcolm's brain. Another swindle? Brilliant!

Ornate and fanciful, graceful and occasionally quite touching, his records seem born of, and underpinned by, the notion of him winning an argument that he may have had, quite probably with himself, about some ill-advised combination of styles. It's possible that, having cracked the problem, he lost interest in seeing each notion through. That would account for the generous portions of filler on the albums.

He was more than capable of arguing with himself. I once called him up about a Sigue Sigue Sputnik-esque hypernotional, musically "limited" girl group that he was managing called **Ping Pong Bitches,** featuring Bobby Gillespie's girlfriend or somesuch. We spoke for an hour or more. I say we but he did 95% of the talking, after I'd introduced myself. It was hugely entertaining and I can barely remember a word of it. I do recall that he rarely spoke of the music, focussing instead on The Point: the impact and the potential of the girls. He was basically delivering the marketing plan. The music would fall in behind it. He talked right through any attempts at pointing out some of the huge, huge inconsistencies in his patter. I gave in after a while because it was just too much fun listening to him, which was the idea, after all. It had turned from a phonecall into a promotional broadcast from McLaren FM.

However the record that people most readily recall and rightly so is his first, *Duck Rock*. Inspired by another field trip to the USA, it's safe to say that when *Buffalo Gals* dropped, no-one was ready for its punched up, scratched beats, chopped vocals, drum effects, electro synths and, um, its spoken line dancing commands. The head-spinning B-Boys in the video were also new to most. It's often mentioned that Punk and Reggae were unlikely but successful bedfellows but Punk made strong connections to early Hip Hop too. They were both super basic musically and didn't call for musical chops as much as having something to say at a volume and speed that encouraged you and the listener to work off your frustrations.

And so the Pistols' manager was behind one of the first Hip Hop hits. *Buffalo Gals* was regarded as a novelty at first in the UK. It was certainly novel. Hip Hop, if it was known at all over here, was limited to a few singles by Grandmaster Flash but mostly from when it was subsumed by a quite disparate bunch of Pop groups. **Adam Ant**'s *Ant Rap*, **Blondie**'s *Rapture* and *Wham! Rap* are not really the high points of those artists' careers but they were massive hits in the UK and showcased Hip Hop to a willing audience. It still seemed like a phase, a craze back then and at first, one that might well seem somewhat hokey in retrospect. *Buffalo Gals*' Smash Hits review, *"this* *week's act of great folly",* was pretty typical of Rap's rough reception from the thoughtful music press. It wasn't until a few years later that a Damascene conversion of the NME staff to loving **Trouble Funk** and **KRS-1,** which started the Hip Hop Wars in the hitherto white music dominated mid-Eighties music weeklies that things changed all that much in that regard.

It would still be twenty or more years before Hip Hop became the dominant sound in Western pop music. Since 2000, R'n'B has rocketed up, back to back with Hip Hop, to take over the charts with its omnipresent and hugely cross-pollinated offspring. Crowbarring a Rap verse to a Pop song used to be somewhat frowned upon. In the Nineties, there were some eyebrows that were raised so forcefully, when **Texas** (or their label) roped in **Method Man** for mumpop classic, *Say What You Want,* that they never came down. Nowadays, adding a rap verse has overtaken "getting your band's song in an advert" as the ONLY likely way to break a new artist.

Duck Rock was the product of McLaren's international travels and the production genius of Trevor Horn. It's not just music from the Bronx; there is a lot of African high life guitar in there, well ahead of Peel's **Bhundhu Boys** phase and **Paul Simon**'s (dis)*Graceland.* You don't really picture Malcolm sweating it out from dawn until dusk in the studio, and indeed it seems he did not. Horn's guest musicians on the record included Anne Dudley and JJ Jeczalik; and the Fairlight noodling about they did in McLaren's absence became the first **Art Of Noise** album, featuring another pioneering proto-Rap/Breakbeat classic, in *Beatbox.* So we have Malcolm to thank for that, albeit by default.

Like Paul Simon, McLaren attracted criticism and, in his case, court action, for appropriating African music without crediting the writers. However, after an out-of-court settlement, all of the songs remain credited to McLaren and either Horn or Dudley.

The Hip Hop, skipping and twangy Country line dancing of *Buffalo Gals* and *Double Dutch* were both big hits internationally and regardless of whether they repackaged an idea and sold it back to its owners, they stand now as important singles, baby steps in the toddlerhood of Hip Hop. And that album sleeve still looks amazing, doesn't it? The cover, by Dondi White, Nick Egan and Keith Haring, looks as exciting now as it did at the time. This, you surmise, is not going to be a boring record. Grafting things together to make mutant fun things is what you see on the sleeve and emphatically what you get on the record.

It's hard to imagine now, how exciting and alien Hip Hop was when it was first heard in the UK. The early Eighties had already been defined by huge numbers of hit singles that sounded compellingly strange, across all sorts of genres. Synthesisers, samplers and bold new ideas rapidly had rendered huge tracts of Rock and Pop music, along with traditional instruments, embarrassingly old hat almost overnight. The early singles by **Grandmaster Flash** and the **Sugarhill Gang** were super fun and catchy Pop songs. Really catchy, though. It's amazing how many people of a certain age will suddenly be able to go word for word with **Flash** when *The Message* comes on at a party. I've witnessed this happening once again in the last month. These were and are populist records, designed to be singsongs, albeit ones with, yep, a message.

It's the same message told by Martin Luther King or Huey Newton, Iceberg Slim or Marvin Gaye; about empowerment, about standing up against being ground down and not being given a chance to get back up by the American government and, let's not overlook, American society. It would be dangerously mad to say that American's endemic racism has gone away. It hasn't. It has improved, though. A little. Societal attitudes now are perhaps less casually vile than they were in 1980, or at least less openly vile. At least in the media or, OK, parts of it and certainly in the big American cities or, OK, parts of (some of) them. It's better now than it was in 1980 and the atmosphere of oppression was better in 1980 than it was in 1950. My mum was 17 when Rosa Parks refused to hand over her seat to a white passenger in 1955. It's really not so long ago. The notion of a black president in 1980 was still not even nearly worthy of serious discussion. It has been said, half-jokingly, that Hip Hop has in fact won now. Weed is legal, Dre is a billionaire (thanks to Apple buying his Beats headphones company) and there's a black president. Despite Obama breaking through that whitewashed ceiling, the statistic about a sixteen year old black boy's chances of seeing the inside of a prison being way higher than the inside of a college dormitory is still a shameful fact of American life. The daily footage of white cops, harrassing, beating and killing black teens tells a very sobering story. The Message has a way to go yet.

So *The Message,* especially in its full version, is a particularly desperate indictment of life in the big city in America. "*You'll grow in the ghetto, living second rate, And your eyes will sing a song of deep hate*". Give or take the jive phrasing, the facts of the song still apply pretty accurately today to American cities outside the sterilised centres of New York and LA.

The genius of Mr Flash and his (let's not overlook that adjective) Furious Five is that this *Message* of – deep breath – slashed public services, prostitution, drug use, repossession, unemployment, inevitable incarceration, poverty, starvation, debt, suicide and the unattainably high price of tickets to sporting events was bolted onto a bouncy tune so infernally catchy that people, who gave not a moment's thought to the plight of Flash and his peers, were singing about it all over the world. Clever.

The first rap hit single had come a couple of years previously. *Rappers Delight* by **The Sugarhill Gang** from New Jersey was based on a fourteen minute party jam of the bassline and guitar riff from **Chic**'s *Good Times*. It's a gamechanger of a record, no doubt about it, but lyrically it is pretty thin, and the delivery really not far off singing in places. Singing! It's a bit of fun, a novelty and the rapping, mainly detailing the derivation of various of the Gang's nicknames, is inoffensive showboating filler; there to keep the bassline popping for a quarter of an hour and not much more. *"Guess what America, we love you"* is not really much of a sexy Malcolm-X-y call to arms.

In the two years since *Rapper's Delight,* Hip Hop developed as something wholly new. It wasn't a commercial enterprise particularly, but more something that black kids could call their own. It didn't require money and training and could be achieved just with dedication, practise and time on your hands. Hip Hop was a public marquee that housed four aspects of street culture, the Four Elements of Hip Hop: Turntablism, Rapping, Breakdancing, and Graffiti. The crucial thing is that all of these things were new, they were made for and by black kids and, pulled together, it lifted early Hip Hop from "a few records by a few guys" to a proudly defended and readily identifiable standalone cultural movement, that grew and grew (and grew) in importance and popularity.

Now, the struggle of black teenagers in the Bronx and New Jersey and the implications of ownership that tagging a building you could never hope to afford were pretty much lost on most British teenagers but the records were dynamic and irresistible nonetheless and these early Hip Hop and Electro records have become classics. It's never the stone cold authentic records that bring in the mass audience though, is it? I can't bear to research it but I suspect Vanilla Ice and MC Hammer did more than Public Enemy and The Jungle Brothers in terms of bringing the wider/whiter audience to hip hop.

There was a great deal of sonic overlap between the strict "two turntables and a microphone" ethos that defined Hip Hop and the growth of Electro. Electro was principally club music, made with synths but tighter and harder than most Synthpop, and pared back, somewhat brutally, to be strictly about rhythm. The odd synthpop record, like **Yazoo**'s evergreen *Don't Go,* would bridge between the styles and Electro bore a strong Kraftwerk influence but this is a parallel thread of Kraftwerk-derived music, eschewing the glistening melodies that caught the ear of Bowie and OMD, and focussing instead on the bluntly functional and repetitive metallic beats that would eventually lead into Techno and House.

The first massive Electro hit is also regarded as one the early Hip Hop classics. *Planet Rock* by **Afrika Bambaata And The Soulsonic Force** (1982) was produced by the former Philly Soul DJ Arthur Baker. Its relentlessly chunky, rather than fluidly funky, beats struck a chord worldwide and it sounds just as fresh and precision-engineered now as it did then. Sampling technology was not widely available back then so painstaking recreations involving scratching and actual cutting and pasting of tape was the laborious way these records came together. The Kraftwerk influence was worn somewhat brazenly and the gentlemen from Dusseldorff quite rightly sued their way into getting their writing credits on the track.

Both Hip Hop and Electro were very much characterised as black music but whereas the Soul and Funk bands of the Seventies were slick and smooth and compromised of "players", seasoned musicians with painstakingly honed abilities to telepathically hold down a groove within a large band; it was perfectly possible to get machines to do most of the heavy lifting on these new records. This meant these new innovations were eminently stealable by any passing bands with an interest in street culture, whose ear was caught by the music and had access to decent studio technology. And white bands have always borrowed "somewhat" from black culture.

There is a tendency among gentlemen of a certain age to rhapsodise about **The Clash** – all misty memories of distant youth and cherished, fading feelings about their motivated and angry young selves. I'll tell you what though: The Clash were an absolutely magnificent band. An album a year for six years and a colossal amount of ground covered. They were vital, questioning, powerful, intelligent, inventive, adventurous, fearless and never less than completely cool – and the songs always came with huge choruses attached. They were also a band aware of rock's history and aware of the way that classic bands map out their place in it. Sore in love with iconography, iconoclasm, themselves and the possibilities of music. They weren't teenagers picking up instruments for the first time like some punk bands. They were fully fleshed out with art school angles, semiotic considerations and, more importantly, time had been served and chops learned (and unlearned) on the Pub Rock circuit. In the past, they had been the longhairs that Punk sought to replace but everyone, from the cornershop to the Cabinet, needed a bit of a haircut in 1975, so let's not be mean.

In 1982, I remember seeing *Punk's Not Dead* regularly and badly graffiti'd around the place; and indeed it wasn't. There were glossy, scruffy Punk magazines in Newsagents. Visitors to That London would send you lovely postcards of the Punks that made their home outside Buckingham Palace. Punks were still everywhere. Pale, spotty young men (there seemed to be a lack of girls, I always thought) lurking about in town, in comprehensively studded leather jackets, scribbly T-shirts and haywire, wire-wool hair. I often wondered what Punks did all day. Not pondering what line of work they were in exactly but, having gone to the trouble of achieving the look and replacing the vegetables in their diet with cider'n'glue, what did they actually do? What adventures did they have? What else, apart from hanging out near record shops and in parks, did they concern themselves with? The Walkman had yet to take hold, so listening to music all day wasn't even an option for Punks, so, having committed to looking the part and accepting the attendant drastic reduction in employment possibilities, they had a lot of time on their hands.

The Exploited had been on *Top Of The Pops* a few months previously with their not-very-classic, angry baby of a single, *Dead Cities* and had hit the Top Twenty in 1981 with their cleverly titled album, *Punks Not Dead.* So Punk was not dead. Except of course it was. I am not about to open the can of scrawny worms that is the What Was Punk Exactly argument but it was obvious that The Exploited were both bad and unoriginal and had only listened to the parts of the Punk manifesto that suited them. Presumably the bits about Punk being loud and angry and fast first and relegating music way down the list of priorities. This attitude is all well and good but it led to teetering piles of similarly shit-sounding records. I have always maintained that Punk's lasting musical message was Anything Goes. As Mick Jones said *"With London Calling we chucked out the Punk rule book. Punk was supposed to be about not having a rule book."* This attitude needs new blood and new ideas to keep moving forward, to stop becoming boring. Stagnation was what Punk was supposed to be fighting. Moving forward, however, was not high on a lot of bands' To Do list.

The Clash had been very angry young men, spraypainting slogans on walls and themselves, armed with slightly tinny guitars in 1977; then slightly less angry young men who'd allegedly sold out a touch by using a rock producer to deploy slightly sturdier guitars (and American radio play) on 1978's *Give 'Em Enough Rope;* and had finally pushed on into the open waters of constraint-free Apres Punk with 1979's *London Calling* (or had hypocritically sold out to American Roots Rock if you were/are sticking by their own 1977 *"No Elvis, Beatles or Rolling Stones"* mantra). London Calling America, might be a fair comment here. And that cover. What a calling card. A lucky last-shot-on-the-roll effort from Pennie Smith, standing side stage at the London Palladium in 1979, who'd kept her eye and camera on an annoyed looking Paul Simonon at the end of the show.

It was a grand double album, which ill-dsicipline itself was a Punk hanging offence, although this was balanced, much to the label's annoyance, by the band's insistence that it was no more expensive than a single album. Take that, The Man.

It's a glorious, towering, all-killer record that uses its wired, testosterone guitars, the telepathic rhythm section of Paul Simonon and Topper Headon, and a love of glorious space in the mix to mutate instinctively from lean and massively anthemic radio-friendly Rock into raucous Rockabilly, supple Ska, deft Soul, **Dr John** style Boogie, Reggae and much more over its four sides. At all times, though, it sounds like the same band playing the songs. Paul Simonon recalls, *"It was all about, What about that sound over there, and that music over there? What if we mix that with this, and then put it like this?"*

London Calling was hugely acclaimed and massively successful (five million sales and counting) because this magpie musical attitude was backed up with super-catchy and intuitively arranged songwriting, covering all sorts of hot potato political and social subjects. All this caused the Punk Luddites a great deal of head-scratching problems. To be fair, many of the Punks I witnessed were scratching their heads a lot anyway; although that may well have been for other, more basic and soap-related, reasons.

Such problems were compounded when the band sailed off forever from old-school Punk and into the distance in 1981. Their reggae leanings were already sketched in from covering **Junior Murvin** on the debut, and working with **Lee Perry,** but nonetheless 1981's straight up reggae classic *Bankrobber* was still a little surprisingly free of Punk Rock, and again, CBS were against releasing it. It was another smash hit.

Along with the reggae, came toasting – basically slightly stoned freestyle rapping over Dub Reggae, originating from Jamaica – and working with Jamaican singer, producer and dub adventurer, Mikey Dread. After *London Calling*'s profit-slicing pricing, the band were talked out of releasing a single every month in 1981 by the suits at Sony. Pause a moment to imagine what would have happened if they had gone ahead and done that? A band at the peak of their powers. Damn you, unnamed suits; it would have been the stuff of legend and you could/would have compiled them for another album.

Instead the band and **Mikey Dread,** under the watchful of eye of Bill Price as engineer and mixer (and maybe just a little bit, producer), had their revenge when they came up with *Sandinista.* This was the first Clash album I bought and I still love it to pieces. All thirty six songs over six sides. The 2013 remastering seems to add a huge amount of clarity and depth to the mix and I am recommending it enormously. It has revealed so much of the detail on the recordings that was previously hidden in shadow. The band insisted it cost no more than a double album too. Bargain! Take that again, The Man.

Having covered America with *London Calling*, they cast their nets yet wider and included a lot of Caribbean music, Calypso, as well as Gospel, Skiffle, military Marching Music and, yes, Hip Hop. The most frequent criticism of Sandinista (and this really is a hugely criticised album) is that it is "all over the place". It is. There you go. Enjoy your win, squares. It was, not uncoincidentally, recorded all over the place; from London and Manchester to New York and Jamaica. The band were so confident and flexible and, let's sum this up in a single, apposite word – talented – that they were capable of subsuming all of the influences of these environments and whatever threads of music's past that was inspiring them into songs that all sounded like The Clash. It turned out that sounding like The Clash could happen in all sorts of new and hitherto unimaginably wonderful places.

Can you imagine how they'd have fared if they stuck at Punk's air-clearing Year Zero, and continued on forever with a two chord racket? Luckily you don't have to: **The Exploited** have contributed the no-doubt-wonderful *Fuck The System* in the Twenty First Century. You might argue that **The Ramones** failed to develop beyond square one but you'd be wrong because they were perfect to begin with and made an artful merit out of maintaining the status quo. See also Status Quo. Actually, don't.

Kicking off *Sandinista* is The *Magnificent Seven*, which is basically a Rap. Even if it's a sort of Rap song that hadn't been heard of before (or since) and features a good deal more than two-turntables-and-a-microphone. The album starts with an alarm call, *"Ring, ring, seven a.m."*, rolling drums and a particularly funky Simonon bassline, before Joe Strummer offers a stream of consciousness lyric, which shows he'd been listening closely to **Grandmaster Flash**, who had been invited to open for The Clash at some of their fifteen night run at Bonds Casino on Times Square in 1981. The Punk fans didn't exactly warm to him but Strummer was obviously a fan. The Magnificent Seven includes among its many non-sequiturs, *"Who's...Flash?"* and a late gambol into some suspiciously Nile Rodgers-esque guitar at the end in acknowledgement to those early Hip Hop records.

The even more Hip Hop leaning 12" remix of *Seven, The Magnificent Dance* was created by Pepe Unidos aka Simonon, Strummer and manager, Bernie Rhodes. A white label was serviced to and adopted by the same New York radio stations that the band had heard playing Grandmaster Flash and the like a year before. That must have been very satisfying, knowing that the DJs had no idea of The Clash's Punk roots.

During the bands' touring in support of their next album, *Combat Rock* in 1982, they hired New York Hip Hop graffiti artist **Futura 2000** (who went on to design Unkle's sleeves) to do live graffiti behind the band onstage. He also worked on the sleeve for *Combat Rock* and designed the sleeve for *This Is Radio Clash*, another Hip Hop influenced slice of brilliance from the band that appeared just between *Sandinista* and *Combat Rock*. Futura 2000 also contributed a rap on *Overpowered By Funk* on *Combat Rock*. Long before *Combat Rock* appeared, the graffiti styled logos had been successfully integrated into The Clash iconography, and they had established a line of credit with some of the key players in New York Hip Hop. It all followed a natural curve from the primitive "actual vandal" sloganeering spray painting of 1977 too. Clever.

The first single from *Combat Rock* was *Know Your Rights*, a melody-free spoken word, or maybe ranted word, manifesto read aloud over clipped, one-note, scorched guitars. Joe Strummer was playing an Orwellian Government character appraising the people of their perceived but unenforceable rights. "*This is a Public Service Announcement…with guitars*" are words that kick off the single and the album. The single failed to reach the Top 40. The two following singles, *Rock The Casbah* and *Should I Stay Or Should I Go* are undisputed classics now, familiar to all but only hit #30 and #17 on release and were the first times that a **Clash** single had seen the inside of the Top Thirty since *Bankrobber* in the summer of 1980. Interesting to note that *Should I Stay* managed a considerably more respectable #1 position when re-released as the soundtrack to an advert in 1991.

It's fair to say that the majority of the Clash's original British fanbase got seasick and bailed on their voyage away from loud Punky guitars and rock music in general. *London Calling* was a platinum (300K) record in the UK but they only managed silver (60K) discs after that. It was a very different story in America where the majority of the record buying public got to know the band via their appearance alongside other funk-influenced British imports like **Duran Duran** in the Club Charts, all broadly considered New Wave, which was a way broader and less judgemental church in the US than it was in the UK. *Rock The Casbah* was an American Top Ten hit right off and *Should I Stay* broke the Top Twenty too. *London Calling* and *Sandinista* had already been Top Thirty albums in the US and *Combat Rock* broke into the

Top Ten. The band toured the album in America with the not-all-that-Hip-Hop **The Who**, whom had not only failed to live up to their youthful promise vis a vis death and aging but also had become somewhat drum solo-y by this point, all of which caused any punks, who had not previously done so, to go grey and start waxing apoplectic at the band's decisions. Cunningly, the footage from their support slots at American stadiums was cut together to make a video for *Should I Stay...* that portrayed The Clash as a stadium band. I certainly believed it.

Unpopular though the move was, I think The Clash deserve more credit for their pioneering work in borrowing from, drawing attention to, and enhancing, in their own small way, the Hip Hop scene in New York. **The Clash** and **The Pistols'** manager as Rap Pioneers? Why not, it's a good story. Malcolm would be proud.

09. NEW GOLD DREAM: THE BIG MUSIC, SHIMMERING + MODERN

Rejecting Rock'n'Roll, the new European Music tilts at stadiums

SIMPLE MINDS THE BUNNYMEN PETER GABRIEL KATE BUSH

The European canon is here. Rock'n'roll ain't noise pollution. Two theories. Both are correct but, in 1980, one of them was sounding somewhat old-fashioned and the other was a statement of intent that was becoming excitingly real very rapidly. By the time they had released *that* song, on 1980's computer perfect *Back In Black*, which is (by now, conclusively proven to be) the best Rock album ever made, even AC/DC had succumbed to the power of the forensic accuracy achievable with modern production techniques. Here in Europe, people were rebuilding rock music from the floor up and it no longer sounded like An American Product. It was not Rock'n'Roll. It wasn't rooted in bruising Blues riffs; instead it was more feminine and fluid but no less powerful or relentless. No longer reliant on thrusting and blunt force, this was muscular and lithe, driving and beautiful. It was not following in Punk's ragged footsteps. It didn't set out to make you mosh or slam into your fellow concert attendee, venting your feelings through your elbows but was instead a new kind of thrill that got the blood moving just the same. It sounded new, lusciously psychedelic and scalpel clean. Ambition in motion, station to station.

Cock-rocking guitars were out, Kraftwerk keyboard drones and washes were in, set with sundry attributes from whichever post-1975 Bowie album was floating your boat at the time, from the sublimely succinct pop of *Speed Of Life* to the exotic travelogues of Lodger to the eerie and experimental hauntings of the second side of Heroes. Rock history and conventional chords were a thing of the past. Originality and creativity were now de rigeur in a race to reinvent and reinvent until your band became something exciting and graceful and new. And huge.

There's no escaping the fact that the infant **Simple Minds** lacked grace. They were the awkward kid in the class. The ones whose clothes didn't seem to quite hang on them properly. They were not a popular band at first. Not at all. Not being popular or having to tour the world to adoring fans meant they had a lot of time to make albums. They released two in 1979 and sneaked a #62 "hit" with *Life In A Day*, which is alas not a brilliant song. They sounded like something less than the jumble of their influences and were trying a Punk-via-Magazine style feisty rock noise. Few people ever really reminisce all that fondly about those first two records.

They were jarring albums, reacting to their surroundings just like punk had taught them to. Glasgow in the Seventies and Eighties was not such a lovely place; divided firmly into two warring "My Jesus beats your Jesus" factions and full of the drugs and misdirected anger that habitually sucked into the vacuums created by Thatcher's evisceration of the northern cities' futures and her obliteration of the dignity of labour. Endless tenement blocks with dripping tap kitchens, studded with peeling paint pubs and cold, broken playgrounds and promises is going to make for angry music.

Jim Kerr says in a recent (MOJO Jan 15) interview "when David Bowie and Roxy Music came to town, they were from another planet, there was no source of reference. I was looking to escape Glasgow, hungry for something more. It enabled me to invent my own world to live in."

A few months later, their third album, *Empires And Dance* (1980) marks a massive change, and you can see the influence of the times, as set by **Joy Division, Bowie** and **Kraftwerk**, pushing synths and soundscapes to the front, at the expense of the jarring Rock tropes. It opens with the smoothly pounding and sweetly industrial sounding disco of the colossal *I Travel*, before opening out into the clean vistas and lazy backwards vocals of *Today I Died Again*, and then the synthetic handclaps and strutting funk of nearly-but-not-quite hit single, *Celebrate*, which probably skews the wrong side of metronomic and nudges into plodding by its close. Letting go of Rock saw them, along with **Ultravox** and others, move up a level, artistically and in popularity.

Simple Minds' first two album sleeves were proggy and minimal, respectively. Quite smart-looking each, they were more successful than the records inside. Malcolm Garrett's sleeve for *Empires And Dance* combines these two traits and follows similar ideas, graphically, to those Peter Saville did, which is not entirely surprising because they studied at Manchester Polytechnic together. **Ultravox**'s *Vienna* and the first **Duran Duran** album would soon make this style massively popular and it soon became somewhat ubiquitous and emblematic of the New Pop. It was quite easy to rip off. All that was needed to simulate this new paradigm was a plain white background, a discreet logo and a few artfully placed parallel bars of colour graphics intruding slightly onto a small photo, lurking asymmetrically in one of the corners. Ideally that would be a monochrome or blurry shot of the traffic at night or a piece of industrial machinery lit by neon lights (or, yes, a band photo if you must, **Duran Duran)**. There was a gradual injection of commerciality/glamour and pop into the chilly template set by Peter Saville's **Joy Division** and **OMD** masterpieces.

This new understated, geometric grammar of glamour was important for bands like OMD, Simple Minds and Ultravox. They were not blessed with six packs and cheekbone razors. I am not sure anyone had six packs then, except on a Friday night. These bands were essentially nerds in big shirts. Making music with synths in those days was not the press-D-for-Dubstep miracle it is now. Oscilloscopes were often used, technical prowess was essential and only earned by putting in the legwork with the bricklike instruction manuals and then losing weeks experimenting; trying, failing and trying again. Such scruffy bookworms were pleased when, in 1981, Utilitarian Chic became very cool and bands started resembling facsimiles of businessmen, mechanics, pilots, spies or other looks all seemingly drawn from Career Advisers' pamphlets. That, and Kraftwerk's uber-functional *Mensch Maschine*, of course. Boiler suits all round.

Sons and Fascination and *Sister Feelings Call* were released as a double album in 1981, presumably in an effort to get on top of the band's prolific output. They brought **Simple Minds** to within a floppy disc's width of the Top 40 with a series of brilliant singles in *The American* (#54 May 1981), *Love Song* (#47 August 1981) and *Sweat In Bullet* (#52 November 1981). These singles displayed a much lighter touch, with no hint of the snotty ruckus that was Simple Minds' early incarnation as Punk rabble, **Johnny And the Self Abusers** left at all and only trace elements of their own first few albums. The new aesthetic was way more indebted to **Neu** and **Georgio Moroder** than it was to **Magazine** and **Wire,** and all three singles still throb and shimmer very brightly to this day.

Tellingly, all three of these singles came with extended 12" versions. This was very much a statement of intent, rather than a standard marketing ploy in 1981. American club culture was coming to Scotland. Kinda. This was a cold, Glasgow-y take on it, rather than the carefree, weekend-starts-here beano, that the city would later become associated with. The band obviously had one eye on the dancefloor but these are Post Punk Proggy Funk jams rather than the clean sun-drenched lines of a **Donna Summer** single. Not that the Moroder influence is remotely hidden on the dikka-dikka-dikka intro to *Love Song*, although Giorgio's next thought probably wouldn't have been some snaking guitar excoriation. The extended versions of these singles have much merit and aren't the three-extra-minutes-of-drums will-this-do perfunctory attempts at lengthening songs that blighted the mid-Eighties and only served to get fans feeling ripped off at buying a second format. It's the sound of a band stretching out (literally), experimenting and absorbing new ideas, rather than crudely Xeroxing them.

However, there's no disguising that the album versions of the songs are the ones that are the definitive arrangements because the real thing Simple Minds were trying out with this inspired sequence of singles is Pop Music. You'd have needed extra strong ESP powers to see that the *Life In A Day era* **Simple Minds** were going to be a fluid, perky and slightly psychedelic Dance Pop group within two years. The evolution was successful because it was gradual and only succeeds because the starting point was so unlikely. The results really shine because you can still sense the Glasgow in these singles and the band's bones, their jagged, hesitant edges are still detectable, submerged just below the polished surfaces, giving the songs a unique rippled and trippy texture.

More importantly, these awkward nearly New Wave geeks were looking like they might finally be picked for the team. Five albums in a little over two years saw them grow in confidence and ambition and, atypically, originality. It was more public than most bands' backroom development but it's fair to say that no-one outside Virgin was taking them that seriously until *Sons/Sisters* reached #11 in September 1981. *Sons/Sisters* showed they'd left Rock and Punk music standing. Instead there were lengthy travelogues, hugely in debt to the European Avant Garde instrumental music of the Seventies, all peppered with bursts of Jim Kerr's increasingly streamlined, fluid and aptly stylised lyrics about travel and foreign cities with sundry dream images of stars and wonder.

It's no wonder that bands dreamed and sang of energy, escape and elsewhere. Getting away from the decaying town or city you were stuck in was high on a great many kids' To Do lists. Anywhere but here, anywhere but here. Travelling abroad was an unknown pleasure to most, with the exception of the little England-On-Sea of the Costa Brava or the end-of-the-ferry joys found in the magical booze hangars of Calais and the neon streets of Amsterdam. The exoticism, history and sophistication of Vienna or Berlin were magnified and filtered through old glamorous black and white films and the muted colours of the foreboding, new glass and concrete post-war architecture glimpsed on the News.

Kerr's dreamy, keening lyrics sounded like they were improvised on top of instrumentals, rather than set to music by the band, and serve to propel the music along as much as anything. The propulsion was palpable in **Simple Minds**. They believed they were going places and they were soundtracking that transition (*"ambition in motion" – Sweat In Bullet,* 1981). The band sounded looser now; freer and very much the better for it. Compared to a lot of their peers, who sounded solidly earthbound and hell-bent on making a racket to reflect Britain's grim reality, Simple Minds were liquefying and becoming something very new, very fast. Escape velocity had been achieved.

As a thirteen year old fan of these singles, I expected Simple Minds to do the decent thing and go fully Synthpop next. Everyone else was. Surely they had a *Vienna* in them? Or a Quiet Life? Just a few months after *Sweat In Bullet* bottomed out of the charts at the end of 1981, *Promised You A Miracle* was released. Produced by Peter Walsh, who helmed **Heaven 17'**s forward looking *Penthouse & Pavement*, it seems likely that having the another hot Synthpop band was Virgin's plan. What I can see now is that the band had already made their adjustments; absorbed synths, taken what they needed from disco and fully tasted that freedom from foursquare guitars but they were not going to be an airbrushed New Pop group.

Contrary to my expectation, *Promised You A Miracle*, the first single from *New Gold Dream* had way more in common with **Associates** than anything or anyone else; the chimes at the start of *Promised* are very similar to those on *Party Fears Two*. The title speaks volumes too, doesn't it? After a few albums of travelling, swiftly but perhaps mapless, they had arrived. It was definitely all new noises and obviously a very catchy song but it was the work of neither hairy rock band nor shiny synthpoppers, and existed purely on its own skewed Pop terms. This was a new European music, gliding serenely in between Rock music and Pop, with hands outstretched to both. Neither throwaway nor, as yet, serious and pompous.

The arrangement sounded like actual humans were playing it, more or less, with duelling mille-feuille synths and intricate Pat-Metheny-style guitars, flowing and interchangeable, clean and vibrant, ebbing and flowing over a rhythm section playing a sort of intense Proggy, fretless Funk. Their intentions in that area were signposted by having **Herbie Hancock**'s Fusion doodlings on the album.

And if that sounds horrible, and I am aware that it does a bit, it was actually a beautiful thing; technicoloured and genuinely exciting. It's quite a hard thing to dance to, this Progsynthfunk, but dance we did. I look back fondly to some of the things my friends and I used to throw shapes to: from the snail's paced dirges escaping from **Sisters Of Mercy**'s Reptile House to reels around **The Smiths'** fountains. Ah, the freedom to dance IN PUBLIC to anything that grabbed your mind; DJs freed from BPMs, dancers free from shame. I do miss that. A bit.

The strutting and sexy, almost (*almost;* go with me on this) **Prince**-like *Glittering Prize* that preceded the album in August was another Top Twenty single. Jim is not quite likening his girl to a Red Corvette here but rather ascribing her some higher cypher, glowing like anthropomorphic jewels. And why on Earth not, eh? Girls do shine; I have seen them do it.

Alas, Jim Kerr was not pin-up material, no matter how sexy and feline the music, no matter how tight the trouser or billowy the blouse; so they didn't make the cover of Smash Hits in 1982. They had to wait another year for that accolade and, my word, it was a shocking image; all light shining from his arse, hands folded like doves and properly nasty white pointed shoes. 1983 had that effect on a lot of people and few made it through unscathed. Ridicule may not have been something to be scared of but it was still going to happen, so you'd best be prepared.

What still impresses about *New Gold Dream* is the band's confidence to leave space all over the record, despite access to unimagined vaults of newly synthesised noises. The songs have a great many parts and instruments but never ever feels cluttered. Unusually for a frontman and hard to imagine, given his later "messiah years", Jim Kerr is happy to take a backseat on many of the songs and the instrumentation is all about sailing out on that locked groove than building to any great crescendos. There are guitars a plenty but there is precisely no Rock'n'Roll on the album and its Jazz curlicues surprised everyone. Listening to Herbie Hancock wiggling unhurriedly away on *Hunter And The Hunted* – it is definitely not the sound of a New Wave band.

By 1982, Simple Minds were sounding European. If perhaps you'd pondered what sounding European was a few years previously, it would have been less easy to define. The success and fallout of Kraftwerk, Bowie and Moroder had drawn a number of different strands together and the European canon was now becoming tangible if not strictly defined. Like Bowie, its essence was found neither in standing still, nor in looking back. It was instead defined by its own questing motion and lack of reliance on roots. A rejection of Rock'n'Roll, of white American music culture and, in its place, a confidence to experiment and stand out. Being a Bowie fan, Jim Kerr knew that *"Everything is possible..."* and **Simple Minds** had decided to throw out the rulebook, ignore expectations and make something big. *New Gold Dream* is a massive album. Not in terms of length (nine songs, forty six minutes) but in ambition and execution. It wasn't meant to shake the walls of the Top Rank clubs of the nation nor was it wholly Pop or kitted out for the dancefloor. It just demanded its own space. The bigger, the better to unfurl; unhurried and graceful, suspended and gleaming.

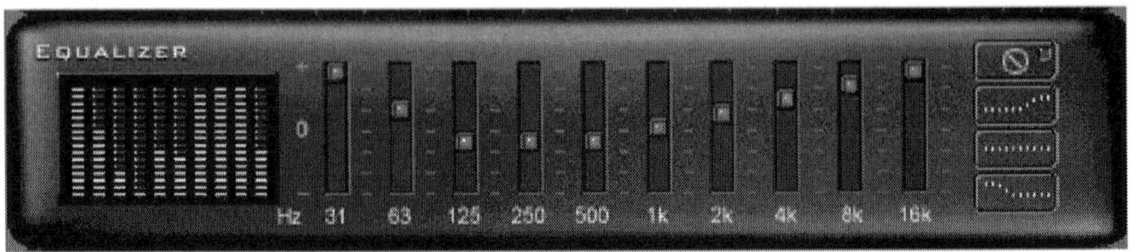

It was made for expensive hi-fis and the new domestic miracles that were Graphic Equalisers. I did not have such luxury toys at the time and would take my copy of *New Gold Dream* to my friend's house. My Word – that seems like a strange notion now, doesn't it, readers? We'd have to make notes of the positions at which the miniature faders were set by his dad, so we could restore the "room-perfect" combination, afterwards. I miss those little faders quite a bit these days.

Hi-fi stereos have little in the way of Tone control these days and if you really want to hear a bit more bassline or lady backing vocals, or indeed cowbell, then you can't. Computer knows best. I don't understand this at all. It seems like a backwards step, like cancelling Concorde or the Space Shuttle (Yes, an error exactly of that magnitude). I have always hated that "Dolby On", creamy smooth sound. Still do. I like sparkling, brilliant things and I like things that cross the line into the red a little. Smooth? Really, no thanks. I prefer just a little crunch. Sometimes colossal, booming dub records with heightened harmonica. Or panned stereo **Beatles** records without George. Maybe I just liked the faders and the producer fantasises they engendered or maybe different kinds of music require different enhancements. Whatever it is; I miss them and I want them back.

So *New Gold Dream* was lavishly and expensively Produced, with a capital P, by Peter Walsh. Its nine sensual songs sounded relaxed, healthy, luxurious and slightly extravagant. There's nothing small, seedy or homemade about it. It doesn't sound like five pale wee guys from Glasgow at all, having more in common with another band who cast a long shadow over the Eighties, **Roxy Music.** Roxy were very much responsible for many of the tics and clichés of actual Eighties (as opposed to early Eighties) bands. That roomy, luxurious production, wafty, glacial synths, almost-but-not-quite funky basslines, clipped thin guitars and that style of crooning that is not so bothered about consonants. Traits that all crept into this record and subsequently infected everyone from **Duran Duran** to **The Police.**

So until CDs were to arrive, graphic equalisers meant many hours were spent excavating and enhancing details and making *New Gold Dream* or *Architecture and Morality* sound bigger, lusher and subtlely different. It was geeky but it was fun and oddly interactive too. *New Gold Dream* really lived up to its name on a fancy stereo. Incandescent, graceful and smart; it moved to the beat of its own very slightly tinny 80s drum.

It's not possible to overlook or overstate this fact: the drum sound is the Achilles' Heel of so many albums of this period, most heinously on the otherwise briskly acoustic and finger snap PERFECT *High Land hard Rain* from **Aztec Camera,** whose panned, reverbed and whatever-they-did-to-them drums sound as bad as disco Linn drums. The single infinitesimal flaw with the miracle of those flat octagonal drumpads and their facsimiles, is that they sounded nothing like drums. At all. They were different and novel and very future and, before you could raise a hindsight-heavy objection, they were everywhere, blotting copybooks and catalogues with their myriad limp impressions and "pooh-p-p-poo-pooh" disco snare sounds. Miking up drums in a studio is tiresome and painfully slow, so I can see the attraction and the novelty of electronic drums but, boy, that escalated quickly. I mean, that really got out of hand fast.

The producer has been the key player of many, even most, fine albums but production is a never-ending process of refinement and, if unchecked by time or budget, it will just keep on going; demanding the editing, polishing and erasing of every flaw and smoothing of every ruffle, until there is little trace remaining of the excitement and intensity of a living band, caught up in its performance.

You can also go too far the other way, even more easily. There are many scrappy, enthusiastic and life-affirming lo-fi records, from **Howling Wolf** to **Ty Segall**, but lo-fi ought to be an unfortunate product of enthusiasm, circumstance and budget, rather than something you purposefully set out to achieve. "Making a lo-fi record" is like aiming to miss. Getting the balance with production is the trick, isn't it? Too little and the bands weaknesses are exposed, too much and the band disappears entirely.

New Gold Dream's layered production flooded my imagination with new ideas and colours, filled every corner of the room and it pushed

Simple Minds further out, weightless and free. There are few feelings like a favourite band's new record pushing past their assumed limitations; unfurling into the next, previously unimaginable and undiscovered level. It's that sense of pushing that is exciting. What would Bowie do? That was the standard question. Clearly he would step out of the comfort zone, make demands of himself and try new things. Oh, and he would succeed each time. The flawless track record. Ambition in motion. *New Gold Dream* nailed all this perfectly and so, to follow it up, the band took a quantum leap to sound bigger, to fill bigger and bigger rooms.

Just as with pursuing lo-fi ambitions, there is a problem with this quest for bigness and luxurious production per se and **Simple Minds** would, in time, to discover this to their cost (and by cost, I do mean in ineffable kudos – their subsequent records aimed for mass acceptance and reaped massive profit). They were not the only ones either. A previously earthbound band expanding into **The Big Music** was a remarkable thing because it represented change and ambition, and it so often saw the music take flight, but starting at that point – starting at big – is a very different thing altogether. This is the problem known as "The U2 Dilemma". With a massively successful album behind them, bands tend to move up to more expensive producers, take longer sojourns in the studio, with myriad distractions (cocaine, international jetset commitments) and emptier notepads of songs.

The phrase, The Big Music came into usage after a rather brilliant, elegiac single by **The Waterboys** in 1984 about having had your ears opened by some sort of divine inspiration and/or "jazz manna from sweet chariots" (-me neither). The sleeve pictures the band playing their instruments on a hillside. It's supposed to signify a pairing of BIG, organic things, a natural sound and a musical connection with Mother Earth. However the notion of a damp drumkit set up on a hillside is, in hindsight, quite a worryingly bullshit one and should have set off alarm bells.

The term was then retrospectively and pretty fairly applied to bands like **Echo & The Bunnymen, The Chameleons, Simple Minds** and **U2.** Indeed Daniel Lanois was quoted on Pitchfork, as saying that "*U2 had been listening to New Gold Dream by Simple Minds as a point of reference*" while making *The Unforgettable Fire*. Simple Minds had become one of those big shirted, billowy, bigness-for-its-own-sake chiming guitar bands by 1985 and would aim for bigger yet, as the Eighties rolled along but in 1982, they were still pursuing Bowie and Kraftwerk's retrofuturistic European canon. It's strange that U2 first channelled Simple Minds *on The Unforgettable Fire*, their first multi-million seller and subsequently Simple Minds seemed to import more and more U2 as time went by, even tackling The Troubles, as they are rather cutely remembered by the media.

These Big Music bands were all from the British Isles, literate, serious and all used atmosphere, keyboards, drones and arpeggiated guitar shimmers to build a stadium sized hum, rather than just cranking up Rock guitars to the front of the mix, as was traditional, and hollering at the audience to "Go crayzeeee". Not that any of them were playing stadiums. Yet.

So, a small confession: I am not going to write much about U2. I am sure you are aware of their catalogue if you care to be. 1982 was the year that made them. They'd been trying to nail that big, lush sound and finally got it on *New Year's Day*, which is a great wee tune with a pleasingly plangent piano motif. Its parent album, *War* and the astonishingly popular live mini-album that came hot on its heels, *Live: Under A Blood Red Sky*, sealed the band's reputation and sent them up to the big leagues. For now though, they were not really as big as **Echo & The Bunnymen** or **The Teardrop Explodes**.]

The Teardrop Explodes were fronted by Julian Cope, who emerged from the same big talking, weed smoking, cosmic Scouse mafia as Pete Wylie and Ian McCulloch. All three were in the barely-real but super-legendary band, **The Crucial Three** and all three sported hefty egos that spun them out in slightly different directions. **The Teardrop Explodes,** like **The Bunnymen** hooked up with Dave Balfe's Zoo records. Balfe ended up joining the band after their first single, *Sleeping Gas*, in the summer of 1979. The band scored an Indie Chart hit with their third single for Zoo, the dreamy'n'swirly *Treason*.

Cope described their music as Bubblegum Trance but those early singles mix the traditional wonky Scouse Sixties guitar influences with a lighter West Coast Beat Group froth. While recording their debut album, *Kilimanjaro*, Cope was introduced to weed and acid and the outlook for the band changed. The infighting, that had already caused some aggressive line-up changes, intensified and members came and went quite rapidly. Cope wrote a couple of books about his time with the band (*Head On* and *Repossessed*) and if you were ever curious what goes on in the head of a lead singer and what tensions drive bands forward and apart or just how mad Cope and Balfe were, then I can strongly recommend them both.

The Teardrop Explodes were really fucking cool, in an NME way, but having their cake and eating it as Smash Hits pinups too. The debut album was a minor commercial success but brought great critical acclaim. Hot on its heels was the brass-topped and copper-bottomed hit single, *Reward*, their best known song and a Top Ten Hit that has propped up Alt-Eighties compilation albums ever since. *Kilimanjaro* was another one of those albums that doesn't contain the hit you bought it for. Sigh. (It does now, by the way). Nonetheless it continued to sell and expectation for the follow up, *Wilder,* was high. Not as high as Julian, though, a man who once claimed that "he felt like he was a city centre" while tripping and that his veins were like the streets and his blood was the traffic. I must say this shocked me a bit at the time. Having been up that flagpole now a few times now, I can only empathise. Acid is really the only drug that hits you with the sort of strange effects that your parents, visiting policemen and really cool Sixties films alerted you to.

I love *Wilder* with a passion and played it TO DEATH on its release. I can still go word for word when it's on, as it is now. Alas, I am no nearer having much of a clue as to what most of it is about. It is, as they say, a bit weird. The band sound completely different on this album, with the exception of *Pure Joy*, which is surely a hangover from the first record. Keyboards, rhythms and textures dominate most of the songs, relegating or replacing the guitars. Arrangements are looser and it feels fluid and clammy, meditative and inviting. And baffling. Cope is crooning his heart out and smearing himself out across all the songs and he takes all the writing credits. On the one hand, it IS better produced than *Kilimanjaro*, but the songs can't resist choosing the path less travelled, or never travelled. *Colours Fly Away* sounds like an attempt to repeat *Reward's* rewards but is scuppered by slightly odd time signatures and a downbeat chorus. *Seven Views Of Jerusalem*'s rhythm sounds sort of Arabic, or possibly just backwards...and impenetrable, with a fretless bass and chanted choral falsetto chorus. *And The Fighting Takes Over* features the most beautiful distant horn section, barely audible but quite magical. I think the lyrics were Cope just downloading his internal monologue unchecked. I am not sure they are cut-up, as was the vogue. Instead they are plain old disorganised and slightly deranged. There are hints of confessions and lots of the songs have bits written in the first person but the whole thing is intentionally elusive.

I am not sure why the brassy *Passionate Friend* was not a big hit though. It peaked at #25 but barely touched the sides when compared to *Reward*. I still can't see why anyone who liked any of their previous singles wouldn't buy it. I did. It does cram a lot into its grooves, a sitar solo here, a *"Hunnunannoo"* there but those Ba-Ba-ba-ba-bas were surely irresistible?

The two most enduring tracks from Wilder are the ones most unlike previous Teardrops songs. *Tiny Children* was supported by radio and was almost a hit (#41), despite being a drumless and chorus free dreamscape. Similarly, if not more strangely so, was *The Great Dominions*, a legendary track despite not being a single. Again, I have no clue what it is about but I can confirm the worry that, *"I don't want to get my laces burned"* can be very real as a similar thing happened to me on the wrong side of the mirror once. They seemed on the verge of crossing over to being an Actually Big Band but of course they split up during the recording of their third album. Cope continues on his singular voyage to this day, releasing album after album of cosmic Head Music of one form or another, from Ambient Drones to Proto-Metal.

As a post script to this bit, I bumped into David Balfe at a party in January 2014. I told him about this book and my misgivings about calling it *New Gold Dream*, which suited the music but came pre-tarnished by Simple Minds' later albums. He sympathised and suggested *Dare* instead. Obvious, really. I am not sure why I didn't think of it myself but, y'know, I didn't. So, Cheers Balfey.

The Teardrop Explodes' great and often quite bitter rivalry with The Bunnymen drove each band on to try and outdo each other. Both bands railed against Rock'n'Roll's clichés, its dumbness and the lumpen weight of its history, but I felt that **Echo & The Bunnymen** still wanted to make the efforts needed to lift audiences up, while still wearing their art prominently on their sleeves, while the Cope took his band on an uncertain and inward journey.

The Bunnymen were fronted by the uncommonly beautiful Gob-on-legs that is Ian "Mac" McCulloch. Spouting snatches of Blake, Bowie and Baudelaire and secretly channelling Jim Morrison and Sinatra from behind a perma-tumbling fringe and leather trousers, Mac was the epitome of Eighties Northern cool. He always had a savage word for other bands and anyone he regarded as lesser mortals than he (ie everyone but Bowie and Iggy) and gave truly excellent copy. His acid wit and cherubic lips guaranteed that girls and boys paid equal attention and it was always worth reading his scabrous and hilarious interviews. Still is.

The Bunnymen were a formidable unit, A Proper Band. Greater than the sum of their parts, thriving on chaos, and, as is often the case, subject to fallings out, drug paranoia, and massive arguments. Unified they were unstoppable, divided they were merely mortal, as made clear by some of the later or solo records. Will Sergeant was Mac's songwriting foil on guitar and Les Pattison provided the punchy bass runs that drove these huge songs along. As per the fashion then, they started with a drum machine before taking Pete de Freitas as drummer before their debut album, 1980's *Crocodiles*, was released. It was produced by Dave Balfe and future Bunnymanager-KLF-writer-guru-crackpot-iconoclast, Bill Drummond, and was a Top Twenty hit for the new label formed around the Bunnymen, the legendary Korova records. Everything about the Bunnymen was legendary, even if, especially if, they did say so themselves. *Crocodiles* is a sparkling debut album that channels the Pop peaks of **Television, Bowie, The Doors** and **Iggy Pop** into new shapes and tops them with Mac's rich baritone voice, pouring lithe, visceral poetry into the mix. You could never be sure what the Mac's songs were about. I have always hoped they were about something rather than just cutting up interesting phrases as per Bowie/Burroughs.

I dread to think what their breakthrough Top Twenty hit, *The Cutter,* is about. Its horrorshow imagery leads straight into *"Spare us the cutter, couldn't cut the mustard"* and thence to *"will I still recoil, when the skin is lost?"* Could be circumcision fears (!), could be pressure to edit songs, could be about being held back by someone, could just be writing about the Cut Up technique. It could, of course, be about nothing. Who can say? I am drawn to things I don't fully understand though and I was so very drawn to the Bunnymen. There was artistry afoot here, points subtlely out of reach, allusions to exciting things; dark romance, myth and sex. They were portentous, pretentious and arrogant and clearly thought that the simple stuff was beneath them. It wasn't a puzzle to unravel like one of Bowie's songs; these songs were wrapped up tight, their dark hearts obscured. Their songs were the seeds of dreams, dark screens to project onto. Like staring into the night, seeing shapes in the dark – one could sense that there were things in there but quite what was real and what was imagined was unclear.

The other thing that registered immediately about the Bunnymen was that Mac sang. Really sang. He might spend his spare time scowling, smoking and chatting up your girlfriend but once he got on stage, the arrogance/shyness would fall back as his instinct took over and his voice completed the band's spirit animal. The Bunnymen were much greater than the sum of their parts and so were never quite the same after Pete's death in 1989. A rare natural catalyst completed the band's magic and released the feral feelings pent up in these songs to prowl the room. Too many bands simpered or muttered into the mike but these tunes were delivered with full conviction and no holding back. It's something to behold, listening to Mac raising the roof, riding high on the back of these melodies.

Crocodiles is a fantastically nippy debut. Seven of the ten songs are under three minutes. Simple yet elegant songs like the excellent *Rescue, Monkeys* and *Villiers Terrace* are fantastic psychedelic pop, flavoured with the timeproof triumvirate of **The Beatles, The Who** and **Pink Floyd**, that have influenced Scouse bands for generations, while others, like *Pictures On my Wall* and *Stars Are Stars,* have a febrile feeling, needled along by Sergeant's spiralling guitar play and Mac's velvety croon, embroidered with yelping, howling and, well, showboating.

1981 brought another album, *Heaven Up Here*, which has the most beautiful sleeve, showing the band, writ small against the landscape of a deserted cloudy, infinite and oddly purplish Welsh beach. Whereas the mainstream bands had everyone's faces as large as possible on the album sleeve, this tiny-band-pictured-against-a-natural-cinematic-backdrop became A Thing (and subsequently a signifier of The Big Music) for the Bunnymen and was appropriated by other bands, most notably U2. Duran Duran would never have been photographed like that. It just shouts "our music lacks artifice and is really fucking BIG", doesn't it? There is a soupcon of "this is all bigger than us" modesty in there too. No wonder it struck a chord with Bono.

It might have been their greatest sleeve and it graced the Top Ten on its release but it's the least of their early albums and just a little rudimental. They've cut all ties with the Sixties and are pushing forward but, with the exception of the silken guitar groove of *A*

Promise, and the proto-Goth tubthump of *All My Colours*, it is all a little flat and grey. After the taut pop thrills of the debut, Heaven Up Here feels a little satisfied and not in the mood to exert itself. I might be in a minority with tis view but I am not alone: Bill Drummond said of it "*The album is dull as ditchwater. The songs are unformed, the sound uniformly grey.*"

The leap between the second album and 1982 single, *The Back Of Love* is astonishing. Produced by Ian Broudie, it is teeming with life and colour and all kinds of odd little art-for-art's-sake cul-de-sacs. It displays layers and layers of studio trickery, backwards bits, dubby breakdowns, fidgety horns and strings. A tight circular guitar riff kicks off the double time bassline and it hits the chorus after twenty five seconds. This is clearly a honed and determined attempt to write a (cool) hit single and one which came together quickly and easily in the studio in London. Strings subsequently became a totem of the Bunnymen after L Shankar had drenched them all over *The Back Of Love*, invoking a frisson of fellow Scousers, The Beatles in their 1967 glory. The term "hit single" doesn't do this brilliantly weird mini-symphony justice however. People who had not heard of The Bunnymen loved this song and Bunnyfans were uniformly pleased with this bright and bruised, darkly colourful new single. It stepped out of the dark shadows of *Heaven Up Here* and into the light. Hero time. It also swaggered into the Top Twenty and brought the Bunnymen legions of new fans.

Its parent album, the magnificent *Porcupine*, was harder going to make and was initially rejected by Korova's parent label WEA for being uncommercial. They subsequently re-recorded it with Shankar's strings added all over it. The album was now so hugely commercial that it burst in at #2 in the UK in February 1983, aided by the lyrically and musically darker hit single *The Cutter*, which had cracked the Top Ten. Bunnymania.

Porcupine brought acoustic guitars to the fore, along with percussion, xylophones and the aforementioned Indian Strings from Shankar. It's hard to understand why *Clay* was never a single. My word – that is a majestic song. No clue what is was about: feet of clay, Cassius Clay, a propensity to be easily moulded? All these and more, no doubt. Soaring and layered, there is something of *Clay* in a lot of Radiohead songs' production. Nigel Godrich must be a fan. Who wouldn't be seduced by the absolutely inspired counter melodies and harmonies resting casually in the mix, deftly woven jarring undertones, bursts of feedback, beautiful strings, tumbling drums and jazzy piano. It has peak after peak and drops back to its knees at least once and, just as it's climaxing, it all washes away. No bogus bonus, no overkill. Perfect. Mac sings a masterclass, rising and falling with the song, never overstepping, breaking for cover on the choruses and then letting the music lead the way. It should have been #1. The greatest non-single ever? Maybe.

The title track is a monolith. Opening like some sort of frantic yet funereal Hungarian folk music and then slow marching to the halfway mark, whereupon it pulls out a gun, steps up and blossoms with angry energy and feels like...well, it always felt like revenge to me. A song on a mission. *Heads Will Roll* starts out picking away like Paul Simon before the band swagger in with another luscious and ever building terrace anthem. There is more light and shade, and WAY more colour, on *Porcupine* than on the first two Bunnymen albums put together. There were so many choices for another single from the album. Cool bands being cool though, these were all eschewed for something new.

Never Stop, from 1983, was the Poppiest single the Bunnymen ever made. The title of the 12" version *Never Stop (Discotheque)* was an unusual suffix for a mardy Northern trenchcoat-wearing bunch. If The Cure could have fun pop singles with xylophones, then so could the Bunnymen. It was another Top Twenty hit. It does feel a little slight now, sandwiched between the twin peaks of *Porcupine* and the imminent and mighty *Ocean Rain*.

Atypically for bands who stepped out into the poplight in the early Eighties, the best was yet to come with the Bunnymen. *Ocean Rain*, the album that they insisted was marketed as "The Greatest Album Ever Made". It is their best and most well known record with *Seven*

Seas and, particularly, *The Killing Moon* living on in multiple soundtrack appearances, notably *Donnie Darko*. If you don't own this album, then you are missing something important in your life.

Another important record in 1982, from a band that were glowing on a similar page, was *Forever Now* by **The Psychedelic Furs**. *Love My Way* and *President Gas* seemed ever present despite not being actual hits. They must have had a lot of radio play and The Furs always seemed quite big to me, even if they were no-one's #1 favourite band. I suppose they were a cult band with the level of presence, via the ads and posters that comes with a Major Label Priority marketing spend. The band's second album had been a minor hit in the US and their subsequent albums were bigger over there and there must have been label pressure to match that in their home territory.

The Furs had started in London in the late Seventies and was based around Richard Butler and his brother Tim. Richard Butler's slightly nasal and weirdly transatlantic vowels gave the band an instantly memorable hook. They were born out of Punk but always included influences from before that Year Zero as evidenced by their name. Chaotic, improvised noisefests across ten minute jams that were, by their own admission, *"equally likely to be brilliant as awful"*, brought them attention and a deal with CBS.

Their first two albums sounded a little like Killing Joke, with one note basslines, intense and furious guitar squalls and dark lyrics. Except the Furs often deployed saxophones and weren't afraid of six or seven minute songs. They managed to score a couple of nearly hit singles with *Pretty In Pink* and *Dumb Waiters*. A re-recording of *Pretty In Pink* became an actual hit single in 1986 after being used in the John Hughes film of the same name but was already quite the iconic Indie disco staple. Aside from a Top Twenty placing on its re-release, they only managed one actual Top Forty Hit with *Heaven* from 1984's *Mirror Moves*.

Forever Now was produced by the none-more-punk **Todd Rundgren**, who had helmed *Bat Out Of Hell*, which was still in the Top Twenty best sellers of 1982, five years after its release. Its sleek, pulsating lines make it sound a little like New Gold Dream but they were still very much a Guitar Rock band, albeit one sufficiently airbrushed to fit onto MTV, amid all the Synthpop bands of the Second British Invasion. *President Gas*, with its massive descending scales-based hooks and thinly veiled rhetoric about Reagan struck a chord in the UK, particularly in the left-leaning music press. Oddly, a quick straw poll among my similarly aged friends reveals that they all thought it was a hit, despite it not even being released as a single. The Furs fitted in alongside, if somewhat behind, Simple Minds, the Bunnymen; as did Manchester's **Chameleons**, who never managed a hit at all but endure as a cult band anyway. A Peel band who never quite made it. If you want to know what a Chameleons album sounds like, listen to an Interpol album. They sound exactly like that but way more graceful and with less of a metaphorical stick up their notional bum.

Another profoundly British artist, who was very much dancing to the beat of her own heavily processed and sampled drum was **Kate Bush**. She is acknowledged now as Living Legend but in 1982, *The Dreaming* was her fourth album in as many years and the first she had produced herself. Its innate strangeness only solidified Kate's reputation as a bit of a nutter and often a figure of fun. Eccentric English institutions, who forever push the boundaries, often endure this "freak" status, coupled with fluctuations in faith/support, along the way to achieving National Treasure status Along with her friend **Peter Gabriel**, Kate was not only entranced by the possibilities of the Fairlight but also in a position to buy or rent one. Like Gabriel, her songs explored a huge variety of topics, factual and fictional, set in different times and countries. *The Dreaming* has songs about Vietnam (*Pull Out The Pin*), Aboriginal Australians (*The Dreaming*), Houdini (*Houdini*) and, oh yes, Stephen King's The Shining *(Get Out of My House)*.

The breadth of subject matter of her songs was more than matched by the beautifully idiosyncratic instrumentation. Some of the early sessions for this album feature traditional Irish musicians like **The Chieftains** and **Planxty**. Elsewhere you'll find field recordings of birds, mangled answering machine messages, lush string quartets, Dave Gilmour humming away and, um, Rolf Harris on didgeridoo. There is a lot of wordless ranting and even processed choirs of people making donkey noises. Kate has described it as her *"I've gone mad album"* and it's tempting to agree; although it is probably better thought of as a record where she was free and able to indulge her fantasies and make music that still sounds as vibrant and vital now as it did then. It certainly doesn't sound like an Eighties record.

It should come as no surprise that **Bjork** rates it as one of her favourite albums. The first single, and album opener *Sat In Your Lap* comes thundering in, atop colossal slightly military drums and only gets more over the top as it progresses, with shrieking and wailing and a thousand variously processed Kates unloading her conflicted feelings about a relationship. On the next song, Kate sings each of the first few lines in a completely different voice, leaning on a sort of mutant cockney accent for much of its length. As deranged as it sounds, which is quite deranged, it is relatively conventional compared to the rest of the record.

Sat In Your Lap reached #11 in the UK but second single *The Dreaming* didn't bother the Top Forty and the exceptionally odd third, *There Goes A Tenner* about some minor criminals getting cold feet, while attempting a bank robbery failed to make the Top Hundred and remains Kate's worst selling single ever. The album fared better and reached #3 but its novel but unsettling sound textures prevented it from finding favour with most of her by now quite large fanbase.

It remains a challenging listen but its sprit of adventure, of experimentation, and of bravely following your heart was very much in keeping with the times and that aspect endures. Kate was an established artist by this time, with the support of her label but, with the strangest kinds of records flying off the shelves, all sorts of artists were being indulged like at no other time. Not fitting in with the pack was regarded as a cherished merit, which sounds like an arthouse wonderland compared to the major label culture of today. Its British eccentricity and blend of accessible songs with outlandish experimentation places it in a select group of contemporaneous albums like *Dazzle Ships, Sulk, English Settlement* and *Fun Boy Three*.

Another artist who was hugely influential in the very idea of the absorption of new musical ideas by previously hidebound guitar bands in the early Eighties and gave many others the courage to try all sorts of new things is someone who has fallen from critical favour now, particularly in the UK. It's a shame really and I am sure he'll circulate back into their good books again at some point because **Peter Gabriel** has had a remarkable career. I have little to no time for his albums fronting **Genesis** and the subsequent existence of **Marillion** alone really ought to have sealed his fate for posterity.

His passion for African Music has made for a phenomenal number of albums on his World Music label, Real World and it seems churlish to be down on someone who has tired of Western Music and taken the time and trouble to discover music from all corners of the Earth, but there is often a slightly dull worthiness to the whole thing that lingers nonetheless.

But two things make Peter Gabriel forever amazing.

Firstly, the amazing range of Doctor-Who-monster outfits he wore onstage fronting Genesis, so a big box of kudos frogs for that.

Secondly, Peter Gabriel's first four solo albums, all called *Peter Gabriel,* are comprehensively amazing. Sometimes known, somewhat unimaginatively as 1, 2, 3 and 4. Also known, more imaginatively, as *Car, Scratch, Melt* and (for reasons I cannot explain) *Security.*

His solo career started off with the brilliant *Solsbury Hill* in 1977, a relatively sane and beautiful song, that sounds like something that Robert Wyatt might be involved with, and, OK, a bit like Genesis too. That first album also contains the significantly more unhinged, *Moribund The Burgermeister*. By 1980's *3/Melt,* Peter was on a roll. *Games Without Frontiers* was one of those hits that lived up to its title and translated internationally and I don't recall a bad word ever being said about it. It's an indisputably brilliant and accessible song. In my head, it is of a piece with **Talking Heads'** *Once In A Lifetime*, despite the fact that *Once* came a year later. Both are mainstream songwriters in some ways, but both are very happy to build a track around unusual instruments on a loping groove, without feeling the need to fill out the track with guitars and neither will do ANYTHING the obvious way and this experimental sensibility means that some of their music can be a bit annoying and some it rides a Pop wave to the stars and makes singles of unparalleled genius, that will live on forever. Such is Art Rock.

Melt features **Phil Collins, Kate Bush, Paul Weller** and **Robert Fripp** among many others. Gabriel, like Bowie, is a solo artist who is happy and able to draft in, say, Paul Weller to play some messy guitar on just one track and this revolving door cast makes for very diverse sounding albums. Phil Collins' big gated drum sounds, used on *In The Air Tonight*, appear here first. It's easy to dislike Phil Collins' music, politics and the way he conducts himself much of the time, but that single was pretty unique and rather great. **PiL** loved it so much they grabbed engineer Nick Launay (subsequently Yeah Yeah Yeahs, Nick Cave etc) for their Flowers Of Romance album and in turn Collins grabbed Launay to help him make In The Air Tonight. Prejudice is a minefield, isn't it?

Songs like *I Don't Remember* and *No Self Control* have no antecedents in Pop music. There is a palpable sense of the unhinged and of being wired here. Squealing guitars from Fripp, all sorts of percussion, and banks of harsh keyboards from Gabriel make for a suitably uneasy backing for the frantic and paranoid songs. 1982's *Security/4* continued Gabriel's quest for new sounds and new technology. It's an early, purely digital recording with most instruments being fed through a Fairlight and sampled and it sounds pretty Avant Garde to this day. Lyrically, Peter has already started his travels here with songs that are nominally about African Drummers (or Jung's views on same (obviously)), Native Americans and voodoo rituals. *Shock The Monkey* was a wonderfully lopsided and powerfully deranged single and I can remember playing it over and over again, trying to work out what the individual instruments were, to no avail. Gabriel was by now a critically acclaimed member of the Avant Garde and, at the same time, a genuine Rock Star. Hence the album had a South Bank Show dedicated to it while *Monkey* was all over Radio One. His next album with its lead single *Sledgehammer* and its classic video would lift Gabriel up to international Pop Superstar status.

If Bowie seemed five steps ahead of the pack in those days, then Gabriel's questing mind and experimentation always placed him maybe only a couple of steps behind Himself. It's odd that they never made any music together. Maybe they don't get on. Or maybe He has just not forgiven Gabriel for Genesis yet.

Britain's latest crop of hot bands, along with its established Punk and Rock stars had rapidly established a brand new, exotic and propulsive music, free of Rock'n'Roll, satisfying on every level and basking in critical acclaim, while accessible enough to keep the singles charts stocked with hits and sell like hot cakes. The European canon was here and its proud independence was something quite magnificent to behold. This, for me, was the real Cool Britannia. But, just as the bands and the fans were getting comfortable with the idea of everything being big and brilliant.....

10. AVALON: IN PURSUIT OF PRODUCTION PERFECTION

Months in Montserrat. Luxury as commodity. The real Eighties kick in.

ROXY MUSIC DURAN DURAN SCRITTI POLITTI THE BLUE NILE

Have you heard *Love Is The Drug*? Of course you have. But recently? What a song. What a record. What a production. Smart, feline, horny, tense and dirty. It's hip-rollingly enticing and packs a chorus that would make a dead man dance. Oh my, reader, **Roxy Music** were an astonishing band. A collision of some very differently minded people that common sense would probably say ought not to have been in the same band. The clash was beautiful and the disparate ideas combined explosively to swagger through a series of five hugely ambitious, experimental and sublime Artpop albums from 1972 to 1975, that all made the Top Ten. Also, they are five of the finest records of the Seventies that were not recorded by David Bowie or someone in skinny black jeans too.

That's five groundbreaking classic albums in three years again, by the way; along with a couple of Bryan Ferry solo records (which also went Top Ten). Seven albums in three and a bit years. Seven! A solid work ethic, right there. Make no mistake, these Roxy albums are weird records, full of awkward corners and jarring, lurching tunes that feel just on the right side of ramshackle, all driven roughly over whatever chaos lay ahead by Bryan's weird vibrato baritone croons, grunts and, ah yes, comedy foreign accents.

But as these gleaming "Rock" records slid smoothly in, alongside **Dire Straits** and *Avalon* on many shelves around the country, surely their luxurious, shagpile production was just an extension of **Brotherhood Of Man** extended reign of polite terror. There was no room for fun or spontaneity or excitement here. Any of these things would necessitate a lot of forms being filled out and way too many meetings. AOR was still reeling from **McCartney**'s reggae section in **Live And Let Die;** and it was still not the time to rock the boat again. Yachts demand that nothing should be rocking too much, after all.

This chapter might seem a bit like I am using slick production as a stick to beat bands with. And I am. It's OK though, they can take it. They're so rich, so they can't feel a thing. They absolutely deserve it too. So many interesting and promising careers were ruined by boring slick production and absolutely massive success. In my defence, I have refrained from mentioning the year's most boring and smug album. Maybe you like **Donald Fagen**'s *The Nightfly*. Millions do. I have heard it a few times and it's just awful. I blame it for encouraging Chris's deBurgh and Rea and a million other crimes perpetrated after its release. I was just grateful **Fleetwood Mac** didn't release a record in 1982. Alas, it turns out they did and I had blanked it out. It's called *Mirage*. Of course it is. It has a vile-looking sleeve and a single called *Gypsy*. *Gypsy!* I can only imagine the atrocities within. But I'd rather not. If I am honest, I am not really one for Jacking, all that much, but I agree 100% with the **Reynolds Girls** brief but heartfelt manifesto, *I'd Rather Jack Than Fleetwood Mac*. Starting a group just to diss Fletwood Mac is a fantastically noble and fun and Pop thing to do, isn't it?

twin peaks

Peter Gabriel brings the weird

·CLOSER·

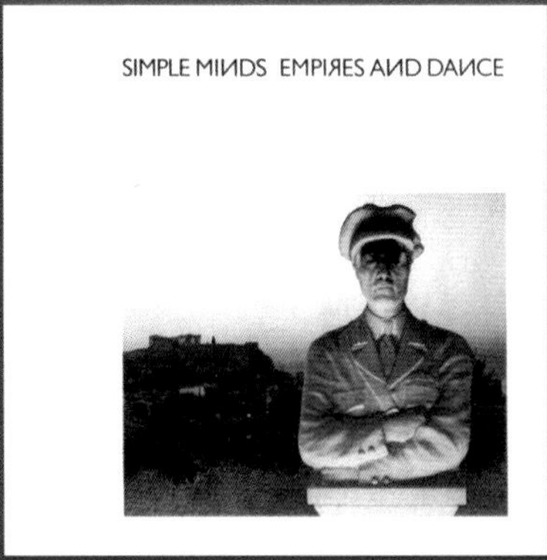

SIMPLE MINDS EMPIRES AND DANCE

ULTRAVOX
VIENNA

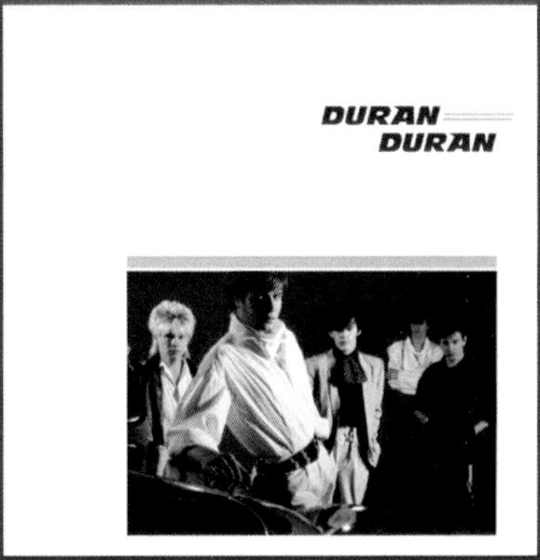

DURAN
DURAN

SIMPLE MINDS
NEW
GOLD DREAM
(81-82-83-84)

Duran get sophisticated

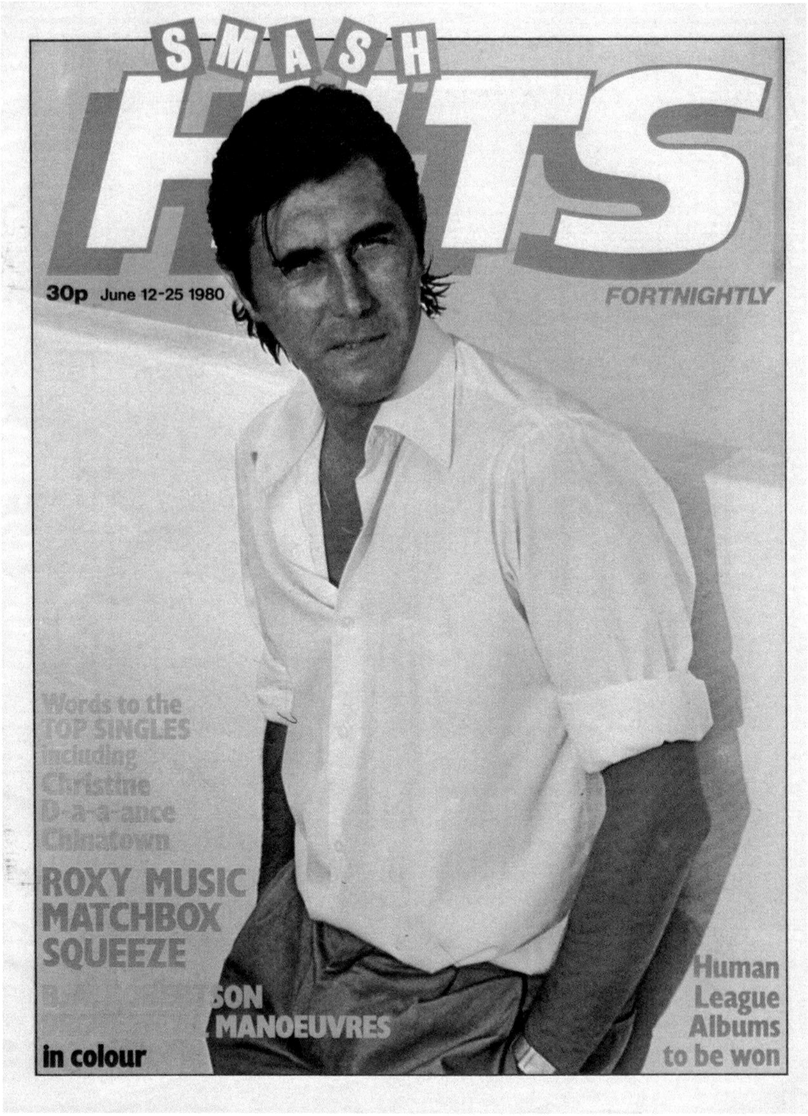

SMASH HITS

30p June 12-25 1980

FORTNIGHTLY

Words to the TOP SINGLES including Christine D-a-a-ance Chinatown

ROXY MUSIC
MATCHBOX
SQUEEZE

SON
MANOEUVRES

in colour

Human League Albums to be won

Scritti Politti

Songs to Remember

art + commerce

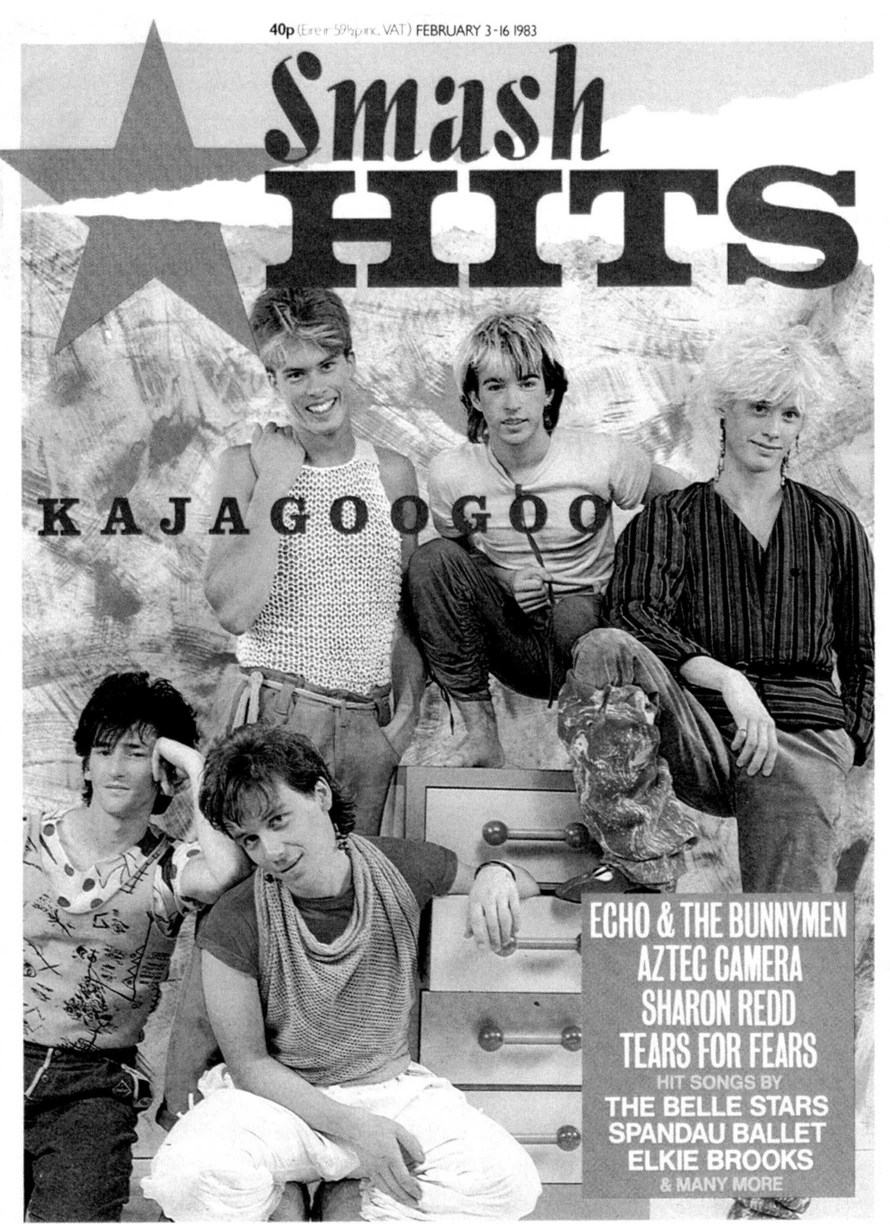
40p (Eire Ir 59½p inc. VAT) FEBRUARY 3-16 1983
Smash
HITS
KAJAGOOGOO
ECHO & THE BUNNYMEN
AZTEC CAMERA
SHARON REDD
TEARS FOR FEARS
HIT SONGS BY
THE BELLE STARS
SPANDAU BALLET
ELKIE BROOKS
& MANY MORE

NO.

DURAN DURAN
DURAN DURAN
SEVEN AND THE RAGGED TIGER
DURAN DURAN
arena
DURAN DURAN
RANNOTORIOUS
DURAN
AN DURAN
DURAN DURAN
STRONAUT

11. THRILLER: ECONOMIES OF SCALE, KAJAGOOGOO VS PRINCE.

It was all over by 1983. The UK offered up Kajagoogoo and Paul Young against the American colossuses. MTV boots DIY visuals out in favour of million dollar videos.

MICHAEL JACKSON MADONNA PRINCE CDs MTV

Kajagoogoo. It's just a word, isn't it? Just a band. *Too Shy* was quite good, wasn't it? Or harmless enough. And Nick Beggs' clickety-clackety hair was just a photoshoot waiting to happen, wasn't it? Hush hush, ooh...hmmmm well, no, dammit, NO. It was all wrong; cynically so and it wore its vacuous heart so proudly on its sleeve that it upset me. This was my first experience of someone, and I am speaking of The Man here, at a big label taking "my" music, missing its point (or not caring about it) by a mile and making a shiny, wipe-clean cardboard cutout version of it.

At the same time that Limahl & Co surfaced, **Paul Young** started making records again. *Where's the harm in that? Nice spiky hair too; I thought you liked that. Covering The Joy Divisions doesn't exactly make him a murderer, now does it?* Well yes, yes it does and murder, as The Clash had helpfully just reminded us, is a crime.

So is it wrong to paint old Paul as some sort of chipmunk-cheeked Antichrist or **Kajagoogoo** as the Five Idiot Horsemen of the apocalypse? Of course it isn't. You've got to go with your gut, right? Is it then too mad to paint 1983 as some sort of Pop Apocalypse? A little, perhaps.

But really – not all that much.

From 1979 to 1982, there had been seismic changes in pop music as we have discovered/remembered over the course of this book. Boring old pap/Pop was out and singles were cool again. Every Tuesday we wanted to know if our bands had gone up or down The Top Forty. If you were not a football obsessive, this was your version of Final Score, after Saturday's matches have shuffled up the Leagues. Hunkered around a contraband radio in the playground, we cheered and booed. Pop music had got exciting and fun by becoming experimental and hip. Old Punks and talented freakshows, lucky lunatics and smart bandwagon jumpers; all manner of seemingly unconventional and unpredictable artists had been flipped into the Top Twenty on the back of a brilliant single or three, an eye-catching haircut and, finally, a primary coloured Smash Hits photoshoot that persuaded Radio One to bring them out from the shadows of Evening Specialist play into the bright lights of Daytime.

A lot of these freshly minted New Pop stars had now gone beyond a few hit singles and were making inroads into America and beginning to unlock untold Billboard riches. The perky new MTV was waking America up from its Heartland Rock reverie and was spraying its face with the technicoloured videos of British upstarts like **Duran Duran, Culture Club, Depeche Mode** and, for some reason, **The Fixx**. The British vanguard were leapfrogging their way to stadium status, platinum records and The Big Time. The British Empire had struck back and begun the Limey Haircut wars, for Uncle Sam, had.

Ample opportunities open up for smart operators at this point. That is the rule of Pop music. The Golden Rule actually. Why waste time and precious money innovating and failing? The sweet spot for the major labels is just after the spearhead. Coming second and winning big. You pay your A&R scouts to keep a keen eye out on what is going on, to take the relevant meetings but do nothing about it. Then, when the hard work is done by others and Some New Scene is blowing up and making headway, it's time to jump in and stage a land grab, while there's still plenty of room.

Major labels do not pay shareholders with critical acclaim nor do they discuss the pushing forward of Art at the AGM. What is that phrase about knowing the price of everything and the value of nothing? There's nothing wrong with that, I suppose, and there's really no pretence to be adding to mankind's cumulative erudition but...but...music means everything to me and I just find it depressing, is all. Oughtn't there to be a point beyond or beside profit? Some meaning to the music....otherwise it might as well be coathangers that they're pimping? A big fat No is, of course, the answer to that question. The other old skool A&R motto that sticks with me, and I forget which major label executive told it to me first, is *"Selling music is the same as selling soap powder. Except it's harder because you don't have to persuade the soap powder to jump into the box"*.

Hmmmmmmm.

So the free-for-all was coming to a close. No more archly bonkers #1 singles for the bass player from The Damned. No more ambient album tracks from Japan clogging up the Top Five. Time for the professionals to step in and round up the strays. The game was, at least partly, up. The bigger labels had been caught on the hop a little and realised that a seismic shift had indeed happened. Not that a great many of these bands weren't already on major labels. They were. It's just that no-one had expected them to become the dominant force in Pop Music and not every label had their own Spandau Ballet and their own OMD. Yet. It even sounds ominous, doesn't it? The rush to sign bands that sound like a set of other bands rarely ends well for anyone. Nobody expected **Duran Duran** to be rivalling **Supertramp** as British exports after a few years in America and when it happened there was a panic. Nobody expected it but, credit where due, Virgin seemed particularly prescient here with **PiL, Magazine**, **Culture Club, The Human League, OMD, XTC** and **Simple Minds,** and, um, **Blue Rondo A La Turk** among others on their books but it was now time for the others who'd passed on all the hot new bands to jump in feet first and throwing cash around at the first band they could find with a stupid haircut and a couple of hummable tunes. Hence **Kajagoogoo,** who were, of course, also on Virgin.

It worked too. *Too Shy* was the debut single and it went to #1. You may have a few pedant points if you can name their follow up singles, which didn't have quite the same impact. Double points if you can name the album. Triple if you're male. So this is how it works. You note what's becoming hip or popular, find a very pale malleable imitation, get it produced by whomever is doing this sort of thing well (in this case Duran producer Colin Thurston and, yes, extra roll, Nick Rhodes) and then squeeze it for all it's worth. All in.

Shit or Bust. The album was called *White Feathers*, by the way and if you remove the band's cheesy logo, it has a curiously 4AD-ish sleeve.

My problem with this; THE problem with this, is that it's all ass-backwards. **Kajagoogoo** were obviously reverse engineered to fit a profile. That makes them pretty much willing cardboard cutouts. When the bass player's togglesome haircut is such a big part of the USP, it's pretty obvious that music is not the driving force behind Kajagoogoo's debut album's existence.

It is in the nature of things but the stunning variety of new sounds: the synthesizers, Gothy guitars, funky bass, Electro-Disco, a half-assed rap, tribal drums, weak Linn drums, lyrics that didn't make sense, muted Nile Rodgers guitars, industrial bleeps and Kraftwerk whooshes was reduced to a checklist. Tick any five, add a handsome singer into the mix, blend to bland and boom, you were away, with a little luck and a huge record buying team. Depressing, isn't it?

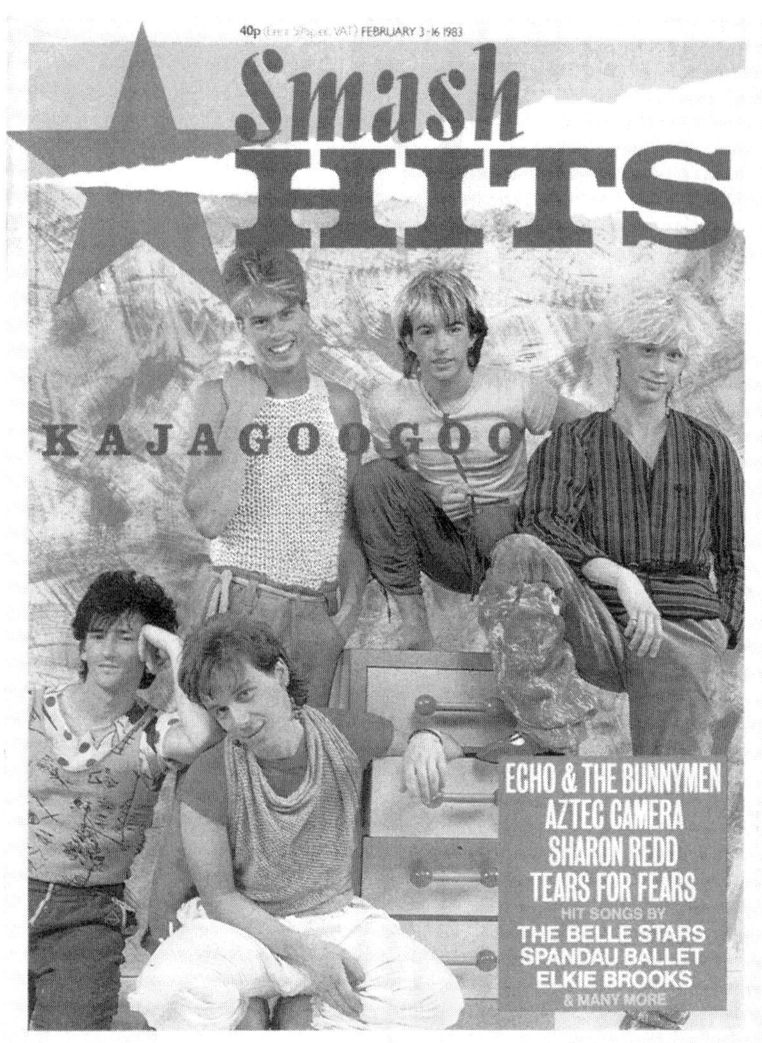

Of course, there were many, many others. It's not all Kajagoogoo's fault. Not personally. They didn't set out to destroy music, they just fit the description on the A&R BOLO and were picked up. After 1982's Pop revolution, Britain In 1983 gave us **Paul Young**, **Howard Jones**, the rise of **The Thompson Twins, Level 42, Nik Kershaw**, even greater bluster from **U2** and **Ultravox**, the remodelling of **Eurythmics** and *Club* motherfucking *Tropicana*. Awful things each. No class, no ideas, but very nicely packaged product that was not going to offend anyone, staffed by professional and reliable musicians. Artless, pointless and, of course, massively successful. Success was the aim, is the aim, of major labels but this was my first glimpse of success as a commodity. Whereas before bands had tried to stand out, to intimidate and to worry people, many of those same looks had now gone mainstream; and Thatcherism was encouraging a lot of bands dress solely for success. Why else would you be in a band? You do *want* to play Wembley, right? Even if it means forgetting your dreams of being a legend? Of course you do. Selling out was fitting in nicely. Being successful was now the sole point of being in a band for many, leaving Artistry sobbing on the hard shoulder, all cascading mascara and broken promises, wondering where it had all gone wrong. This New Pop looked cool and hip and lucrative. Everybody wanted a slice and would take whatever short cuts that their managers and labels asked of them to achieve that aim. Never mind having something to say, or finding an interesting way to say it or any of those old-fashioned rebellious boat rocking notions that made being in a band exciting in the first place.

So that was the British labels' response to 1982 and it was piss poor. Flooding the market with dreck that could only screw everything up. I dunno – maybe Nik Kershaw changed your life? I doubt it somehow though…

There are four other factors that made 1983 the beginning of the end for New Pop…or at least for its dominance of the charts. I should point out that some of my favourite records came out in 1983. Wah! The Smiths! REM! The return of Himself! Some of my favourite records have come out every year from 1956 right up until this week. Music still amazes me. But after Christmas 1982, things were different, less unpredictable and maverick, more efficient and boring. Here are those four factors…

1. The luxury gap. Most of the acts who made great records in 1982 that sold well went on to make much, much worse records the next time around.

2. America was not idle. The tail end of 1982 saw three hugely significant records by acts that would go on to dominate the whole world for decades. **Madonna**'s debut single, *Everybody; 1999* by **Prince** and *Thriller* by **Michael Jackson**.

3. Now That's What WE Call Music. The Pop compilation becomes a ready-to-wear monster.

4. Compact Discs. Oh baby, that feels good.

1. The Luxury Gap

Let's look at some of the key albums that we've talked about. *Dare, Rio, Sulk, The Lexicon Of Love, Rip It Up, Dazzle Ships, Combat Rock,*

The Hurting etc are all iconic records bursting with ideas and creativity. They were all very successful too, with the possible exception of *Rip It Up*. But let's roll forward a year or so and ponder again this new list: *Hysteria, Seven And The Ragged Tiger, Beauty Stab, Texas Fever, Junk Culture, Cut The Crap* and *Songs From The Big Chair*. These are not iconic names with the same Proustian rush at all. The melting pot of creativity and the exchange of ideas of 1981 and 1982 had thrown up all kinds of wonders. These bands had experimented with Pop and each found their sweet spot. Everything was golden. So what happened? It's not Difficult Second Album Syndrome, by and large, because most of these bands had long passed that point. So how come their next records were so disappointing?

There is always pressure from the labels not to rock the boat. Why not stay on in that sweet spot? More of the same and quickly would be ideal. Equally there must be pressure from themselves to, ahem, *"always believe in your soul";* to better their previous successes and move themselves on, creatively and artistically. These bands had all been praised and rewarded in the first place for breaking the mould. Each had great critical acclaim to go along with their gold discs and thus two very demanding and distinct masters to serve. The success of their previous records will also have brought bigger shows and a lot more money in their pockets, which opens new doors to ever more exclusive distractions. Buying a house, a nice car, nicer clothes, more expensive hotels and restaurants, cocaine, models and buying bigger houses. A better car. Yachts. And then there are Compass Point, Montserrat and Nassau. Being megastars, they'd need to escape the media attention and, what with the press and fans following you around, bursting your creative bubble and being weird, there's no way you are going to record your next masterpiece over three weekends in some Industrial Estate in Hackney. No indeed, it's four months in Nassau for you, arriving on a chartered plane with considerably more instruments than songs to bed in at your studio/villa complex. Yes indeed, the last piece of the puzzle of the drop in album quality…is ego.

Your hands might be able to record the album in East Acton but your ego needs to hear the tropical breeze and to feel the ocean waves lapping at your cocktail, in order to harvest the exotic fruits of your mind. Also, having been proven right once, no-one – not the manager, not the bass player and least of all some suit at the label – is going to tell your ego that your next cluster of songs is not quite as great, or indeed just plain rubbish.

After *Dare*, **The Human League** did lengthy sessions with Martin Rushent again, followed by Chris Thomas, who both walked out, and then they finished the record up with Hugh Padgham. Those are all very expensive gentleman to hire and that adds up to a lot of very handsomely appointed sessions in expensive studios with assistant engineers, tape ops and expenses and whatnot... that came to nothing. *Hysteria* arrived two and a half years after *Dare* and it just wasn't as good. It IS pretty good but 7/10 is a long fall from 10/10. Anything seems like a big drop from 10/10 and bands are judged critically as much against their last album as against the competition. How do you top a world-beating album? Do you go the OMD/Radiohead direction and get all experimental? In many ways, that is the easier path. Setting yourself up to fail, or conspicuously not trying to succeed in the same way, takes the pressure off. That is the problem with hitting the jackpot by breaking the mould with an album of hummable tunes. The mould cannot be rebroken; so more of the same ends up being so much less. *Dare* had inspired a generation who had taken its ideas and run with them, taking them into new places, and *Hysteria* was, well, just more of the same. Too little, too late. Cool sleeve, though.

Associates similarly went through a series of studios and producers, also including Martin Rushent, and took nearly three years to release *Sulk*'s follow-up, *Perhaps*. Even as a lifelong fan of Billy, it's hard to describe this record as anything other than patchily interesting. *Breakfast*, the magnificent Scott-Walker-sings-Nina-Simone piano ballad and, oh dear, single failed to break the Top Forty, but justifies the album's existence and opening single *Those First Impressions* is an elegant and swoonsome Pop song, which fell on mainly deaf ears. A hundred times less mental than anything on *Sulk*, it was certainly weird to see Associates not being weird. Starting the follow-up in late 1982, the initial album's master tapes disappeared in Billy's care and it had to be re-recorded from scratch and took a further couple of years and many suitcases full of cash for *Perhaps* to be completed by which time, everyone but Billy had left the band. Having worked with Billy in later life, I am familiar with his dissatisfaction with his own work. He always wanted more, always wanted something new and often turned on what he'd just recorded.

Duran Duran had long since been believing their own bullshit. You could see it in their eyes. According to Le Bon, *Seven And The Ragged Tiger* is "*is an adventure story about a little commando team. 'The Seven' is for us — the five band members and the two managers — and 'the Ragged Tiger' is success. Seven people running after success. It's ambition. That's what it's about*." The band were tax exiles for most of 1983 and started to record the album in the South Of France. They moved on to Montserrat and finished up in Sydney, nearly a year later, and at no point did anyone convince Simon that half of the songs were irredeemable rubbish that no amount of mixing would fix. So it goes. They did finish up with enough singles and earned their first (and only, thus far) UK #1 album and went on to be a big band but the peak of Duranmania was behind them.

OMD had scared off most of their fans with *Dazzle Ships* and *Junk Culture* was only a minor hit. That's a shame really because it's a strong album, mostly. It is a successful blend of the experimental ideas on *Dazzzle Ships* and the golden Pop nous of *Architecture & Morality*. The band had acquired a Fairlight and were able to combine their twin traits much more convincingly than before, allowing each to comfortably inhabit the same song. It feels like a more complete album and it's just bad luck that a year after *Dazzle Ships,* fans were still licking their wounds. They should have probably ditched one of either *Talking Loud And Clear* or *The Locomotion* (both singles) in place of something less twee and more strange. That would have helped.

Orange Juice deployed a mini album, *Texas Fever* before their next and final album, *The Orange Juice*, by which time, Malcolm Ross and most of their direction had left. *What Presence?* is still a late career high for the band, and would be for any band. **The Clash** had become Joe Strummer's personal domain. The rest of the band had been sacked, for various offences, from being a hopeless smackhead to always disagreeing with Joe. Their manager, Bernie Rhodes, completed the final album alone with session musicians, synths and desperation. Despite the rather brilliant opening single, and annual state of the nation address, *This Is England,* the whole album is so awful that it makes me cry a bit and should have been put out of its misery, rather than resuscitated. **Tears For Fears** set out to be the biggest band in the world and pretty much succeeded. *Songs From The Big Chair* was colossal but, despite a couple of excellent songs, the whole thing was just too bright and breezy (for me). Too damn smiley. Where was the angst and confusion of *The Hurting?* The fears and tears had all ironed themselves out evidently but this sunny outlook didn't do it for me and they sounded like a different band. A much more appealing band, as it happened. Their subsequent efforts to become the (new) Beatles and the painfully slow and heartbreakingly pricey attempts to better *Sergeant Pepper* on *Sowing The Seeds* led to even bigger success. By that point, however, I just couldn't see a single element that had first attracted me to the band left. So it goes. In the interests of research I listened to *Sowing The Seeds* just now. I won't get that time back. Don't be tempted.

2. America Was Not Idle

After the free-for-all, the successes and the failures of 1981 and 1982, it felt like there was really only one genre left standing. This was no longer Synthpop, Magpie Pop or Post-anything. The gaps between all these new vibrant genres and been filled and cross pollinated and it had all been swallowed up, whizzed up into what we know now just as Eighties Pop. The net result was a shiny robot monster; empty and avaricious, expensively shod and with Raybans bolted on, to conceal the dollars in its eyes. Soon we would read Martin Amis' *Money* and meet Tony Montana and Gordon Gecko and amid all the champagne cork popping and the major labels' buoyant domestic and export successes, the idea of challenging yet accessible pop music was largely driven back underground. The new batch of groups in 1983 just did not have the staying power or breaching–the-gates hunger and in the time we spent waiting for The Human League, Tears For Fears and the like to return, the Americans woke up and took over. Martin Fry of **ABC** says that *"The reality was that **Madonna, Prince** and **Michael Jackson** did it better, bigger and more global than a lot of British acts".*

And there's the rub. I love **Madonna, Prince** and **Michael Jackson**. I really do. They made not just some of the very best Eighties Pop records, but some of the very best Pop records ever. They WERE Eighties Pop's royal family. They were very carefully thought out, very expensively produced and unbelievably driven as artists. They were going to succeed and so they did; on such a colossal scale that they took out much of the competition. Why like five quite promising bands when you can love Prince for ever? There was no room for risks and quirks in the face of *Thriller*. These acts had no dilettante-ish side projects. They'd never split up. They were going to be unstoppable. They had bigger budgets, bigger videos and a professionalism that made a lot of British acts look small time; and all for a bigger prize. *The* big game: World Domination.

It's probably not a coincidence that they were all solo artists. There is no one to argue with, no-one to fall out with, no-one to blame when you are on your own. There's no idle banter, no waiting around for the drummer and no bunking off to the pub to talk about the singer either.

Michael Jackson WAS quite famous before *Thriller*. That sounds a little disingenuous, doesn't it? It's accurate though. He'd been a child star, in the public eye since he was five and been in **The Jacksons** since the Sixties and had gone solo in 1971at the age of thirteen. His band had their own TV show and he had released the greatest Disco album ever (his fifth) in *Off The Wall* and it has (now) sold twenty million copies. So yes, he was quite famous but *Thriller* took it to a new level.

By 1984, Michael was Elvis famous, Beatles famous and given that, for most Pop fans, those were somewhat old hat as references and didn't necessarily mean much to them, Michael was only slightly less famous now than Jesus. Lennon had joked that **The Beatles** were *"bigger than Jesus"*. Michael wasn't joking. He had told his new manager, John Branca, that he wanted to be the biggest star in the world *"and the wealthiest"* and he wasn't joking about that either. **The Beatles** had grown famous during the Sixties and because the Sixties came to life around them, over a series of records. Michael's uberfame went stratospheric over one album in a little over a year. One of the first things he bought with his money was The Beatles, or at least their publishing rights. That's an aggressive corporate takeover; a particularly bloodless one given that he outbid his mate, Macca, who had guested on *Thriller*.

Thriller despatched seven of its nine songs to the tops of the charts worldwide. Hit after hit after hit. Can you imagine? It's time to pull a seventh track from Thriller, Michael? OK, how about the title track, with say, a million dollar werewolf film, directed by the super hot guy who did *An American Werewolf In London* to promote it? Shock and awe, baby, shock and awe.

After *Off the Wall*'s massive success in 1979 and 1980, Michael had retreated and thrown himself into his work. What else would he do, right? *Thriller* took two years and an eye-watering three quarters of a million dollars to make. It drove Quincy Jones half mad and Michael more so. The nine songs, mostly by Michael and British writer Rod Templeton, formerly the drummer in **Heatwave**, who had also contributed three songs to the previous album (including *Off The Wall* and *Rock With You)* were meticulously crafted pop, rock and soul and you know them all. It continues to sell. It sold another million plus copies the year Michael died, washing up as the 14th Best Selling album in America that year.

Thriller is a business. A multi-platform entertainment project. It employed twenty nine musicians, other than Michael and Quincy Jones and the whole thing was a money-no-object mission to make the biggest album ever made. It's big business and it worked very effectively and it makes *Seven And The Ragged Tiger* look a little small time, doesn't it?

Michael's videos were mini-movies. They were not shot in an afternoon in a warehouse in South Central LA. Hollywood directors bring Hollywood production values. The video for *Thriller* itself is over ten minutes long and had a colossal cast. The idea was to be so big that no-one could compete. Mission accomplished.

Prince Rogers Nelson was signed as a very precocious teenager to Warner Brothers in the Seventies. It's slightly exciting to picture the teenage Prince, all afro, afghan, arrogance and raw talent. His first four albums *For You, Prince, Dirty Mind* and *Controversy* were written, produced and played largely by **Prince** himself and the funk auteur had had a run of American hits right from the off. *Soft and Wet* from his debut had made #82 and *I Wanna Be Your Lover* from *Prince* had reached #11 but he was pretty much unknown outside America except among the funkiest funk afficianados, who had got *I Wanna Be Your Lover* #41 in the UK in 1980. It's a bit unfair to call these first albums funk. They were quite a bit more than that – **Prince**'s musical DNA stretches back through **Sly Stone** to **Jimi Hendrix,** and he really rocked out at live shows.

1982's *1999* was a masterstroke though. A party in itself. The confident double album consisted of what came across like 12" versions of its eleven songs, only one of which is under five minute long and it is a statement of intent by its name alone. It was looking proprietorially to the future. The title track is a millennial party anthem, written eighteen years upfront. That is some cocky behaviour, which was ultimately borne out by the fact that not a Millenium party on the planet would have passed without playing that song at least once. The glitter carnival of *1999* brings in more Disco and Rock to the mix than before and offered a series of anthems that everyone could get behind, that is to say they were not as overtly sexual as previously and white people bought them. It was a huge success. It was a Top Ten record in America and the fifth biggest seller there in 1983. The single edit of *1999* was a Top Thirty hit in the UK but even after a couple of releases, *Little Red Corvette* failed to replicate that.

Back in the still rather segregated Seventies, white people mainly bought rock music and so, in a move that seems to parallel *Ziggy Stardust*, Prince's next move was to imagine himself as a guitar-humping Rock Star. *Purple Rain* was the semi-autobiographical, semi wish-fulfilling story of himself, starting out in Minneapolis, getting a band and making it big. It's probably fairer to say it was a mixture of *Ziggy Stardust* and *Saturday Night Fever* and one gigantic ego. The film is, depending on your mood and your irony levels, either colossally terrible or terribly colossal. A bit of both really. It was a box office hit around the world. **Prince**'s sixth album, nominally released as the soundtrack to the film and his first with a band, **The Revolution** was enormous. Single after single came out. Hit after hit after hit. Tracks from *1999* came back and were proper hits in the UK. The whole world bought into this magnificent record. *Purple Rain* was THE phenomenon of 1984. It won Grammys, Brits, and even an Oscar. It spent twenty four (!) weeks at #1 in the US charts and sold thirteen million copies in the US alone, including a million and a half in week one. A million and a half! That means Warners probably pressed close to three million copies. Imagine!

Oh and it's brilliant. *Like Thriller,* it has nine tracks and feels no need to pad it out to ten. Nine perfect songs, each of which could be a single. That was Michael's plan for *Thriller* and it was **Prince**'s plan for *Purple Rain* too. Michael had brought Hollywood production values to *Thriller*'s clips and Prince had gone one further and made a hit movie. And it's definitely a movie, not a film, before you start.

They both understood well the ways of the entertainment world and both had applied the still young Hollywood tentpole blockbuster logic and economics to music. Spend big to get big. Open big and stay big. This was mass marketing on a global scale. There was nowhere on earth that didn't know *Thriller* and *Purple Rain*. Total market penetration. There were stars and there were superstars like **Bowie** or **Mick Jagger.** This was bigger, this was the age of the megastar. One perfect album and no end of money behind it to keep milking it until the artist called time on it. For new markets/fans and for those with a short memory, these albums became Greatest Hits collections, all on their own, generating more bangs for your buck than your average Pop star.

Madonna was a little behind these two gentlemen and was only just releasing her first single at the end of 1982. It was the first pulled from her forthcoming debut album, *Madonna*, and by the end of 1983 she had pulled four more and had had a Top Ten album all over the world. Her moment also came in 1984 with *Like A Virgin*, which went toe to toe with *Purple Rain* as a globe straddling brand phenomenon giving her another five massive hits. She had been watching Prince and Michael and wanted the same for herself. Her videos were events, her primary weapon was sex and it does seem quaint now that her bellybutton and nipples caused such a massive fuss back then but they did. She played it perfectly and hit a run of perfect pop singles that lasted for a decade. Her first Hits album, the justifiably titled *Immaculate Collection*, which captures that imperial phase has sold over thirty million copies. THIRTY MILLON!

I am not sure why Britain never matched these icons in the Eighties. The budgets were huge but so were the rewards and it's the same labels, CBS and WEA, here as there. I guess after having their arse handed to them a little in The Second British Invasion, the Americans put their heads down, pulled in all of their experts (or not, in Prince's case) and, as Martin Fry said, they just did it better. *Like A Virgin, Thriller* and *Purple Rain* are great albums. You know that, though, right? Right?

Prince, Madonna and Michael Jackson took over pop. The self styled king, queen and, you-know-what of pop. They ate or steam-rollered much of the competition. If *Purple Rain* was the number one album for months on end, no-one else was going to get that accolade. It's total market domination, strength in numbers and Pop taking on a new, bigger mass market and fighting with the economies of scale. In terms of warfare, these were not wars of attrition, or skirmishes; they were atomic bombs. Instant, effective, long lasting and what the hell else were you going to be talking about after they'd gone off? Such Eighties.

3. Now That's What We Call Music.

It was time for the small players to be squeezed out as the Pros took over. This New Pop music was a fine commodity and plenty of new customers wanted to buy it. Time for the big labels to figure out a new way of selling it. One of the first stages in this consolidation by the majors was the *Now That's What I Call Music* series. Compilations were nothing new but we were still sleepwalking through the era of BBC's *Top Of The Pops* compilations, which were inexplicably popular albums with a nice partially dressed Page Three Stunna type on the front along with a list of song titles aimed at the casual pop fan. The very casual pop fan, who was so relaxed and half-interested that they didn't mind that these were not even the original songs but weak and vaguely similar cover versions by nameless session musicians. It doesn't seem possible, does it, readers? They were helpfully priced quite cheaply because they weren't seen as proper albums. I never had one. Did you?

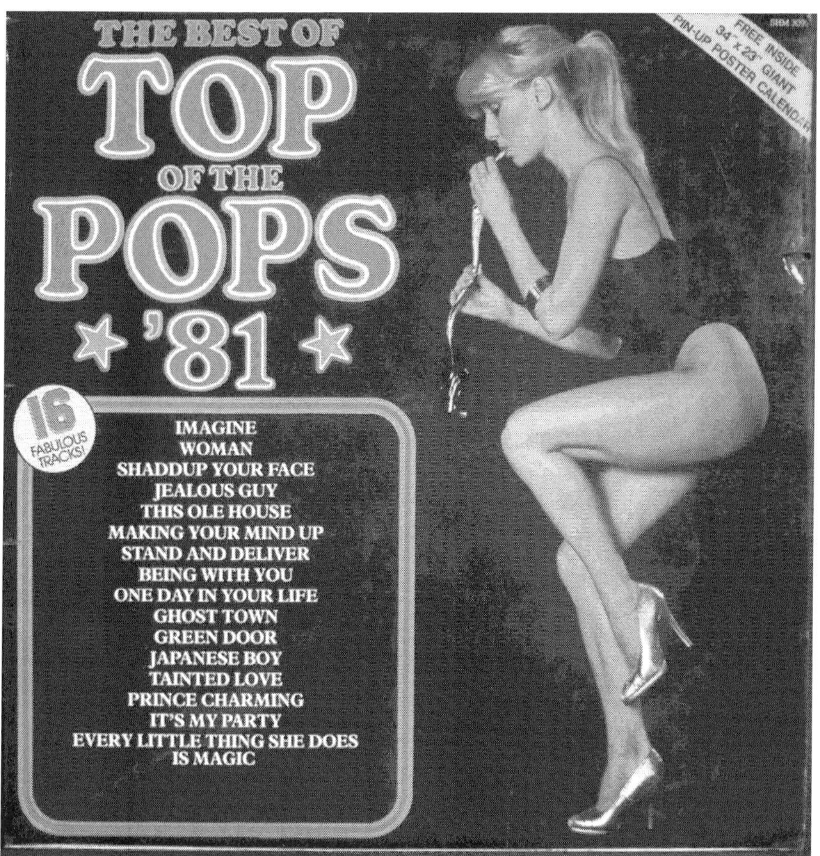

The new *Now That's What I Call Music* albums were invented by a couple of executives at Virgin, Steven Navin and John Webster, and celebrated the renewed love of Pop music and also the key fact, which they had spotted which was that many of these music fans were not accustomed to and/or did not want to buy lots of singles, either because they were older album buyers lured back in to the Top Forty by the explosion of amazing singles, or because they were kids being bought birthday and Christmas presents. The other bigger, shinier idea was that the albums were made in co-operation with other major labels so had access to a broader range of hits. Albeit a broader selection of hits from bands that the labels themselves were pushing as priorities. They were super-current, hence being called *Now*; and also they were double albums and thus *more* expensive than albums. Clever. They were an instant and massive hit.

Guess who had TWO singles on the first Now record? Yep, **Kajagoogoo**. THREE if you count the Limahl solo single on it too. And you should. Just saying.

The problem was that a lot of people, particularly older people, just stopped buying singles and waited until the next *Now* because it would have all the best/big ones on there. A million Pop buyers buying their singles 30 at a time makes for very, very homogenous tastes. It excludes mavericks and new ideas and concentrates attention, and thus individual album sales on fewer and fewer acts. So, after a few quite interesting and tempting selections, they were mostly pushing rubbish. I bought the first three, as I recall. After that, they just weren't speaking my language. Man.

The labels who weren't involved in the series soon grew their own. CBS/WEA launched the *Hits* albums, and MCA/Chrysalis came back with their version, the not entirely originally named, *Out Now*. The *Hits* records lasted out the Eighties but gradually *Now* subsumed labels and songs until it dominated. There can be only one. That tagline from *Highlander*, was a none-more-Eighties notion indeed, wasn't it?

They've shifted over a hundred million *Now* albums since 1983, with bespoke editions in dozens of countries. A HUNDRED MILLION! There have been two or three a year since 1983 and they are always,

always huge. I think the next one due is Now 91. They still crash in to #1 in the charts today. Although now they have their own chart in the UK. That series of albums being Number One for ten, fifteen or more weeks a year, stopped a lot of artists having the hugely marketable accolade of "a number one album", so they invented the Compilation Chart in 1989. Probably just as well now because while album chart toppers VERY rarely break into six figure sales in a single week, the *Nows* will shift a quarter of a million sales in week one, without fail. *Now* would be number one in the real album charts for most of the year now. Sigh.

4. Compact Discs. Oh baby.

Quality is an odd word, an abstract noun. We all know what it means but it means something slightly different to each of us. *Thriller* is a good quality album, you might say. The workmanship, musicianship and song-writing is undoubtedly good quality. The production is consummate and state of the art. It took two years to make. There are no bum notes. There are no bad songs; aside from the Macca one. And the last one obviously. We've probably all had a good bit of use out of it and we all probably still like some of the songs and so it still works today. It was built to last. That must be a sign of quality. If you don't like at least *Billy Jean*, then you are in the wrong book, so clear off and thanks for buying it.

The newly minted Eighties Music fans liked "quality albums". Quality album. This phrase annoys the pants off me. Aside from the fact that I am a grammar snob – when I choose to be innit – and it has turned an abstract noun into an adjective; my main issue with it is that it is just risible bollocks. I know what people mean by it. I just don't agree. Applying these rules, it seems that if *Thriller* is a quality album, then perhaps *The Clash* is not. That would mean that *Sergeant Pepper* is better quality than *Help!,* which is obviously madness. Furthermore it implies that *Brothers In Arms* is better quality than *Sergeant Pepper.* I am joking of course. Except I am not. Not at all. They are both rubbish.

The pursuit of production perfection is one of the worst legacies of the Eighties. In 1981, the big albums discussed earlier were fizzing, very slightly awkward or imperfect but human and pulsating with life. By 1984 the big sellers were Quality Albums. And by 1985 they were albums that you just "had to have" on CD. Paul Young, Sade, Sting, The bloody Police, Dire Straits, Queen, Lionel Rich Tea and U2. And, oh my god, the return of Tina Turner, Billy Joel, Elton, Eric and Rod. These were top quality album merchants, apparently. That list of artists is also pretty much what you got to hear on Live Aid, from the UK's end anyway. Live Aid was the last boot in the face of New Pop. I am biased, just like you but, whatever your definition, this was just not the best quality music available. Just agreeable expensive sounding albums from Rock's journeymen. This was music for you dad, surely. I mean, if you were under twenty and this was what was doing it for you, you needed to have a long hard word with yourself. And if you are still listening to it now, please seek help.

It seems Lionel pulled the biggest crowd at Glastonbury 2015. FFS.

So where am I going with this? The pursuit of production is not wrong but it seemed to me that people were buying records because the production was "quality". I have no words to answer that kind of attitude. I don't get it. It is not an appreciation of music. I hear exactly the same snobby nonsense today from glitch-heads into **Boards Of Canada** or niche German techno labels. If the best you can say about something or the first thing you say about something is to marvel at its production, to praise the grain of the hi-hat, or the eerie clicking noise under the keyboard washes that you can only hear on headphones, then you have this whole thing upside down. You are just like a Prog Rock fan, and where's the fun in that? And where does all this leave *Upside Down* by the **Mary Chain,** eh? Answer me that. Actually, don't. For what it's worth, I think *Upside Down* has an incredible production from Joe Foster and is one of the best Pop singles of the Eighties and it still crackles with life and visceral power today.

Expensive Nassau production, Pino Palladino bass playing and Bob Clearmountain mixing demanded and was granted a new expensive luxury – a premium format. Gatefold vinyl was not enough. CDs arrived in 1982, took off in 1984 and went ballistic in 1985 on the back of **Dire Straits'** *Bastards In Arms,* which word-of-mouth held as something you just couldn't appreciate unless or until you heard it on CD. Hmmmm. I did try, at the time, in the interests of being able to slag it off knowledgably. Not really for me. There's a nice chord change in the *Theme From Local Hero,* if that helps. Was that on there? I forget. *(It was a B side).*

As *The Matrix* was to DVD and *Avatar* was to Blu Ray, so **Dire Straits** became the sine qua non of CD. Which was annoying because *The Colour Of Spring* was just around the corner and that is the one that shows off the magic and depth of CDs. That is the one that should have sold twenty bazillion copies. Can you imagine?

Once people had experienced *Brothers In Arms* 100 times on this new and genuinely amazing format, they wanted more. More quality albums. More Sting, more Tina, more Sade and once they had been baptised into Eno's production pool with *The Unforgettable Fire*, lots more U2. Big, expensive albums from megastars beat experimental and forward looking albums from restless Pop upstarts into a not very close second place. Aspirational consumerism was upon us.

These days CDs are the dominant force in album sales. Oh yes they are. At least here in the UK. At least for now (in 2015). Digital formats are fast catching up and have overtaken in some genres. Vinyl is enjoying a productive retirement but still only accounts for about 2% of album sales, so let's not have that pointless argument. In five years, I suspect things might be different. In five years, the notion of sales will seem quaint, I expect.

I just don't understand the race to annihilate CDs. They are great. Didn't we love them? All of us. They sound better and more detailed than vinyl. We were all clear on that. They don't scratch, skip and bump after twenty plays. And if you spill curry on them, you can wipe it off with no ill effect. Amazing, no? Although, if you are spilling curry on your albums, you may need to have a firm word with yourself.

The one huge obvious downside to CDs was that they were digital recordings. And by about 1995, you could make perfect copies of them with CD Burner units for your hi-fi and this, along with broadband, led to the acceptability of illegal downloads, a decimation of sales and the destruction of the entire music industry; all of which made a lot of people happy and a few people very sad and unemployed.

Taping an album was just fine but it was a stopgap. It most definitely didn't sound as good as a record. Or a CD. And if you put the Dolby on, it was like wearing a woolly hat over your ears. What was all THAT about, Dolby? It's surely easier to tune out the hiss than muffle the music. Ah but Dolby ON meant increased "quality". Hmmmmm.

So we all loved CDs and threw our vinyl out. I didn't. Then we all hated CDs and wanted the analogue warmth (distortion) of vinyl again but at four times the price. So we threw our CDs out and digitised and had just a very few chunky 180gsm albums, all of which were doubles because CDs had led to longer albums that wouldn't fit on two sides of vinyl. I didn't. I buy a lot of records in secondhand shops, charity shops, eBay and Amazon Marketplace, seeing as hardly anywhere else sells them. This lurching from one extreme to another is causing these people in Oxfam all kinds of problems with regard to racking and pricing, so please make your minds up. This copy of **Neil Young**'s *Harvest* on vinyl. Is it 99p or £15? Original pressing with the who-cares-what coloured label or new'n'mint – which is better? Who can say anymore? (me, new pressings sound better). It's pot luck now. Picking up CDs for a pound, as I do every week, is amazing though. Having lived through the time of £15 CDs in the Nineties, I just cannot resist. It won't last. Someone will decide that up is down again and they'll be collector's items once more. Except for the endless supplies of Mel C and Robbie Williams CDs in Poundland. They'll never run out. I remember working at the famed (but now sadly dwindling) second hand record shop empire, *Record & Tape Exchange* in London in the early Nineties and seeing people told that their copies of *Brothers In Arms* and **Sade**'s *Diamond Life* on vinyl were worth 2p. Sad faces all round but we had literally thousands of copies out the back. I hope they kept them; I dare say they are premium items once more.

I have a lot vinyl. Most of it bought in the Eighties. When CDs came in, I was mad for them. They do sound better, on the whole. Clearer, brighter and better. You can hear the full frequency range. Old familiar albums were revealed to have hidden secrets when heard on CD for the first time. And some digitally remastered CDs go even further. *Avalon, The Stone Roses, Bummed, "Heroes", Sandinista* and plenty more have had a whole new lease of life as remasters round at our house. I will grant you that a lot of modern electronic music, with its intricately sculpted sub bass, does pop and bounce a lot harder on vinyl. So there you have it, some things sound better on CD, some on vinyl (at least the first dozen plays anyway) and nothing sounds great on MP3 ever, especially if it's below 320kbps. MP3s are just for browsing. Most of the frequencies are changed to mono to save space. It's heartbreaking to think people mainly listen to music on MP3. Through laptop speakers or phones. There is a reason why an MP3 is 5 Megabytes and a "full fat" studio quality WAV or AIFF is 50 Megabytes. Most of the music, or at least most of the detail, has been stripped out. Imagine you bought a Millennium Falcon toy in Toys R Us (for a child, of course. Obviously). A big one. It had ladders and lasers and radar dishes and opening hatches and ramps and turrets and guns and bleeps and flashing lights. All would be amazing. Hours of fun would ensue. Now imagine you saw one in a boot sale. All the little bits were missing, and nothing flashed or bleeped. It's still recognisably a Millennium Falcon, of course. But it's clearly not nearly as good, is it? Well, that is how I see MP3s.

And don't pretend you like crackle. It makes you look stupid. I am aware of Peel's much repeated comment about life having surface noise and it makes NO SENSE AT ALL. I don't see anyone taking a pin to their albums to add crackle.

The other problem with CDs has to do with *Thriller*. Michael and Quincy sat in darkly plush rooms for years and whittled down what they had recorded, some thirty songs, all the way down to nine. It runs to forty two minutes and fits on a vinyl record without the need to lose any sound quality. Michael didn't want a double album any more than Spielberg wants a five hour film. CDs almost doubled this capacity and to add to the woes of these *quality* albums, we now had quantity. No more self-editing. Record and release everything to capture the rapture of the artist's newfound fecund genius. The debate about albums as an artform is for another day but forty-few minutes, while it was arbitrarily decided by the format, is a good length. It requires and rewards discipline. Even after months on a tropical island, bands had to wake up to themselves just a little bit and bin the lesser tracks. For everyone's sake. Perhaps an album is not supposed to last over an hour. Mostly. Perhaps it's too much, too long and no-one cares. Perhaps not enough modern albums are making it into the canon due to excess filler. What if they made CDs that last three hours; and in DVDs, they have. Why no three hour albums? Because no-one wants them, Silly Billy. And by Billy, I am in no way reaching out to Billy Corgan here but, if you are listening...please stop now, Billy. How many listens did you give **Outkast**'s *SpeakerBoxx / LoveBelow* all the way through? Slightly disingenuous question, I know because it is two solo albums put together but you take my point? Right? Do you? Maybe it's just me.

CDs are great but, just as with fridges, they work better if you don't feel the need to fill them right up.

So to recap, the music from 1980 to 1982 was amazing and popular and hip. John Peel gave bands with interesting ideas a session and a year later they had sold 300,000 copies of their brilliant, innovative and colourful debut album. Amazing scenes. Truly. This music was birthed by Kraftwerk, Bowie, Punk and Thatcher and it was killed, on purpose, by Kajagoogoo, Prince, CDs and, again, Thatcher.

I miss the days when pop stars couldn't dance and didn't care about it.

My Ten favourite singles from 1980-1982

1. New Order: Ceremony
2. Associates: Party Fears Two
3. The Specials: Ghost Town
4. Echo & The Bunnymen: The Back Of Love
5. Blondie: Atomic
6. Malcolm McLaren: Buffalo Gals
7. Indeep: Last Night A DJ Saved My Life
8. OMD: Souvenir
9. Prince: Little Red Corvette
10. Japan: Ghosts

Yours?

12. ALL YOU NEED IS NOW

1980-2015-20??: The persistence of Duran Duran and the perpetual Eighties revival

LCD SOUNDSYSTEM LA ROUX HOT CHIP THE KILLERS

Duran Duran's Synthrock, hair and shameful clothes are so inescapably, inexcusably Eighties that the band ought to have been marooned there; drinking pink champagne on a perpetual Concorde flight, as music and fashion swooshed past them in the opposite direction on their way to somewhere newer and cooler. Sure, they have sacks full of brilliant singles but their innate Duranity really ought to have boxed them in and held them back as times changed. And changed again. And again.

It didn't though. Perhaps it was because they had never tasted cool, that they could never lose it. And perhaps, once they realised that, they were free to experiment, flirt with ridicule and acquired a certain psychological Kevlar; safe in the knowledge that their colossal international fanbase would be loyal and the critics would laugh at them, whatever they did.

Their debut album is one of the key releases of the early Eighties and one of my favourite records of all time. Preposterous Pop and a landmark Synthpop document – it's constructed entirely from Bowie style cut-up lyrics, luxuriant Kraftwerk whooshes, dikka-dikka Moroder keyboards and Chic basslines and packed with so many great potential singles. All killer, no filler. (Except maybe *To The Shore)*. If you haven't had the pleasure, go listen to *Friends Of Mine* – a lost Duran anthem, or better yet, Duranthem that they still play at shows. They followed it with a classier image revamp and the jet-setting Lifestyle Pop of *Rio*, which helped to define/inspire the decade's conspicuous consumption and gave the wardrobe department of *Miami Vice* something to work from. Then came their first British #1 single; and their worst song yet, which I will admit to liking but being a bit baffled by at the time. *Is There Something I Should Know?*, has the winning line, *"You're about as easy as a nuclear war"* and remains a generation's go-to example of wordplay so stupendously clunky, that even the infant **Kasabian** might conceivably rub it out and have another think. It was such a travesty that they left it off their third record, *Seven And The Ragged Tiger*, whose sparkly singles belie the tosh that makes up the rest of the album, and where its inclusion might have proved helpful, frankly. *Seven* was recorded over many, many months around the world as the band ~~went on a massive holiday~~ become tax exiles and it sounds like it. It's mostly awful. Nobody noticed this, however, and the band grew bigger than ever. After two singles from *Seven,* they were about to get even bigger with three of the decade's defining global hits.

The Reflex is a brilliant and groundbreaking, if truly vacuous, single that sounds like an edit of a quite merciless 12" remix – which it is, courtesy of **Nile Rogers**. The club versions of singles were still a minority interest, which received little radio play, although they had proved the gateway into America, via Billboard's Club charts. Nonetheless, it was a bold move to incorporate those sounds into the actual single. It sounded pretty out there on first listen. The band had wanted it to be the album's lead single but its stuttering vocals and computer edits scared the label. They needn't have worried. It hit #1 at home and in America, where it conspired with *When Doves Cry* to keep Bruce Springsteen's poppiest, and most brazen single, *Dancing In The Dark* off the #1 spot.

The Refle-fle-fle-fle-flex might be a bit vacuous (as is much astonishing Pop, all the way from *Love Me Do* to *Bad Romance*) but it is a magnificent single that has become one of the decade's most enduring and endearing hits. It also sucked the band into a musical vortex, where clashing ideas from different band members, adventurous Pop production, ridicule and the genuinely appalling were forced closer and closer until they reached a singularity and fused together to create the smoking gun that is *The Wild Boys* (which I notice that they have been opening shows again with in 2015, including hipster electronics festival, Sonar).

Even by Duran's sky high standards, this is a silly song. The video, shot by Russell "Highlander" Mulcahy, manhandled the song way past silly, along the corridor of people shouting "please don't do this" and out of the window-of-no-return. If you have never seen it, you are in for a treat. The band look like they had been kicked off the Mad Max set for drinking cocktails instead of beer and the video involves dwarves, mutants and Simon strapped to a huge windmill's sail that dunks his head in water as he sings, along with a greater than average amount of smoke, fire, chains and billowing curtains. And capes.

The notion of trying to drown Simon as he sings struck home with many, no doubt. The band had stretched Adam's maxim on ridicule to an undiscovered level – surely he hadn't meant one should actively aim for ridicule?

The single was again produced by their hero, Nile Rodgers, and it was stuck in the middle of the worst cash-in live album I have ever heard, *Arena*. **Duran** live is a truly fun experience but I am not sure many go to re-hear what clunky new arrangements the band have conjured for their many hits, especially if they are recorded on a microphone that has been sealed in a biscuit tin. By any reckoning it ought to have finished the band off. The shark was consummately jumped. "*Wild Boys fallen far from glory*" indeed. Yet both the single and live album were massive hits again and instead of ending them, the band got away with it and managed to survive by tactfully disappearing.

How to come back from a single like that, with everyone still sniggering at you? Well, it turned out that James Bond was stuck in a similar Eighties limbo, seduced by technology and overdosing expensively on special effects. Perhaps meeting in some Global Brand Rehab centre, where **Chic** were also staying, they all crossed their streams and came up with *A View To A Kill*. It had many of the same production tics, this time courtesy of Chic's Bernard Edwards, but was a little more restrained and had an air of classiness, presumed to have been left behind on a beach in Sri Lanka a few years previously. Likewise, the film toned down the special effects in favour of using **Grace Jones**, who was just as good as CGI and probably cheaper. **Duran Duran** had made it through a black hole of crazy and come out smelling of roses, more or less. They did the smart thing and disappeared for a year. During which time, they also did the other smart thing and split up; although hiatus might have been a better word. The band's relationship was under the usual strains and different members wanted to move in different directions. Andy was becoming more Rock, or perhaps Rawk, and wanted to be that Wild Boy, full time.

The inevitable side projects appeared and, again, the unrestrained indulgence should have done for them but it didn't. Their critical rating had never moved much above zero so they had nothing to lose or prove. Simon, Nick and Roger formed **Arcadia**, which was basically Nick Rhodes' blurred Polaroid vision of a keyboard-centric Duran Duran. Their *So Red The Rose* album is actually rather lovely, in its way and much better than *Seven And The Ragged Tiger*. John and Andy borrowed **Robert Palmer,** bits of **Chic** and pursued a harder Funkrock to construct The **Power Station**. 1985 should have been Duran's Naughty Step year but both side projects were successful commercially and by no means terrible, musically. Could it be that Duran Duran were somehow untouchable?

The answer seemed like a yes when they emerged a year later in 1986, minus Roger, Andy and their management; with black suits, more reasonable haircuts and calmer demeanours, filtered via a nice monochrome Anton Corbijn-ified look. Classy. Grown up. Less Mental. That was the new message. The music was produced by Nile Rogers again but this time on a more collaborative and organic footing. All was well in the Duran garden; now that they had downsized Andy Taylor's rockery.

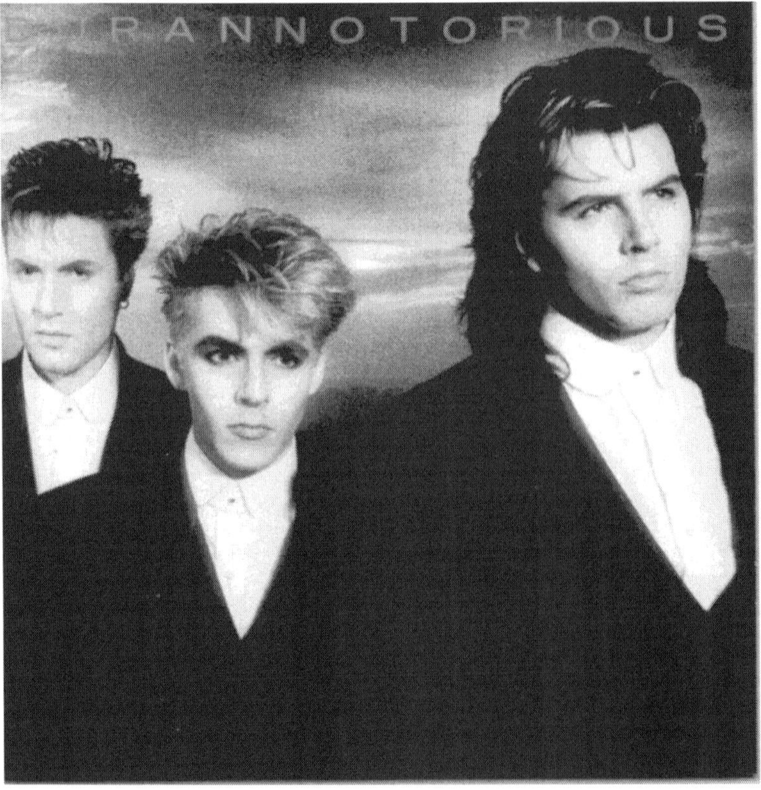

After a trio of ear-bogglingly frantic singles, this was a languid take on Duranfunk with a hint of late-period **Roxy Music**. The title track was a huge hit worldwide but the album only got to #16 in the UK and subsequent singles, including the stunning *Skin Trade*, the first Duran single I can imagine someone covering successfully, failed to break the Top Twenty. The album still went platinum in the US but *Notorious*

marked the end of Duran's bulletproof Imperial Phase. What follows at this point with Pop bands is a thinking gap and then a really bad album that no-one buys. And so it came to pass. Twice. *Big Thing* (or Big Thinig if its sleeve is to be believed) and *Liberty* were not great records at all and although the band had enough of a hardcore fanbase to get them Silver discs, that is not much consolation to a (formerly) huge international Pop group. The dumper tapped its watch, beckoned them in and ticked their name off.

In 1993, the band confounded expectation once again and played the self-titled comeback album card, which is musical shorthand for "this album has all the things that you liked about us and none of the silliness of that last record", although silliness is a vital cog in the Duran machine. The *singles Come Undone* and, particularly, the wonderful *Ordinary World* were massive international hits and Duran were up and running again, racking up platinum albums. Time, you'd think, for a measured response and another hit album with an appropriately hot producer. Sadly not.

Buoyed perhaps by the surprising fact that no-one had had them murdered for what they did to **The Velvet Undergound**'s *Femme Fatale* on that self-titled comeback record, they reached for the next card in the Legacy Band Ideas Pack for their next trick: The Covers Album. Self-produced, naturally. This is a safe and standard ploy for a big band. You won't win prizes but there is no shame in the move and you get to show off or recast your cool influences. It gets the catalogue moving and you can tour it if you fancy extra cash. Duran's greatest hits effort *Decade* had been released in 1989 and was still selling well, giving them yet more platinum discs from all over the world despite its heroically ugly sleeve. What could go wrong?

Alas, *Thank You* is to covers albums as *Arena* is to live albums, only way more so. In May 2006, Q magazine named it as "*the single worst album in the history of recorded sound*". So I suppose Duran Duran were topping charts again. The band's egos seemed back at full power and there was no stopping them. Opening the album with an almost nu-metal take on **Grandmaster Flash**'s hip hop classic, *White Lines* set the tone nicely. The anti-cocaine stance of the song apparently sailed through their irony filters, unchallenged. Elsewhere **Public Enemy, Led Zep** and **Dylan** all took one for the team. You have not really lived and died until you've heard their Beck-ish bluegrass take on *911 Is A Joke* by **Public Enemy**. Surely, you'll be thinking, if anyone truly understands the deadly consequences of the poor response times of the emergency services in the ghetto, it's Nick Rhodes and Simon Le Bon. In their hands, the line "*call a cab cos a* *cab will come quicker"* comes super close to sounding like *"well, duhhh"*. I have a weakness for cover versions and for Duran Duran but I have a bigger place in my heart for truly heroic failures so I love this truly "special" record but am never less than boggled by its defiant existence. I've just discovered that the Japanese version has a quite stupendously bad cover of *Diamond Dogs*. You shouldn't look. But you do.

A final album for long term label EMI in 1997's *Medazaland* sunk without trace and was buried. Possibly in a grave next door to whoever designed that sleeve. It remains their only album that seems to have been deleted. The appetite for Duran was far from over though. In 1998 EMI released another hits compilation, *Greatest*. It sold a million copies in the UK and the same again in America. That is a LOT. Greatest Hits packages are supposed to capitalise on the success of a band but rarely do. The trick is release one that captures interest in a band coming from a new audience, otherwise you are relying on a fanbase to buy what they already have once more. Duran must have managed that – I guess *Decade* was a hit on cassette, and *Greatest* was a fat double CD VFM phenomenon. The DVD version is pretty brilliant and an essential purchase.

2000's *Pop Trash* for Hollywood records sold as dismally as *Medazzaland*, millions of sales of *Greatest* notwithstanding, but a new deal with Epic and the regrouping of the original Fab Five put 2004's quite-good-actually *Astronaut* back in the Top Five in Britain with a Gold record and a world wide arena tour to boot. Duran were officially big again. It didn't stick and their second effort for Epic, 2006's *Reportage* was announced and then shelved amid more fallings out with Andy, with the label and with the modern world. The book of Pop Rules would suggest again that this should mark the end for the band. For real, this time. Absolutely – time to turn off the machines.

Instead they teamed up with R'n'B superproducers **Danja** and **Timberland** and an at-the-peak-of-his-fame **Justin Timberlake** chimes in on a couple of tracks. Justin was three months old when *Planet Earth* was released and had yet to go to school by the time Duran's 1st flush of success was over. *Red Carpet Massacre* reportedly has some of the songs from *Reportage* and the band have variously said that the decision to work with Timbaland was theirs and also one foisted on them by the label. It's a pretty perky album and a relatively successful attempt to update Duran for the 21st Century. One might argue it was the first time in a long time that Duran had made some smart moves and made concessions to the modern world. It bombed, of course. A damn shame, if you ask me.

However four years later, in 2011, they returned with **Mark Ronson** who, after his production success with **Amy Winehouse**, could have chosen to work with anyone he pleased. Ronson gave interviews saying he was a big fan of classic Duran and set about reviving their glory days. Perhaps because Mark was a kid when Rio was in the charts, he had a feel for what they should sound like. What seemed to me like a recipe for (another) disaster produced the best Duran Duran album since *Notorious*. Indeed it sounds like it could have been the album that followed it, way back then. It was released on the thirtieth anniversary of their debut album and it's genuinely brilliant. *All You Need Is Now* got Duran the best reviews of their career and the appearance of **Kelis, Scissor Sisters** and Arcade Fire's string arranger, **Owen Pallet**, demonstrate the multi-generational appeal of the band. The album made #11 in the UK and broke the Top Thirty in America but didn't add any further Gold discs to the wall. The title track is as good a single as any from their heyday and both *Girl Panic* and *Safe,* the track with Ana Matronic, should have been proper hits. The six-minute-plus, *The Man Who Stole A Leopard* is wonderfully, perfectly daft and features Owen Pallet adding movie strings to the song, which slinks along like *The Chauffeur*, and might or might not be about a leopard theft.

They have yet to do an acoustic album, so there is that to worry about but it is a wonderful thing in 2015 to be considering that the new Duran Duran album, *Paper Dolls* might well be something to look forward to.

Duran have racked up thirteen studio albums and that makes for a large chunk on fans' album shelves. Such dedication takes faith and persistence, on behalf of the band and the fans. OMD have twelve albums, Simple Minds have seventeen although they did have kind of a head start. Marc Almond's work ethic continues to impress: the five Soft Cell albums sit alongside eighteen solo records, putting him roughly equal with David Sylvian and Gary Numan, in terms of shelving inches; although few can match Gary's tally of twenty bloody three live albums. Those are enviably long careers.

Of the twenty three* acts to adorn Smash Hits' front cover in 1982, almost half (eleven) were also NME cover stars that year; and all but six made the NME cover within 6 months of 1982. *[*OMD, **DEPECHE MODE, JAPAN, HEAVEN 17, ABC, ALTERED IMAGES,** DURAN DURAN, **BANANARAMA, HAIRCUT 100, YAZOO,** TOYAH, BELLE STARS, **FUN BOY THREE, SOFT CELL, MADNESS, ASSOCIATES,** MARI WILSON, **SPANDAU BALLET, CULTURE CLUB, BAUHAUS, ORANGE JUICE, DEXYS MIDNIGHT RUNNERS,** TEARS FOR FEARS]*. Pub fact: NME never put OMD on the cover. That seems a damn shame, especially for Dazzle Ships. They really were on the naughty step with the Hip Police.

The gap between cooler, underground music and the Top Twenty had more or less completely closed by this point. So the cool kids and chart kids were buying much of the same music. It was an unprecedented, and, as yet, unique situation wherein the narrative of innovation and development in music was played out in the Top Forty, as opposed to via John Peel and Import record shops. The cool new records were hits. The records were selling in great numbers in the UK, as well as around the world. These bands were beloved household names – and so many of them still are. Life-changing, game-changing records are not going to be forgotten. Accordingly, the majority (seventeen) of those 1982 Smash Hits cover stars (OMD, Depeche Mode, David Sylvian, Heaven 17, ABC, Duran, Toyah, Bananarama, Nick Heywood, Alison Moyet and Vince Clark, Marc Almond, Madness, Spandau, Culture Club, Pete Murphy, Edwyn Collins and Dexys) have released records in the last few years; more than three decades later. Amazing longevity. Will Kasabian still be releasing records in 2034? We can but hope not.

Regardless of whether you are as kind as I am about **Duran Duran** (and I do love them), it is boggling to think that the singers from the likes of **Soft Cell, Japan** and **Tubeway Army** et al would still be pumping out interesting and well-regarded albums three decades down the line and still be able to sell out big rooms, when they fancy it.

To say "when they fancy it" is disingenuous. Keeping the flame burning for this long takes a mixture of bloody mindedness, reinvention, business acumen and the good fortune/sense to surf the periodic waves of revival-related relevancy, when the opportunity presents itself. Increasingly, such Legacy (shoot me) Bands aren't reliant on major labels and instead head up their own cottage industries, many of which are booming now, as acts re-inherit control of their catalogue from completed record deals and use the income from live shows to kickstart records and/or labels. Investing in a record label might seem counter-intuitive in the current market but if you know you are going to sell a certain number of records *and* you know who is going to buy them (and have a list of their email addresses), then selling albums is still very profitable. The difference between selling a new album direct to fans at shows, via mail order or digitally and keeping 100% of the ten pounds income is stark when compared with major label royalties of 19% on the five pounds that HMV pays the label for a new record, freeing up less than a pound per record sold. Even that rather paltry level of return is based on the assumption that you have recouped your advances and are not paying off the debt of a previous album.

The Record Business is dying now, killed by downloads, greed, stupidity and bad music. Fewer and fewer acts are getting the major label push that drives most artists past the tipping point on the way to fame and fortune. This means that there are fewer and fewer bands coming through that graduate to be That Band for a new generation. It's easy to measure this decline when one witnesses how few bands are able to sell enough tickets to be considered bankable Festival Headliners, hence the alarming frequency with which the same handful of acts top bills year in, year out.

That might be boring but it is very reliable. It's true that many festivals, usually new ones, in the UK go under each year but the bigger ones almost always sell out, to ever-increasing crowds and revenues. Glastonbury sells out in under an hour on a wintry Sunday, months upfront and with no artists announced. Meanwhile medium sized festivals tap new demographics; targeting families, clubbers, metalheads, Goths or even people who only like tribute acts. The live music business is booming. The market is expanding, new younger fans arrive every year, of course but it is maintaining its hold on an aging , eternally adolescent audience who will still ante up to see **Echo & The Bunnymen, The Human League** or **ABC**, year in and year out, and do not need a new album to motivate them to do so. They are also happy to pay premium prices. As CDs and download prices slip lower and lower each year and music is regarded as a free commodity by the kids; a ticket to see a band who can be relied upon to play enough of the hits to satisfy the fans seems to skyrocket each year. Phil Oakey said in November 2014 in the Metro, *"I'm not sure there is now such a thing as a commercial album for a long-established group. You just do songs and hope they'll get used in a film or on a TV show."*

Once an act reaches "Arena level" for a couple of albums, once they are That Band for enough people, it is possible now, with careful attention and curation of the catalogue, to keep them operating at some substantial version of their peak indefinitely; an ongoing bonanza. It's not an easy balancing act however. You can easily over-milk a legacy or the stored goodwill of fans' memories. Filling out a band with some young kids who'll play for chips, beer and a bed; and then running perfunctorily through That Album three times a year up and down the country to pay the mortgage will soon do that.

Understanding the cyclical nature of the music business is the key to success here; and similarly adjusting your tactics as popularity waxes and wanes, to avoid over-exposure at one end of the spectrum and being totally forgotten at the other. The trick is also to bank some cash when the going is good and live off it, when the needle swings away again, as it surely will. However that is much, much easier said than done, especially if you have latent tastes for expensive things.

Some achieve this by disappearing for long periods, giving fans time to miss them and allow their hearts to grow fonder. Others just retreat to the fringes of the spotlight; diversify into other artistic endeavours; such as acting, writing and grinding out underwhelming solo albums. Such simmering on the periphery gently reminds people that you exist and gives the Brand Name a rest. It also unlocks the bonus level of successful, parallel careers.

Releasing what is essentially the same album, again and again, is another fate that some acts are trapped within by their audience's demands (or by their rejection of anything that tries something new). Others seem to repeat themselves of their own free will, whether by if-it-ain't-broke design or an inability to conjure forth any new ideas whatsoever.

There are several bands by now that take up space in my record collection with a lot of quite similar albums that don't see play from one year to the next. This is the way it goes for most bands, whose career sees out a decade, I suppose. I have come to terms with the fact that Duran Duran's *Big Thing* and **Flaming Lips'** *The Terror* are probably never going to get played again. Few artists have a gift for reinvention and the good fortune to have an audience who will roll with it. Fewer still have the sort of critical currency to have the whole process rubber stamped and legitimised. It only works if you have a clearly defined aesthetic, within a world of your own creation that dictates which projects are appropriate and which are not

Nick Cave has a legendary work ethic and is quite the polymath. Although there are often four years between **Bad Seeds** albums, he also releases albums as part of **Grinderman**; he has written screenplays (The Proposition, Lawless, the heaven-set but rejected Gladiator II), scored other people's films and plays (almost one a year since 2000) and contributed to dozens more. He has written several books, acted in films and as a voice artist and in 2014 released a "fictionalised autobiographical documentary" in *20,000 Days On Earth*. If you are a Nick Cave fan, there is always plenty to keep you interested and he has not made the mistake of releasing endless identical Bad Seeds albums that sound like the good old bad old days. Instead Cave has varied and developed his sound, periodically essaying a bar room crooner, Grand Guignol Vaudevillian ringmaster or unchaining the apoplectic hellfire preacher that you can always detect, bubbling away beneath his dark eyes. It's not an unblemished track record but his missteps are few and far between. Even Bowie Himself is the father of quite a few (later) albums that are not going to be added to the pantheon.

Sometimes however, mainlining the status quo is all that is ever asked of a band. Some, like The Ramones, turned it into a self-reflexive artform that became a meta-joke which embraced the Scooby Doo nature of the band (and indeed bands in general). Others pay lip service to artistic development but have huge fanbases who just want to hear fifteen songs from the first couple of records and any seven later ones that are supposed to represent a progression but always end up sounding much the same but less so. And much longer. And that is why **Oasis** will be able to reform every ten years and play stadiums as long as they live, which, as they made clear ages back, is going to be forever.

David Bowie is the Lifetime President of career reinvention. He remains relevant, absorbs new sounds and patronises (in the nicer sense) the more interesting new acts from **Goldie** to **Suede, TV On The Radio** to **Arcade Fire,** despite some less than stunning albums from Himself along the way. Not that there are not wonders on each one but every album since *Tonight* has been at least three songs too long. *1. Outside* is 74 long minutes and *Black Tie White Noise* is almost that. It seems not to matter, though. His legend grows apace.

His consistently elevated presence in the Pop firmament today is still something to behold. Every few years there are vaguely substantiated rumours of a potential world tour by Himself that people desperately want to believe are true. Thousands of people quietly practicing quick draw moves on their credit cards. Austerity busting ticket prices for superstar comebacks have soared in the last few years and the more mercenary, or tax burdened, artists realise that people will pay pretty much anything for one last hurrah. Bowie could charge whatever he pleased for a ticket and they'd be snapped up in seconds, I am quite sure.

His albums will always clutter up the endless, endless Top Hundred Albums listicles and today's cool and interesting new bands are still inspired by Him and His music. And damn, if it isn't always the clever ones. What these smart cookies take from Bowie is that there are no rules, there is no cool and that you can and should pursue your own strange ideas to the limit. The stranger, the better. The wonderful **St Vincent**, in conversation with *Pitchfork* at the recent Bowie exhibition, said that He taught her *"what a rock star looked like"* and inspired her to explore and pursue the theatrical side of herself and to embrace performance and showbiz, *"Bowie is like a natural extension of showmen like James Brown and Little Richard"*. **Thom Yorke**, discussing seeing the *Ashes To Ashes* video for the first time, said (in an HMV advert) that *"the other kids thought it was just too weird and I just thought, I wanna do that for a living"*. ***James* Murphy**'s recent (and brilliant) remix of *Love Is Lost* is clearly a labour of love, referencing **Bowie**'s *Fashion* (and Steve Reich). The passion shines out of every beat. **Beck** recorded a ten minute symphonic version of *Sound & Vision* a few years back. If you have not seen it, put the book down and do yourself a favour. **Nirvana**'s soul-skewering take on *The Man Who Sold The World* seemed to take Bowie's imagined fiction and make it seem purely autobiographical. Funnily enough, I have been in a Youtube wormhole for the last three hours because every single cool act I could think of, has recorded a Bowie cover. Even **Prince** recently covered *Let's Dance*. I don't think that needs further comment. Try it for yourself.

So His presence is still everywhere to such a bedded-in degree that He chose to sit out the media circus entirely for his 2013 comeback, *The Next Day*. This aberrant behaviour is (more or less) unheard of and might be seen as promotional suicide. However it is one of the curses of long-established artists that the press will want to talk about ancient history and publish pictures (and magazine covers) of the glory days over newer photos of lived-in faces. Perhaps sensing this, Bowie uttered not one word to the media during the whole campaign. He let no-one lose the fight for exclusive interviews and thus every publication won. It seemed that all the magazines in the world ran cover stories featuring His face, usually the image from *Aladdin Sane*'s cover, which was also used to publicise the huge *David Bowie Is* exhibition, which is now travelling the world, exactly in the way that He isn't. Clever old Him. He took the "Less Is More" maxim to its logical conclusion. It seems like an obvious move now, doesn't it? That's the thing with genius – doing something new and making it seem obvious in retrospect. It's a great record, too. The man knows what he is doing.

Conversely, **Duran Duran** seem to have gone out of their way to avoid longevity at times, committing many gruesome crimes against sense and taste – repeatedly flirting with career suicide. They have embraced becoming a reboot of a parody of a deconstruction of themselves so many times now, that down ought to be the new up for them but this overlooks three factors:

1. They were quite silly to begin with.

2. They have left reasonably dignified gaps between their albums through luck, judgement or being dropped by various labels and they always leave enough of a gap between tours to still play arenas. When was the last time Duran played a theatre in the UK*? [*that would be October 2003 at the Kentish Town Forum, which only served to drive ticket sales for four nights at Wembley a few months later].

3. The seemingly perpetual Eighties Revival. Every few years there is a new crop of bands name-checking Duran from Franz Ferdinand to Gwen Stefani, from The Killers to Justin Timberlake to La Roux to a succession of bands now forgotten; or never noticed much at the time beyond ephemeral New Band pieces in the press.

Why do "they" keep reviving the Eighties?

"They", being the high street fashion barons and trend-orientated music journalists, bloggers and radio programmers, who constantly reject things that look or sound too six-months-ago. This keeps things moving along at such a dizzying rate that the future often can't keep up with demand. The past is thus aggressively strip-mined to make up the shortfall and things are revived now with alarming regularity; although this doesn't account for the fact that the Eighties' sounds still crop up in the Top Ten way more often than the Sixties, Seventies or Nineties. The richness of the charts in the first few years of the Eighties and lack of an overall defining sound, as opposed to when bands "went dance" in 1989-1990 and ended up sounding rather similar, means that there is ample treasure to plunder.

DFA, the New York label built by James Murphy around his **LCD Soundsystem** project, runs at a constant medium to extremely cool level and can be viewed as a tribute to the early Eighties. The label takes influence from the stripped back New York dancefloor-centric bands from the 1979-1981 No Wave scene and **Talking Heads**' rounded but stuttering funk, along with visual cues from Factory Records' ethics and aesthetics, particularly **New Order / Joy Division's** wry attitude and minimalist artwork. Most of the DFA bands are tightly bound to club culture and they frequently remix each other and none of them make lavish and lush records. Everything seems to come via a back-to-basics filter that cuts out any fat.

LCD Soundsystem also got tangled up in the 2007 Punk Funk revival along with **Radio4, The Rapture, DFA 1979** and more, since forgotten. These bands' sacred texts were Talking Heads and Gang Of Four albums. With more cowbell. This meant fast, tight exciting singles with clipped guitars and stuttering funk, whose open grooves translated to quite lengthy remixes and an explosion of similarly themed club nights in New York and London. Everyone seemed to be slightly suspiciously au fait with **Gang Of Four** overnight, just as they had been with **Wire** during Britpop, despite a virtual media blackout around the bands, both before and afterwards.

Prior to DFA's emergence/existence as a label, New York, along with Berlin, were the twin crucibles for Electroclash scene centred around **Adult, Fischerspooner, Ladyton, Peaches** and **Tiga**, which cherry picked bits of No Wave, Eighties Disco, European Electro and Synthpop to make a series of no-frills bangers, that were pretty fun for a while, but didn't blossom into crossover success, although everything Peaches does is worth a listen. It's not just Electropop and Punk Funk that fuels the sense of an omnipresent Eighties revival. The doomy chords, slow grooves and baritone vocals lifted from **Joy Division** and **The Chameleons** gave **Interpol** and then **Editors** a starting point for their 21st Century makeover. **Goldfrapp** updated the Synthpop Duo and the 2010s (Tens?) brought a further wave in **Hurts, Little Boots** and **La Roux**, who surely looked to **Yazoo, Pet Shop Boys** and **Soft Cell** as role models.

There were a lot of Duran copyists in the Mid-Eighties but most disappeared without trace and this template proved more and more unreliable and uncool as time passed. Once the statute of limitations passed, however, all such crimes were declassified and all bets were off. **The Killers** owe a huge debt to Duran Duran. Their early demos were very closely modelled on Duranesque arrangements. At first, no labels were remotely interested in the band and they were derided somewhat in UK A&R circles. Support in the UK clubs and from the NME started to change that and when the public at large heard the singles from their first album, there was nothing but green lights for the band. This Duranity does make their subsequent dabblings with U2 and Springsteenisms all the more confusing but it marks another milestone for the very idea of Duranity. I am sure I can detect something of the Simon Le Bon in Kiwi singer, **Ladyhawke,** who has made some absolutely fantastic singles in *Magic* and *Black, White & Blue*. Simon is a guest vocalist on a **Charlie XCX** song on the new *Hunger Games* Soundtrack, so don't rule out another gazillion selling Duran compilation in the near future as yet another generation warms to their charms. As to **The Deftones**' cover of *The Chauffeur*, well, that is yours to discover, eh?

Ditching guitars for electronics is one of the many options for bands now, from **Bright Eyes** to **Radiohead.** It's an accepted choice now, like doing an acoustic album. It just another way of paring back an artist's music or muse and starting from scratch.

Those massive Hits from the early Eighties really did represent a Year Zero for music and the beginning of the modern era in Pop Music. The triumph of the machines over musicians and the end of the longhairs. So it's not so much a revival, when the familiar synth washes or taut drum machines take over the charts once again, but a massive jab at the Reset button. A reboot. Back to basics.

Back, even, to the drawing board. Some of those Eighties singles are mini-symphonies, benefiting from years of classically trained musicianship, basking in layered production. So many more, from OMD to Depeche Mode, The Human League to Soft Cell are very raw and spare arrangements, primitive even. Simple melodies that get by on the throbbing repetitious electronic beats that modern dancefloors cannot do without. Hitting the Reset button on a tired genre and returning to First Principles, boosted with innovative future sounds or production techniques, will revitalise music and re-energise records every time.

All modern Pop records can trace their roots back to this explosive period of electronic music and its spirit of adventure and freedom. Hip Hop, R'n'B and all manner of EDM records are all brought to life by the heartbeat of the electronic drum machine and rise on wave after wave of synthpads. There was so little of such music before 1980 that it's just not relevant. Is Beyonce going to dive into the sounds of 1973 for her next record? Will Kanye go looking to Haight Ashbury for new ideas? Is Lady Gaga going to embrace Tony Bennett's crooning records? OK, that last one was a bad example but you know what I mean.

The thing to take from this is that the early Eighties really is as far back as it's relevant to go for modern music. Back to the drawing board. Back to the original template. The oldest of the new school.

You might just have to get used to the idea of a constant Eighties revival.

PHOTO CREDITS

The photographs used in DARE remain the property of the rights holders.

I strongly urge you now and within the body of the text to buy all of the records discussed in this book.

Cover: David Bowie, still from Ashes To Ashes video, RCA records

CHAPTER 1

David Bowie, b/w still from BBC documentary, Cracked Actor.
David Bowie colour still from BBC documentary, Cracked Actor.
Kraftwerk, Sleeve detail from Trans Europe Express, EMI.
Kraftwerk packshot of Autobahn, EMI
Kraftwerk packshot of Radio-Activity, EMI
Kraftwerk packshot of Man-Machine, EMI
Kraftwerk packshot of Trans Europe Express, EMI
Kraftwerk sleeve detail of Man-Machine, EMI
Synclavier, vintage photograph, origin unknown
Moog, vintage photograph, origin unknown
Donna Sumer, I Feel Love cover, Casablanca records
Donna Sumer, Love To Love You cover, Casablanca records
Donna Summer and Giorgio Moroder, mid 70s. origin unknown.
Sparks, mid 70s promotional photograph, origin unknown
Blondie, Best Of cover, Chrysalis records
Blondie, Heart of Glass cover, Chrysalis records
Blondie, Sunday Girl cover, Chrysalis records
Blondie, Dreaming cover, Chrysalis records
Blondie, Atomic cover, Chrysalis records
Blondie, Parallel Lines, sleeve detail, Chrysalis records
Blondie late 70s photo, origin unknown
Disco Sucks bumper sticker, vintage photograph, origin unknown

CHAPTER 2

Brixton Riots, 1981, vintage photo origin unknown
Port Talbot Steelworks, origin unknown
Brotherhood Of Man, late 70s TV still
The Jam, b/w vintage photo, origin unknown
The Style Council video still, Polydor Records
2 Tone Logo, Chrysalis Records
Ska badges, vintage photo, origin unknown

The Special AKA, LIVE EP, 2 Tone / Chrysalis Records
The Specials Do Nothing Advert, 2 Tone / Chrysalis Records
Fun Boy Three, Smash Hits cover, Bauer media
Adam And The Ants Dirk Wears White Socks cover , Do It Records
Adam Ant, vintage photo, circa 1980, origin unknown
Adam Ant Smash Hits cover, Bauer Media

CHAPTER 3

Vintage Synthesizer Ad, Origin unknown
Ultravox "Vienna" video Still, Chrysalis records
The Human League "DARE", LP cover, Virgin Records
Phil Oakey, Smash Hits Cover, Bauer Media
OMD, Architecture + Morality, sleeve, Virgin Records
OMD Promo Photo, Smash Hits, Bauer media
OMD Dazzle Ships, sleeve, Virgin records
Dazzle Ships In Dry Dock, detail, Edward Wadsworth.
Soft Cell, live Top Of The Pops 1981, BBC
Soft Cell, Non Stop Erotic Cabaret, sleeve detail, Some Bizarre
Spandau Ballet, To Cut A Long Story Short, sleeve, Chrysalis records
Spandau Ballet, Musclebound, sleeve, Chrysalis records
Spandau Ballet, The Freeze, sleeve, Chrysalis records
Spandau Ballet, Journeys To Glory, sleeve, Chrysalis records
Spandau Ballet, promo photo, 1980.
Gary Numan, live photo, 1981, origin unknown
Ultravox, Smash Hits cover, 1981, Bauer media
Visage, Smash Hits cover, 1981, Bauer media
Steve Strange, promotional photo, circa 1980.
The Human League, Don't You Want Me?, advert, Virgin Records

CHAPTER 4

Ian Dury, promotional photo, circa 1979
Gang of Four, live photo, origin unknown
Talking Heads, promotional photo, origin unknown
Talking Heads live photo, origin unknown
Orange Juice, Rip it Up, advert, Polydor Records
New Order live photo, circa 1981, origin unknown
New Order, Blue Monday live, Top of the Pops, BBC
Orange Juice, Rip It Up, sleeve, Polydor records
Pete Shelley, Homosapien, sleeve, Active Distribution
Iggy Pop, The Idiot, sleeve, Virgin records
David Bowie, "Heroes", sleeve, RCA records
Joy Division, Closer, sleeve, Universal records
PiL, Second Edition, sleeve, Virgin Records
New Order, Ceremony, sleeve, Universal records
ABC, Tears Are Not Enough, sleeve Universal Records

ABC, Poison Arrow, sleeve Universal Records
ABC, The Look of Love, sleeve Universal Records
ABC, All Of My Heart, sleeve Universal Records
ABC, The Lexicon Of Love, sleeve Universal Records
ABC, Smash Hits cover, 1982, Bauer Media
Associates, Sulk, sleeve, Warner Brothers
Associates, 18 Carat Love Affair, sleeve, Warner Brothers
Associates, Smash Hits cover, 1982, Bauer Media
Blancmange, Happy Families, sleeve, Universal
Aztec Camera, High Land Hard Rain, sleeve, Warner Brothers
Talk Talk, The Party's Over, sleeve, EMI
Tears For Fears, The Hurting, sleeve, Universal Music

CHAPTER 6

Japan, promotional photo, circa 1978, Hansa
David Sylvian, promotional photo, circa 1981, Virgin records
Japan, Ghosts, sleeve, Virgin Records
Japan, b/w Promotional Photo, 1982, Virgin records
Japan, Oil On Canvas, sleeve, Virgin Records
Japan, Tin Drum, sleeve, Virgin Records
Japan, Smash Hits cover 1979, Bauer Media
Japan, Smash Hits cover 1981, Bauer Media
Grace Jones, Nightclubbing, Island Records
Grace Jones, Island Life, Island Records

CHAPTER 7

Five goth girls, origin unknown
Three Imaginary Goth Boys, origin unknown
Siouxsie Sioux, Spellbound, live, Top Of The Pops, BBC
Bauhaus, promotional photo, Beggars Banquet
Maxell Tape advert, detail, Maxell.
Andrew Eldritch, origin unknown
Sisters Of Mercy, WAKE, live still, Warner Brothers
Merciful Release logo, Merciful Release
Two Goth boys, origin unknown
The Cure, Killing An Arab, sleeve, Polydor
The Cure, A Forest, sleeve, Polydor
The Cure, candid photo circa 1981, origin unknown
The Cure, Pornography, advert, Polydor Records
Robert Smith, promotional photo, circa 1982, Polydor Records
Bauhaus, Smash Hits cover, 1982, Bauer Media

CHAPTER 8

The Clash, Smash Hits, cover, 1981, Bauer Media

Malcolm McLaren, Smash Hits, cover, 1982, Bauer Media
The Great Rock'n'Roll Swindle, poster, SMV
Malcolm McLaren, Duck Rock sleeve, 1982, EMI
Grandmaster Flash, The Message, sleeve, Sanctuary
The Daily Mirror, cover, 1976
Sid Vicious, still, The Great Rock'n'Roll Swindle, SMV
The Clash, Promotional Photo circa 1979, SONY
The Clash, Sandinista advert 1981, SONY
The Clash, Promotional Photo circa 1982, SONY

CHAPTER 9

Simple Minds, Promotional photo, circa 1981, Virgin
Simple Minds, Sons And Fascination advert 1981, Virgin
Graphic Equalizer, origin unknown
Echo And The Bunnymen Promo photo, circa 1982, WEA
Echo And The Bunnymen silhouette Promo photo, circa 1982, WEA
Kate Bush, The Dreaming, advert, EMI
Echo And The Bunnymen The Back of Love 7" sleeve, WEA
Echo And The Bunnymen The Cutter 7" sleeve, WEA
Genesis live, mid-70s origin unknown
Peter Gabriel, 1, sleeve, Real World
Peter Gabriel, 2, sleeve, Real World
Peter Gabriel, 3, sleeve, Real World
Peter Gabriel, 4, sleeve, Real World
Joy Division, Closer, sleeve, Universal
Simple Minds, Empires And Dance, sleeve, Virgin
Ultravox, Vienna, sleeve, Chrysalis
Duran Duran, Duran Duran, sleeve, EMI
Simple Minds New Gold Dream, sleeve, Virgin
Duran Duran promotional photo circa 1982, EMI

CHAPTER 10

Green Gartside / Scritti Politti, promotional photo circa 1983, Virgin records
Roxy Music, For Your Pleasure, sleeve detail, Virgin
Bryan Ferry, Smash Hits cover, 1980, Bauer Media
Scritti Politti, The Sweetest Girl, sleeve, Rough Trade
Scritti Politti, Faithless, sleeve, Rough Trade
Scritti Politti, Aylums In Jerusalem, sleeve, Rough Trade
Scritti Politti, Songs To Remember, sleeve, Rough Trade

CHAPTER 11

Kajagoogoo, Smash Hits cover,1983, Bauer Media
Kajagogoo, White Feathers, sleeve b/w, Virgin Records

Top Of The Pops, The Best Of, 1981, BBC
Now That's What I Call Music, Various Artists, EMI.

CHAPTER 12

Duran Duran, Duran Duran sleeve, EMI
Duran Duran, Rio, sleeve, EMI
Duran Duran, Seven And The Ragged Tiger sleeve, EMI
Duran Duran, Arena sleeve, EMI
Duran Duran, Notorious sleeve, EMI
Duran Duran, Liberty sleeve, EMI
Duran Duran, Big Thing sleeve, EMI
Duran Duran, Duran Duran sleeve, EMI
Duran Duran, Thank You sleeve, EMI
Duran Duran, Pop Trash sleeve, Hollywood
Duran Duran, Medazzaland sleeve, Hollywood
Duran Duran, Astronaut sleeve, SONY
Duran Duran, Red Carpet Massacre sleeve, SONY
Duran Duran, All You need Is Now sleeve, Skin Divers

INDEX